John Davies

Sermons on the manifestation of the Son of God

With a preface, addressed to laymen, on the present position of the clergy of the

Church of England

John Davies

Sermons on the manifestation of the Son of God
With a preface, addressed to laymen, on the present position of the clergy of the Church of England

ISBN/EAN: 9783337104764

Printed in Europe, USA, Canada, Australia, Japan

Cover: Foto ©Lupo / pixelio.de

More available books at **www.hansebooks.com**

With the writer's love, to h...

Kate Hurd.

With love & appreciation,
Emily Davies.

SERMONS

ON THE

MANIFESTATION OF THE SON OF GOD.

July 10th 1916

SERMONS

ON THE

MANIFESTATION OF THE SON OF GOD:

WITH A

PREFACE, ADDRESSED TO LAYMEN,

ON THE

PRESENT POSITION OF THE CLERGY OF THE CHURCH OF ENGLAND

AND

AN APPENDIX,

ON THE TESTIMONY OF SCRIPTURE AND THE CHURCH AS TO THE POSSIBILITY OF PARDON IN THE FUTURE STATE.

BY THE

REV. J. LLEWELYN DAVIES, M.A.

RECTOR OF CHRIST CHURCH, ST. MARYLEBONE,
LATE FELLOW OF TRINITY COLLEGE, CAMBRIDGE.

London and Cambridge:
MACMILLAN AND CO.
1864.

The Right of Translation and Reproduction is Reserved.

LONDON
R. CLAY, SON, AND TAYLOR, PRINTERS,
BREAD STREET HILL.

PREFACE.

THE Sermons in this Volume were written and are published under a strong persuasion that the subject with which they deal, the historical manifestation of the SON OF GOD in the person of JESUS OF NAZARETH, is not only one of never-fading interest as the foundation of the Christian Church, but is that which claims our most anxious consideration at the present time. Those who think that the great question of the day is whether the Bible is infallible, or contains an undefined admixture of error, will do right in throwing their energies into the conflict about Biblical inspiration; but I confess that I share the feeling of those who regard this controversy with some impatience, and who deem it expedient no less than manly to accept the challenge of inquiry as to the very ground of the Catholic Faith, the Incarnation of the Son of God.

This feeling is not excited only by such phenomena as the avidity with which M. Renan's book on the "Life of Jesus" has been read, or the sceptical professions of a part of our periodical literature. These things are indications that the doubt of the age must be dealt with openly and directly. But the tacit and sometimes unconscious unbelief of Christians is a fact which concerns us more than the open denials of unbelievers; it is of vaster dimensions, and touches our honour and our safety more closely. It is a more serious thing to a clergyman to fear that whilst he is using the language of the Church the people are only half believing it, than to know that a few educated persons are proclaiming a total unbelief. And it must be remembered that the clergyman will partly infer the want of faith of the people from what he is conscious of in himself; there is no gulf fixed between the minds of the clergy and of the laity. When therefore it is affirmed in such a manner as to excite general attention throughout Europe, and with no one knows how much acquiescence, that Jesus of Nazareth was only a remarkable man, and not the Son of God, we are led to ask ourselves with what degree of positive belief the Lord Jesus Christ is actually recognised by Christians as the Living Ruler of the World. The inquiry, to be worth anything, must be addressed to the philosophy, the literature, and the politics of our time, as well as to its theology. It is not necessary to obtain a precise answer to such a question. No one will doubt that the world would be a very different world if the Gospel were really and heartily believed by all who call themselves Christians. It may be that there is not less faith now than in former ages; perhaps the proportion of assured belief to indolent acceptance was never large in Christendom. If it be so, we know that in every age the real conflict between the Gospel and the world has centered about the person of Christ. The peculiarity of our own day is that the denial which in other times would have been either coarse or silent is now expressed in religious language and by those who have cordial sympathy with Christian sentiments.

The recent judgment of the Privy Council in the case of Dr. Williams and Mr. Wilson, which secures liberty of teaching to the Anglican clergy on the subjects of Biblical inspiration and of future punishment, may seem to have diverted the attention of the Church and the country for a time to questions which, however serious, are confessedly subordinate to that of the Incarnation. I do not underrate the importance of that judgment; its effects, gradually increasing with time, will make it one of the historical land-

marks of the English Church. But its greatest effect **will** be to concentrate our interest upon the Gospel in its simplicity ; to displace certain beliefs from their **usurped positions** as the fundamental dogmas of the Church, so as to **leave the** witness concerning Christ and His work the Corner-stone of the Faith. It may **be desirable to** illustrate briefly this tendency of the **judgment.**

The judgment, strictly considered, relates to the obligations of the clergy. The question was whether a beneficed clergyman might propound certain opinions without subjecting himself to the loss of his benefice. But the laity, it need hardly be said, have the most direct interest in the liberty of teaching allowed to the clergy. To hold a benefice means to **be** the appointed clergyman of a parish, and to have possession of a church, from which the unanimous opinion of the parishioners accounting the incumbent to be heretical would be powerless to dislodge him. It is only reasonable, therefore, that the laity **of** the Church should make anxious inquiries when a lati**tude** which many had thought forbidden has been judicially allowed to clerical teaching. As to the liberty given by the recent judgment, it is unquestionable that it had been openly used to some extent in every age of the Church; but it had been pertinaciously affirmed to be illegally used, and it is not at all surprising that the judgment should have spread abroad a general impression that through the accidental want of sufficient strictness in our Church formularies, an indefinite licence of opinion has received judicial sanction. This is a very mistaken impression; but it is true that the immediate effect of the judgment has been to declare the clergy *free* on certain points.

The clergy of the Church of England are free, then, to an extent which has proved startling to the general public. The idea of a State-Church had become associated in some minds with a necessary and peculiar bondage of persons ministering in it.* To be subject to the law of the land seemed to be a more crushing restriction than to be subject to the opinion of a congregation or an ecclesiastical body.

---

* See Professor Goldwin Smith's recent pamphlet on the Abolition of Tests. The deplorable apology contained in the following extract has peculiar claims on Mr. G. Smith's consideration. "Henry Ward Beecher was asked at one of the meetings in London at which he spoke, 'Do you admit negroes to seats in your church?' and the question was evidently made a point of. But it was a most unfair one. For a church here is as much a private affair as a club, or as a private house. In countries *where there is any sort of connexion between Church and State* such a question would be pertinent: but we might as well ask you, with a censorious air, if you admitted

But it is now made plain that the Church of England is the freest religious communion in the country. Freedom in the direction of a Romanizing theology,—freedom in the direction of Evangelical Dissent, had already been asserted with practical success. The doctrinal cord had stretched without breaking for Dr. Pusey and Archdeacon Denison on one side, for Mr. Gorham on the other. Tractarians and Evangelicals have now found, to their united horror, that the same cord will stretch in another direction. Judicial investigation has ascertained that the Church of England has not forbidden her ministers under penalties to say that the Bible may contain errors, and to express a hope that the curse upon those who die impenitent may not be irreversible. We clergymen are free either to maintain that there is no error of any kind in the Bible, or to confess that there *is* error, according to our judgment and belief of what is true: we are similarly free either to teach that

Hodge, the plough-boy, to the privileges of the Reform or the Oxford and Cambridge Club; much better, for he is of your own race. All our churches are built by people who like to worship together, and though no one is excluded from them, not even negroes, only people of approximately similar social positions are likely to be found in the same congregations. So as our pews are as much our own as our parlours, we don't have the negro in the one any more than we do in the other."—*Letter from* "*A Yankee*," *in the* "*Spectator*," *for Feb.* 27, 1864.

God's forgiveness can never come to a sinner in the future state, or to give utterance to a hope that those who repent after death may not find repentance rejected.* We are not tied up to one given doctrine on these points by any explicit assertion in the Anglican formularies.

What is the meaning of this freedom, so manifestly great and striking, in the eyes of many so fatal? Does it show that the formularies were blunderingly expressed, so that they may be evaded by cunning artifices, like an ill-drawn Act of Parliament? or that the law as to clerical conformity is not sufficiently stringent? There is no sign that our freedom is due to either of these causes. It is perfectly plain that the Church has not attempted to set forth a dogma as to the nature of Biblical inspiration, or as to the final condition of human beings. There is every appearance that the Church has deliberately abstained from dogmatising on these points. Nor is there any sign of weakness in the law. If the Judicial Committee could have persuaded themselves that Dr. Williams or Mr. Wilson had contradicted any

---

* I have appended to this volume an inquiry, the substance of which has already been published in a pamphlet, as to the arguments on both sides of the question to be drawn from the Prayer Book and from Scripture.

single express proposition in the formularies, a verdict of guilty would have been followed by prompt and severe punishment. A recent lamentable case has sufficiently proved that a clergyman of exemplary character may be turned out of his living, if the Judicial Committee of the Privy Council cannot reconcile some statement of his with some statement in the Thirty-nine Articles. The only reasonable conclusion is that the legislators of the Church did not agree with Dr. Pusey and his allies as to the doctrines to which assent was to be absolutely required.

It is only necessary to read the Articles, and the Creeds to which the Articles refer, to see on what subjects the Church of England has been explicit and prescribes conformity. It is the old faith of the Church Catholic, the faith of the Primitive Church, for which our own Church has been jealous. The modern High Churchmen who wish to enforce a dogma contained in no Creed of the Church pay less deference than the Reformers to Catholic antiquity. The Nicene Creed is the great symbol of the Church, —the primitive baptismal confession which emerged from the prehistoric period of Christianity, enlarged by the authority of the greatest Church Council. This is the summary of our Christian belief, which the law of England would not allow a clergyman to contravene. "A poor defective summary," say Presbyterians and Evangelicals, "occupying itself wholly with the nature and the work of God, and scarcely laying down a single doctrine about the human soul. It has nothing about the inspiration of the Bible, nothing about justification by faith, nothing about the punishment of man's sin in the person of a substitute, nothing about the condition of mankind in the endless ages, nothing about the date or manner of the creation of the world." This is a true account. Rightly or wrongly, the Church Catholic, followed by the Church of England, has felt that the great business of a Creed was to set forth the Revelation which God has given us of Himself. Other matters relating to man may not be unimportant, but they are subordinate; they are governed by, and to be deduced from, what is made known to us in the Son of Man. If it is a superficial part of the Faith that God revealed Himself in the Eternal Son who took our nature and died and rose again, and that a Spirit has been given to men who is one with the Father and the Son,—then the theology of the Church of England is defective, and, the foundations which modern religious opinion has lent us being withdrawn, we necessarily totter to our fall. But is not the whole testimony of earnest modern inquiry declaring to us emphatically that *this*, the genuine historical manifestation of God, the incarnation of the Son, is the question of questions, that all controversy is superficial which does not reach to this?

Let the laity, then, learn from the very judgment which has excited their surprise, that Anglican theology, instead of being a blundering congeries of religious traditions, is a firm and definite *theology*, a Gospel concerning God. If we are reproached with having no dogmatic system of metaphysics or of cosmogony, we must admit the defect. But we, at the same time, can claim the liberty of not committing the Gospel to any denial of modern science.

To those who, renouncing the old method of Christendom, have made the infallibility of the Bible and the irreversible perdition of unconverted sinners the grounds of their religious system, the judgment must inevitably be alarming. We know these modern schemes too well. We know how fundamental these two principles have been made, the one for doctrine, the other for practical preaching. "We have a Book, every word of which is true. Whatever it says is to be believed, because it is in the Bible." "All mankind are naturally on the way to an eternity of misery and rebellion. But, during this life, every one who hears the Gospel has an offer of escape. Death fixes the unchangeable doom. Who will be so mad, as not to seize upon his chance of escape whilst yet there is time?" The logic is in each case short and effective. Those who have known no other scheme from their infancy, may well be excused for thinking it impossible that religion can exist upon any other hypothesis. But now the judgment declares to all, with its imperturbable judicial authority, that this is not the dogmatic teaching of the Church of England. The Church allows those opinions; but its own cornerstone is the witness that God has revealed Himself to us in Jesus Christ, Son of God and Son of Man.

The faith of the Church of England, then, is in the strictest sense a historical faith, and we must take it with the disadvantages, as well as advantages, which attend such a faith. The fact that we should profess to believe not merely what our fathers believed, but what a certain number of persons in the third century believed, appears to some philosophical minds infinitely ridiculous. To others, that we should attach our faith to an event, appears inconsistent with the very idea of religion. It is quite true, as a philosophical writer objects in a recent number of the *Revue des Deux Mondes*, that a church which, like the Church of England, has to do with geography and history, does not offer scope to "*le libre élan d'une logique hardie.*" We clergymen are debarred from constructing systems like the scheme of Theodore Parker, which was so elaborately exalted the other day by a writer in *Fraser's Magazine*, to the discredit of our Christian and Anglican theology. We are heavily weighted in our speculations by conditions of time and place. We cannot pretend to be independent of what other generations have felt and thought. Our theology rests upon the asserted fact that the Eternal God manifested Himself eighteen centuries ago, in the person of a Galilean Prophet. We were taken, before we could think, into an ancient society, which began with the acknowledgment of Jesus of Nazareth as its heavenly Lord. If He had no title to be the Lord of the spirits of men, if He was not really the Son of God taking our flesh upon Him, the Church of England proclaims a delusion. When the people of England are satisfied that there has been no manifestation of the Son of God, they ought to sweep away the Church with indignation and shame. And therefore, whatever it may be to Religion in the abstract, to us the historical reality of the story of Jesus of Nazareth is a vital matter. The constant endeavour of half-hearted believers and half-hearted unbelievers has been to persuade themselves, that neither one thing nor the other is true, that they may be more liberal than those who actually believe in Christ, more reverent and christian than those who deny Him. Who can say how many of the educated laity are at present aiming at such a position? Those who feel how insidious and weakening such scepticism is, may be thankful to M. Renan for his plain-spoken theory of the Life of Jesus. It is something that he should honestly have endeavoured to realize to himself a Jesus *not* Divine; we want to know what we are to think of Christ, if we do not receive the Gospel account of Him. But it has also been felt at once that M. Renan's theory is a striking reaction against the prevailing sceptical opinion of the age. The notion that the real Jesus was a mild moralist, and that everything extraordinary in the Gospels was legendary, has not commended itself to M. Renan as the true way of accounting for the Evangelistic life of Jesus. Speaking with the authority of a finished modern critic, he says that large portions of the Gospels, which had been most confidently pronounced to be mythical, are unmistakably authentic. He exposes himself to the contempt of the most advanced school of critics by accepting even the Gospel of St. John as the work of the Apostle. He perceives the weakness of mere morality to move mankind; a message from heaven, a revolutionary announcement, is what stirs the hearts of men. He holds, therefore, that Jesus really did proclaim Himself to be the Son of God from heaven; that He really did assume to do mighty works; that He preached a revolution affecting the whole earth in the name of the eternal God. He did all this, M. Renan thinks, at the price of His personal integrity and perhaps of His sanity. Of course His pretensions could not be true : but if He had not pretended, He could not possibly have produced the effects which are visible on the face of history. M. Renan's account of the *pretensions* of Jesus is instructive, and might help us to a truer conception than most of us entertain of His actual work.* The great controversy with M. Renan is, that where he sees false pretences, Christians see truth.

---

* The most needed reform in the study of the New Testament is the recognition of the place which the Kingdom of Heaven, as brought in by Jesus Christ, occupies in all its history and doctrine.

It is clear that nothing can exceed the importance of the four Gospels as bearing upon this question. But at the same time there is great danger of too narrow a treatment of their office and authority. We are strongly tempted to affirm *à priori* their absolute truth, and to ground our belief in Christ upon this assumption. Such a method is extremely welcome to unbelieving critics. They on their part seize upon the conclusion, that if any portion of the Gospels can be called in question, we are deprived of our only standing-ground. This is not true: and we ought to prepare ourselves — not, indeed, without anxiety — but without fear, to see the subject of inconsistencies in the Gospels treated in the popular manner of Bishop Colenso's work on the Pentateuch. We have not received Christ on the mere authority of the four Gospels; although, if the record of Him in the Gospels could be shewn to be absurd and impossible, our faith in Him would be rendered indefinitely more difficult.

It is a great advantage* to present clearly to our minds the circumstances of the Church in the first century, when there was no New Testament, in the

---

* Mr. Westcott's excellent book on "The Bible in the Church," puts this in every one's power.

canonical shape, existing. The Church was founded and guided for many years, by oral testimony, and with the **help of** records and letters upon which no **stamp of** sacredness had yet been put. The Gospels and Epistles come to us as representatives of that Apostolic teaching, by the living energy of which the **Church** of Christ was founded. It is not by any means a necessary or even a reasonable presumption **with** regard to them, that they should be preternatu**rally** exempt from error. If you consider them independently of such a presumption, their intrinsi perfection is likely to make the profounder impression.

And here, in the reverent but searching study of **the** sacred writings, there is some humble place for **sermons** and sermon-making. I am not unconscious of the power which tradition and professional duty have over the clerical mind, nor am I prepared to deny the charges of lifelessness and other faults often brought against our sermons. But I know that I **have** questioned no other writings so closely as I **have been led by the** duty of writing sermons **to question those** of the New Testament, and that I **have never had a** stronger sense of responsibility at any moment than when I have been preparing to expound them in **the church.** I say this not merely for myself, but in the name of the clergy generally. And I also say that, apart from the minor critical questions with which few of us have concerned ourselves, the more we study the Gospels, the more we wonder at the subtle harmonies which disclose themselves to us. Are these books, seen in the light of reason and science, casual legends which have succeeded in imposing upon the world? It is precisely when we are opening our minds to light most anxiously that such a notion seems the most monstrous to us. St. John's Gospel is the one which is most contemptuously treated by sceptical critics,—in which the Straussian school detect a mere forgery of the second century, which M. Renan holds to have been written by the Apostle John when his mind had been bewildered by the theosophy of Asia Minor, to gratify a personal dislike to Judas and a personal jealousy of Peter. Now, to speak honestly, I find it difficult to preserve a decent respect even for the intellect of the man who does not recognise in the writings of St. John the sublimest and yet the most human theology which has ever found expression in words, and an account of the nature and thoughts of Christ at once the most utterly unworldly and the most profoundly and intensely consistent. It would be no wisdom to cast away abiding impressions like these at the bidding of a philosophy which affirms acts that we call miraculous to be impossible, or of a criticism which has detected variations in the Gospel narratives. And the proper way for a clergyman to encounter the destructive criticism of the Gospels appears to be to seek, for himself and for his hearers, a more thorough knowledge of their higher qualities.

We may suppose ourselves to be reading the New Testament, by an effort of thought, *as if* we were acquiring from it our *first* knowledge of Christ. The is no doubt that we must owe to its books our deepest and most accurate knowledge of Him. But, as a matter of fact, some image of Christ has been previously present to the mind of every Christian who has ever read the Gospels. Properly speaking, we worship the Christ of whom an unbroken tradition in the Church,—a tradition including the sacred volume,—has borne witness to us. When we endeavour to describe the *real*, and not the logical, evidence on which we believe in Christ, we find it exceedingly difficult to be either strictly definite or exhaustive. Early instruction, the example of the good and wise, the authority of the sacred books, the heavenly glory of the person of Christ, the influence of voices seeming to be from above, the conscious cravings of our own souls, the wants of the world, the spiritual vitality of belief, the results of unbelief, the character of alternative speculation — these and many other reasons blend with one another to create a strong but not always definable pressure upon our minds, and to make us cry out, "Lord, I believe; help Thou my unbelief." This recourse to what is called cumulative evidence, accompanied by a refusal to construct a logical scheme with defined logical supports, is baffling to an opponent, and may look like hiding oneself from attack in an atmospheric cloud. But in confessing the power of such influences, we are only following the reality of things instead of bending reality to the exigencies of argument. On the opposite side to our own, the causes which produce unbelief are also much stronger than the arguments of unbelievers. We know that in demolishing the mythical theory, or the forgery theory, or the insane enthusiasm theory, we are not conquering infidelity. Unbelief, as well as belief, is "in the air."

The character of the evidence which we might expect to have may, perhaps, be brought into a clearer light, by putting our belief in the form of a *hypothesis*. Let us *suppose* the Catholic Faith to be true. Our assumption will then be to this effect. **There is** a living God **in** heaven, whose children we **are, whose** relations with us are spiritual or belong **to the** affections and the will, and who is training us by invisible influences to a childlike knowledge of Himself. There is a Father, a **Son,** and a Holy **Spirit.*** The Son took our whole nature upon Him in the person of Jesus of Nazareth, was visible upon this **earth,** and through death and resurrection re**turned** to the Father. Then He founded a universal society, resting upon the acknowledgment of Himself, and quickened by His own Spirit. Thus He opened avenues by which we are invited to come to **God.** By believing in the Son of God as our Divine Head, and submitting to the Divine Spirit—the one Spirit **of** regenerated humanity as well as of God—

---

* Miss Cobbe has shown forcibly how a negative zeal for the Unity of God may overleap itself and lead to a belief in *Two* Gods. "The Unitarians have given to Christ that position which, practically to us as moral beings, *is* a Divine one; namely, that of our Moral Lord and Teacher, and future Judge. This doctrine involves in itself the essential evil of Trinitarianism; nay, goes beyond it. . . . **To** present to our minds a second Lord, another Master, **Teacher,** Judge, destroys for us the whole *moral* value of the doctrine of the Unity of God. Nay, with all respect, I would urge the question on Unitarians, whether they do not here **fall** into an error worse than that of the Trinitarian? If we are to believe in two Moral Lords,—a great Lord and a lesser Lord,—a King and his Viceregent,—is it not better to believe that these two are one and the same Lord?"—*Broken Lights,* page 96.

we receive the spiritual life which is intended for us. God is great, and has His own methods with His creatures. Is it not clear that, according to this hypothesis, the inducements which create faith in us are likely to be of an extremely subtle and varied kind, and will appeal much more to the conscience and to the affections than to the calculating reason? You have a right to object to the hypothesis; but, as it stands, we are plainly called upon to submit to a living Being, and not to construct an impregnable scheme; and the means must have a natural relation to the end proposed. So that it is an additional argument in favour of the truth of the Gospel, that it depends for its reception on living and spiritual influences rather than upon specific demonstrations.

It is the clear vocation of the Anglican clergy to bear witness to this Gospel of the manifestation of the Son of God in our flesh as God's great Word to men. They are to preach it, if they can, as Divine truth, and to rely upon its truth for its power. Their principle must be that which St. Paul (before modern science had taught men veracity) stated so nobly: "We have renounced the hidden practices of shame, not walking in craftiness, nor handling the word of God deceitfully, but by manifestation of the truth commending ourselves to every conscience of men in the sight of God." Πρὸς πᾶσαν συνείδησιν ἀνθρώπων. **Here is** large scope for our appeals; and the wider **that scope** the more necessary it is that we should ground ourselves on the Living Truth. Of all persons we are perhaps the most sacredly bound not to repudiate free inquiry. The notion that in receiving holy orders we abjured the right or renounced the duty of asking, What is true? is one which ought to excite indignation in our minds. And the larger the freedom of opinion which the formularies of the Church allow, the more we ought to feel bound in honour to be true to our serious convictions. "But the consequences?" **Of** course we must take the consequences. If a clergyman cannot honestly proclaim that the Eternal God sent His Son into the world for the redemption **of** mankind, let him withdraw, whatever it may cost him, from the service of the Church. No doubt, with **this** contingency before us, we are heavily ballasted for free inquiry. If we make any **great** change it **will** not be from levity, but from a sense of duty. But it is the Divine ordinance that **serious acts of** loyalty to conviction should generally involve sacrifices. To give up money and social position is a hard thing, but it sometimes is the duty of other persons as well as of clergymen; and these sacrifices are not by any means the only painful accompaniments of a great change of convictions. Nor ought we in the interest of the Church to deprecate in the slightest degree such faithfulness to truth as might involve secessions. It would be far better that we should have **fifty or five** hundred secessions, if they took place not under persecution but from a sense of honour,* than that we should live in an atmosphere of mistrust.

The two questions with regard to the position of the clergy which are most definitely brought before the public mind by existing controversies are these: How do the clergy stand with reference to the Bible? And how do they stand with reference to the Prayer-Book?

(1) **As to the first of these**, the recent judgment has secured to the clergy the exercise of a freedom which

---

* I do not believe that the Clergy of the Church of England are deficient as a body in honourable feeling. The leading members of the liberal school are certainly not in the habit of *under*-stating their divergences from the received orthodoxy. The tone of their writings has been such **as to excite** ungrounded suspicions, amongst admirers no less than opponents, **as** to their real belief. Any one will see this who compares the impression made by the Essays on **so** fair and sagacious **a** reader as Bishop Thirlwall with the explanations given by Dr. Williams and Mr. Wilson in their arguments **before** the Privy Council.

the great body of the laity supposed them not to possess. It is evident that a clergyman may hold any opinion about the Scriptures which a believer in the Creeds can reasonably desire to entertain. Biblical criticism ceases now to have any special terror of its own. If the critical study of the Scriptures leads a clergyman to disbelieve the Gospel, his difficulty with regard to the law will be not that he rejects the Scriptures, but that he rejects the Gospel. It may be hoped that the sense and acknowledgment of this freedom will give calmness to the searching study of the Bible, without making it less serious. A clergyman ought no longer to be tormented by the fear that if he discovers any error in the Bible he will have to give up his calling and his religion. On the other hand he is not bound to see errors in the Bible. It will be very strange if, not coming to the New Testament with the previous assumption that its great story is impossible, he does not gain a continually increasing impression of its virtual perfectness.

(2) As to the formularies of the Church of England, the whole judgment in the case of the Essayists, including Dr. Lushington's with that of the Privy Council, has shown that they are not so restrictive as many persons had fancied them to be. We have, it

may justly be maintained, formularies of unexampled liberality, with a subscription offensively stringent indeed in the letter, but universally, and therefore honestly, interpreted in a reasonable sense. Whether much is to be gained at this time by liturgical reform is a question upon which different opinions will be entertained. It is absurd and unwise to talk as if our Prayer-Book were too sacred to be touched even by the most reverent hands. But if it come to be admitted by all parties, that the cardinal principle of the Church of England is that which is formulated in the Creeds, the revelation of God in His Son—a principle so central that every other doctrine or institution is subordinate to it and moulded by it—and that by this the Church must stand or fall; it will be felt that this principle will supply an important interpretative power in judging of the sense of formularies, and that, when reform is to be attempted, the true method will be to proceed from this centre outwards to less important details, rather than to attempt to frame new forms of words to meet this difficulty or that.

A critic sitting on the outside of things, and looking round upon the world, will see a number of ecclesiastical communions, each with its formularies, and it may make him smile to observe how each offers its own little book as the solution of the problems of existence. Well: it may be a matter of interest to him to ascertain what amount of agreement there is in these various solutions. On the part of the Church of England, those who are content to be its loyal sons may justly plead that, with the least addition or alloy, this Church has embodied the Catholic Gospel in a national form of worship; and that look where you will, to Italy, to Germany, to America, the old Gospel is still justifying itself, and the national form of worship winning new recommendations. We hardly know what to say to those who regard considerations of history and geography as degrading to religion; we must address our appeals to those who will recognize in history and geography the signs of a Divine Providence.

It is often assumed that the discoveries of modern times, and especially of the present century, have made the old Christian faith untenable. If the Bible, and the Bible traditionally interpreted, were the Christian faith, it might be shewn, it is true, that notions formerly held as matters of faith had been made incredible by the progress of science. But it is clear, for one thing, that many such notions were rather the forms of the imperfect science of the day, than deductions from the simple Gospel. And if we take the Creeds—say, again, the Nicene Creed—as expounding the Christian faith, it is not obvious that it is touched by modern discoveries. Even those which are most disturbing, such as the profoundly interesting and important researches relating to the antiquity and origin of man, come into no direct conflict with the message that God has sent His Son into the world, and has poured out a life-giving Spirit. If I may venture to judge from my own experience, the real and trying "difficulties of belief" are such as have belonged to former ages as well as to this. The knowledge of one city or of a single family-circle is as apt to suggest scepticism as the contemplation of all Asia, Africa, and America. The great moral problems do not require extension of surface for their display. And if new occasions of scepticism have arisen, I am inclined to think that they are more than counterbalanced by the accession which time has also brought to the arguments in favour of faith. The inextinguishable vitality of the Gospel, which is one of its strongest evidences, becomes more remarkable with each new phase of philosophy or social organization which it produces or assimilates. It was said after a visit to Rome, "Christianity *must* be true, or it would have perished under the corruptions of its ministers;" and so we may say, "The Gospel *must* be true, or it would not now be the one most fruitful source of spiritual life in a hundred separate forms."

When we are considering the sceptical tone of our current literature, it is well to remember that Christianity won its way from the first *against* such scepticism. It was not "literary criticism" that made the world Christian. Put our newspapers and magazines in Palestine eighteen centuries ago, and ask yourself what their tone would have been? We have too much of modern Pharisaism; we cannot be without modern representatives of the old Sadduceism. That air of worldly wisdom, which is so thoroughly Sadducean, is peculiarly engendered by the institution of anonymous journalism. A writer who writes in name of a literary "staff" is not at liberty to express his own private beliefs; he must carefully tone down his language to the average level of conviction. And to adopt a modest style when speaking as "We," would be uncomplimentary to his colleagues; the humblest contributor may consider himself bound to represent duly the collective omniscience. Anonymous journalism is, in truth, a perfect machine for grinding out Sadduceeism; and this partly accounts for the remarkable difference that may be perceived between the theological liberalism of the higher class of periodical literature, and the temper shown by the laity in other ways.

For there is very little ground for charging the laity in general with being too speculative in religious matters. There is much greater danger from their want of knowledge and of courage. It is not wonderful that laymen, who are busy with other things and cannot study, should cling with a natural and English conservatism to traditions which they have been taught to respect. The fear is—and there is nothing which we have to dread more at this time—that they may retain this English conservatism when it has become utterly hollow. It is already notorious that men of no genuine belief will adhere outwardly to some peculiarly narrow-minded form of religion as a kind of protection to themselves from the trouble of inquiry. I am persuaded that, much as we all have to fear a "cloke" of religion, there is even more danger of it amongst the laity than amongst the clergy. Certainly the clergy are the most responsible, and will be judged the most severely. We have not only to learn ourselves, but also to help and exhort the laity to learn. I do not say to "teach" them; the laity may learn from the same sources as ourselves. But we are bound to testify that to wrap oneself up, privately sceptical, in an exterior of patronizing conformity, is a very different thing from learning. And it would be a blessed thing if Englishmen generally were awakened to a hearty inquiring interest as to matters of faith. What an encouraging stimulus would thus be given to the clergy! What a different thing would the study of the Bible be! How much more interesting would it be to expound it! Such an awakening may come; there are some symptoms of it now. May God hasten it; and so give the sacred records of His Revelation an honour amongst us which the most idolatrous tradition would be unable to confer!

As regards the following sermons, I feel the impulse, common to all publishers of sermons, to make apologies for them; but as I have nothing special to say, I refrain. I have abridged them to some extent, by omitting almost every thing of a hortatory character, and might perhaps call them lectures rather than sermons.

CONTENTS.

PREFACE. v

SERMON I.

THE JEWISH EXPECTATION OF THE MESSIAH.

ST. MATTHEW XXI. 5.—Tell ye the daughter of Zion, Behold, thy King cometh unto thee. 1

SERMON II.

THE PREACHING OF THE KINGDOM OF HEAVEN.

ST. MARK I. 14, 15.—Now after that John was put in prison, Jesus came into Galilee, preaching the Gospel of the kingdom of God, and saying, The time is fulfilled, and the kingdom of God is at hand: repent ye, and believe the Gospel. . . 16

SERMON III.

THE UNFOLDING OF THE FILIAL GLORY.

ST. JOHN XX. 31.—These are written that ye might believe that Jesus is the Christ, the Son of God. 32

SERMON IV.

THE KINGDOM OF THE SON OF MAN ESTABLISHED.

ST. LUKE XXI. 29—32.—And he spake to them a parable: Behold the fig-tree, and all the trees; when they now shoot forth, ye see and know of your own selves that summer is now nigh at hand. So likewise ye, when ye see these things come to pass, know ye that the kingdom of God is nigh at hand. Verily I say unto you, This generation shall not pass away till all be fulfilled. 50

SERMON V.

THE POWER OF THE DIVINE INFANCY.

St. John I. 18.—No man hath seen God at any time; the only-begotten Son, which is in the bosom of the Father, he hath declared him. 66

SERMON VI.

THE TWO COVENANTS.

Hebrews XII. 24.—Ye are come . . . to Jesus the mediator of the New Covenant. 78

SERMON VII.

JESUS IN THE MIDST OF THE DOCTORS.

St. Luke II. 46.—It came to pass, that after three days they found him in the temple, sitting in the midst of the doctors, both hearing them, and asking them questions. 93

SERMON VIII.

THE MIRACLE OF CANA.

St. John II. 11.—This beginning of miracles did Jesus in Cana of Galilee, and manifested forth his glory. 109

SERMON IX.

THE TEACHING OF JESUS NOT HIS BUT HIS FATHER'S.

St. John VII. 16—18.—Jesus answered them, and said, My doctrine is not mine, but his that sent me. If any man will do his will, he shall know of the doctrine, whether it be of God, or whether I speak of myself. He that speaketh of himself seeketh his own glory; but he that seeketh his glory that sent him, the same is true, and no unrighteousness is in him. 124

SERMON X.

WHY JESUS SPOKE IN PARABLES.

St. Luke VIII. 10.—Jesus said, Unto you it is given to know the mysteries of the kingdom of God: but unto others in parables. 141

SERMON XI.

THE FEEDING OF THE FIVE THOUSAND.

St. John VI. 5.—Whence shall we buy bread, that these may eat? 15

SERMON XII.

CHRIST THE BREAD OF LIFE.

St. John VI. 35.—Jesus said unto them, I am the bread of life: he that cometh to me shall never hunger; and he that believeth on me shall never thirst. 174

SERMON XIII.

DISCIPLES DRAWN TO JESUS BY THE FATHER.

St. John VI. 44.—No man can come to me, except the Father which hath sent me draw him. 189

SERMON XIV.

FROM THE FATHER AND TO THE FATHER.

St. John VI. 61—63.—When Jesus knew in himself that his disciples murmured at it, he said unto them, Doth this offend you? What and if ye shall see the Son of Man ascend up where he was before? It is the Spirit that quickeneth; the flesh profiteth nothing; the words that I speak unto you, they are spirit, and they are life. 204

CONTENTS.

SERMON XV.

REVELATION THE GROUND OF PRAYER.

St. Luke xi. 1.—It came to pass, as he was praying in a certain place, when he ceased, one of his disciples said unto him, Lord, teach **us to pray, as** John also taught his disciples. 221

SERMON XVI.

THE SHADOW OF THE PASSION ON THE LIFE OF JESUS.

St Matthew xvi. 21—24.—From that time forth began Jesus to **shew** unto his disciples, **how that he** must go unto Jerusalem, and suffer many things of the elders and chief priests and scribes, **and** be killed, and be raised again the third day. Then Peter took him, and began to rebuke him, saying, Be it far from thee, Lord: this shall not be unto thee. But he turned, and said unto Peter, Get thee behind me, Satan: thou art an offence unto me: for thou savourest not the things that **be** of God, but those that be of men. Then said Jesus unto **his** disciples, If any man will come after me, let **him** deny himself and take up his cross, and follow me. . . 238

SERMON XVII.

THE ORIGIN AND AUTHORITY OF THE GOSPELS.

St. Matthew ix. 9.—**As** Jesus passed forth from thence, he **saw a man named** Matthew sitting **at the** receipt of custom: **and he saith unto him,** Follow me. And he arose, and followed him. 253

SERMON XVIII.

DIFFICULTIES OF BELIEF.

St. Mark ix. 24.—And straightway the father of the child cried out, and said with tears, Lord, I believe; help thou mine unbelief. 270

SERMON XIX.

ONE GOD AND FATHER OF ALL.

EPHESIANS IV. 6.—One God and Father of all. 286

SERMON XX.

THOU SHALT LOVE THE LORD THY GOD.

ST. MATTHEW XXII. 37, 38.—Jesus said unto him, Thou shalt love the Lord thy God with all thy heart, and with all thy soul, and with all thy mind. This is the first and great commandment. 303

APPENDIX.

THE TESTIMONY OF THE CHURCH AND OF SCRIPTURE AS TO THE POSSIBILITY OF PARDON IN THE FUTURE STATE. . . 319

NOTES 363

I.

THE JEWISH EXPECTATION OF THE MESSIAH.

St. Matthew xxi. 5.

"*Tell ye the daughter of Zion, Behold, thy King cometh unto thee.*"

It will be my endeavour on the Sundays of this Advent season, to sketch rapidly some of the broad historical aspects of that great event which we call the Advent into the world, or the Incarnation of the Son of God.

The appearing of Christ in the world is not an event which can be treated with indifference even by those who see in it nothing specially Divine. As an element in the outward history of mankind, the faith of Christendom is mightier and more commanding than any other of the constituent facts of history. As a system of belief, Christianity claims the attention of the student of philosophy, not only because it is the greatest religion of the world, but because of its present life and pretensions. When historians or philosophers go back to the origin of Christianity and the first germs of the Christian Church, they find a wonderful Life, wonderfully recorded, a Life which inspires such awe and reverence that it easily vindicates its place at the basis of the Christian Church, a Life which is accounted for with simplicity by Christians as being Divine, and for which those who refuse this account of it have to seek some other explanation. This Life of Jesus, narrated in the Four Gospels, what was it? How did it come to pass? What is the meaning of it? What was its direct bearing upon the history of the world?

These are questions which we who are assembled here cannot attempt to discuss in the spirit of historical critics. We cannot see them discussed by others who do not share our belief, without being somewhat pained by the treatment which things most sacred in our eyes are made to undergo. But it is better that sacred names and events should even be pulled to pieces, in attempts to make them fit this theory and that, than that they should be consigned to neglect and contempt. In our day, there is a good deal of such pulling to pieces of those scriptural records which we have been taught to regard as Divinely authentic. Let us believe that, when truth is honestly sought, the seeking will not go unrewarded; and let us be thankful when we are led, even by speculations with which we cannot sympathize, to give livelier attention to the things we reverence, or to see them under some new and instructive aspect.

In all the endeavours that have been made to account for the Life of Jesus without admitting Him to be truly the Son of God sent from the Father, it has been necessary to bring into view with care and emphasis whatever there was in Jewish history and belief and literature, to *prepare* for such a character as that of Jesus. It has been shewn that there was much in the history and writings of the Jewish people, which might under favourable circumstances tend to the production of such a personality as that of Jesus, whether Jesus was a real historical person, or lived only in the popular imagination. Now, all information of this kind ought to be most welcome to us. It does not in the slightest degree enhance the glory of Christ's appearance in the world, to suppose that it was abrupt and had no relations with what was going on before. So far as the Bible is concerned, every part of it bears witness in behalf of order and gradual progression. The more we can discern of connexion and preparation in the whole sacred history, the more we enter into God's true method of revealing Himself. We can well afford to be thankful to any one who will make out most satisfactorily that the condition of the Jewish world when Jesus appeared was exactly that into which His appearing would fit. All such preparation of the world for Christ we may contemplate with interest and profit: it is quite another thing to believe that the preparatory conditions of the world could of themselves *produce* Christ, however ready they were to receive Him from heaven.

It is to the preparation of the world for Christ that I desire to lead your attention this morning.

It would be possible to notice movements in the *Gentile* world, as well as in the Jewish, which led up naturally to the appearing of Christ. But these are so much less conspicuous and less important than those which belong to Jewish history, that it will be better for us to pass them by. Amongst the Jews, the grand preparation for the appearing of Christ was the direct expectation of the Messiah, with the ideas which attached themselves to that expectation.

We can see from the Gospels how deep and general was the impression amongst the Jews of our Saviour's age, that the Messiah was shortly to manifest himself. This expectation of the Messiah had come down through several centuries.

We trace the first conscious and lively expression of it in the writings of the prophets of the kingly period of Jewish history. David and his successors, reigning by God's appointment over his people, were regarded by the prophetical mind as images of an Invisible King, the Son of God, reigning in Zion through His visible representatives, and likely to manifest Himself in some heavenly glory. In the older generations of Israelite history, hints were given from time to time of a Mediator, through whom the Absolute God spoke and acted. But in the kingly period the idea of a *King* ruling and triumphing— an unseen King using visible persons as his instruments—grew into some distinctness.

The great Captivity, when the people were carried away to Babylon, had a remarkable effect upon the prophetical anticipations of the Jews. Their thoughts were then fixed upon their restoration to their own country. The sufferings which they had to endure deepened and purified their feelings, and the hope which belonged to the children of the Covenant burnt only the more brightly amidst the gloom which surrounded them. A future glory of their race was continually before their eyes. Israel was to be exalted through the favour of Jehovah, and the other nations of the earth were to pay willing homage to the seed of Abraham. By the Prophets of this age, the worth and glory of suffering, especially of voluntary suffering for others, were more clearly discerned; and in them the hints of a suffering Messiah are most abundant.

The captivity was followed by a restoration, of which we have some account in the books of Ezra and Nehemiah. A portion of the people were brought back from Babylon, and settled in their own city and land; and there the worship and customs of their fathers were re-established. Ezra bore a very important part in this work of restoration. It was he who collected and arranged the sacred books of the Old Testament,—those at least which were then in existence,—and fixed them in what we call a canon for the reverence and the study of the people. This was the beginning of that careful professional study of the Scriptures which was one of the characteristics of our Lord's time. The old language in which the Scriptures were written was rendered into the vernacular. A body of men called Scribes devoted themselves expressly to the copying and illustrating of the sacred books. The people learnt to make much of the law which had been given by Moses, and to follow with careful precision many of its enactments.

The Jews acquired a pride in their *religion*, which took the place of the older pride which had rather made the national glory its object. After the captivity, they fell no longer into imitations of the idolatries of their neighbours, such as had so continually called down the anger of Jehovah upon them in former ages.

For about two centuries after the restoration, Judea was subject to the Persian Empire; and during that time we find no strong development of the expectation of a Messiah. But the whole character of the religion which prevailed at Jerusalem and in Judea in our Lord's day,—the use of synagogues, the reading of the Law and the Prophets, the minute study of Scripture, and of traditions which grew up beside it,—was matured during this period. And you will easily remember how largely the life of Jesus Christ was affected by the religious institutions and habits amidst which he lived.

The period of Persian dominion was followed by a century and a half, during which Judea was subject to the Greek sovereignties which grew out of the conquests of Alexander the Great. During this time the Jews were widely dispersed in Asia. Their Scriptures were translated into Greek, and the doctrines contained in them were brought into contact with Greek thought. Alexandria in Egypt became a very important centre of Jewish action.

This Greek period is chiefly characterized by the rise of those sects which are so familiar to us in the pages of the Gospels. Not much is known about them, beyond what we learn from the New Testament. The Sadducees were the rationalists, or extreme liberals of Judea,—breaking loose from the narrow bondage of the ritual law, proclaiming a philosophical liberty, and prone to intellectual pride and to unbelief. The Pharisees and the Sadducees were correlative to one another: we could hardly understand the one sect as existing without the other. The Sadducees protested against the narrowness of the Pharisees, against their bondage to rules, against their Jewish exclusiveness. The Pharisees maintained with a religious jealousy the sacredness of the law and of the Jewish worship, and were urged by the dangerous laxity of the Sadducees into still greater strictness. A third sect arose about the same time, which is not mentioned in the New Testament, but is called by the name of the Essenes. This sect is worthy of our notice, because it has been often said that Jesus was himself an Essene; and it is certain that in many respects he must have had more sympathy with the Essenes than he could have with the rest of the Jews. The Essenes formed themselves into communities living in a simple unworldly manner, withdrawn as much as possible, though not entirely, from the business and cares of the world, occupying themselves with spiritual religious exercises, and making much of mutual love and brotherhood. They represented the whole monastic tendency of Jewish life, with very much that was beautiful and good in their ways,—with the one radical fault, to which Jesus never gave the slightest countenance, of separating themselves from the calling and the interests of their brethren, and choosing a vocation for themselves.

The Greek period, we may say then, besides its effect in *dispersing* the Jews, and blending them with other nations, left these *sects* as a legacy which the age of Jesus inherited. But it was not in the nature of the life of this period to stir into activity the national expectation of a Messiah. This hope must for a while have slumbered.

Then followed another period, marked by struggles for independence, under what are called the Hasmonean or Maccabean Princes. It is always to be observed that the prophetical aspirations of the Jews correspond very closely to the circumstances of their history. This is one sign of the *order* of God's revelations. No prophecy came coldly down from heaven as a mere enigma for the time at which it was spoken. It effervesced rather out of the hot agitations of a patriot's heart. So it was during the Maccabean century of the Jewish history. It was at this time, when the hearts of true Israelites were most stirred by the old national faith, by the old hopes of the covenant, that the expectation of the Messiah took shape and utterance in the universal heart of the nation.

It is supposed by many, that it was at this time that the book of Daniel appeared. There are great difficulties as to the age and character of this book, which all who have studied it are willing to admit. It seems undoubtedly to profess to be written in the days of Nebuchadnezzar, Belshazzar, and Cyrus. But there are very strong arguments for placing parts of it, at least, in the age of which I am now speaking; and one of these is, that the character of its predictions resembles the whole class of aspirations, which unquestionably belonged to the age of the national Jewish struggle against the successors of Alexander. There is another book, similar in some remarkable respects to the book of Daniel, in which there is the same account of the Messiah which appears first in the book of Daniel. This book—the book of Enoch, —is still extant; and it is believed to be that from which St. Jude quotes in his Epistle. "Enoch also, the seventh from Adam, prophesied of these, saying, Behold, the Lord cometh with ten thousand of his saints, to execute judgment upon all." The books of Daniel and of Enoch contain the Messianic ideas, or the conceptions relating to the nature, the office, and the work of the Messiah, which were current in Judea at the time when our Lord came, and which are, to so large an extent, taken up in the New Testament, as fulfilled in the Advent of Jesus Christ, the Son of God.

Thus, the name by which Jesus chose oftenest to designate himself, is that of the Son of Man. Now this is one of the titles of Messiah in both these books. Daniel says, (vii. 13,) "I saw in the night visions, and, behold, one like the Son of Man came with the clouds of heaven, and came to the ancient of days." The following passage from the book of Enoch embodies the same thought. "I saw in heaven one, ancient of days, and his head was white as wool; and with him was another, whose countenance was as the appearance of a man, and full of grace, like to one of the holy angels. And I asked one of the angels who went with me and showed me all hidden things, of that Son of Man, who he was, and whence he was, and wherefore he went with the ancient of days. And he answered me, and spoke to me, This is the Son of Man, to whom righteousness belongeth, with whom righteousness dwelleth, and who revealeth all the treasures of that which is concealed, because the Lord of Spirits hath chosen him; whose lot before the Lord of Spirits hath surpassed all, through his uprightness for ever. And this Son of Man, whom thou hast seen, shall raise the kings and mighty men from their beds, and the powerful even from their thrones; and shall unloose the bands of the powerful, and break in pieces the teeth of sinners."* The Son of Man, we are told in this book, was hidden with God before his manifestation. "Aforetime he, the Son of Man, was hidden, whom the Most High kept in the presence of his power and revealed to the elect." He is also "the Righteous One," "chosen of God for his uprightness," "the Elect One, according to God's good pleasure:" "the Anointed," "the Son of Man," "the Son of Woman," while also still "the Son of God."

The advent of this Messiah is to be in majesty and glory, to deliver the good, and to overwhelm the

---

* The quotations from the Book of Enoch are taken from Mr. Westcott's Introduction to the Study of the Gospels, Ch. II. The Sermon was preached before the publication of Part IV. of Bishop Colenso's work on the Pentateuch.

evil. "In those days shall a change be wrought for the holy and the elect; the light of day shall dwell upon them, and majesty and honour shall turn to them. And on the day of distress, ruin shall be heaped upon sinners."

We find in the book of Enoch many passages that remind us of the great predictions of Jesus, uttered concerning Jerusalem and the world, and also of the prophecies of the book of Revelation. Thus the seer beholds a period of violence, a time of "the sword," which will precede the final establishment of Messiah's kingdom. "The sword is given that judgment and righteousness might be executed on them who act with violence, and the sinners given over into the hands of the righteous." " And the hearts of the saints were full of joy that the number of righteousness was fulfilled, and the prayer of the righteous heard, and the blood of the righteous required before the Lord of Spirits." After this "the former heaven shall vanish and pass away, and a new heaven shall appear, and all the powers of heaven shall give light for ever sevenfold. And after that shall be many weeks without number in goodness and righteousness, and sin shall be no more named for ever and ever." "And it shall come to pass in these days, that the elect and holy children shall descend from the heights of heaven, and join their Lord with the children of men. And from henceforth there will be nothing that corrupts any more; for He, the Son of Man, has appeared, and sits upon the throne of His Majesty, and all evil shall vanish and pass away before His face." "And the chosen One shall dwell among His chosen people." "And they shall be arrayed in the robe of life; and the Lord of Spirits shall dwell with them, and they shall dwell with that Son of Man, and eat with Him, and lie down and rise up for ever and ever."

It is rather startling, at first, to find phrases like these, which we are accustomed to associate exclusively with our sacred books, existing before in a book which is not included in our sacred volume. But, as I have said, there is nothing really to disturb us in finding that the teaching of our Lord and of His Apostles is not abruptly severed from what had before been occupying the minds of the people. What we have to observe is this, that our Lord took to himself the name about which associations like these were already clinging. When He appeared amongst His countrymen, instead of saying, I am one of whom you never heard before, and going on to explain who he was, he quietly spoke of Himself as the Son of Man. The generations before our Lord came had been thoroughly penetrated by the expectation of One, such as the book of Enoch describes, who should come to execute judgment in the earth. Many of their notions might be mistaken; these might be corrected; but on the whole, the expectation was a right one, sown in the minds of the people by God Himself, and Jesus of Nazareth when he came was the fulfilment of it.

It is an undeniable fact of history, that this expectation of the advent of a regal Son of Man, was the occasion of many a pretended Messiah rising up and claiming to be the Prince who was looked for. The New Testament mentions some, and refers to others. It is, therefore, an easy thing for an unbeliever to say, "Jesus of Nazareth was one of these. Others failed to establish anything like a successful position. He happened to succeed." Yes, but the question is, why he succeeded when others failed? Are the facts of his history and character symptoms of a pretender, or signs of one who was true? The history of the age, as we have seen, offers us a choice of alternatives. The whole mind of the people was bent on the coming of the Messiah; the sacred books were searched in the narrow spirit of the Biblical study of that time, for minute tokens of place and circumstance by which His coming might be interpreted. Pious men and pious women were waiting in clear anticipation for the vision of Him who was to come. The common people had some notion that, when the Messiah came, He would appear in the clouds of Heaven, clearing them asunder with a glorious apparition, and descending in irresistible might upon the earth. All the Jews believed that the advent of the Messiah would be for the glory and deliverance of their nation.

At the crisis or in the midst of this general expectation, one appeared who openly professed to be the Sent from God.

Was He the mere product of the popular longings?

Was He the genuine fulfilment of a Divinely inspired hope?

These are the questions which the world has to answer. They were propounded first to the Jesus of the time. "Art thou He that should come, or do we look for another?" This was the question which openly or silently was addressed to Jesus by Scribes and Pharisees, by devout Essenes, by common Galilean multitudes.

The correspondences which I have just been bringing into view, do not at all enable us, of themselves, to choose our answer. Suppose that they were closer than they are. Suppose there was hardly a word in the Gospels which was not to be found in other books like that of Enoch. The unbeliever might say, 'We see nothing original in this professed Advent. It merely attempts to meet the popular expectations.' But we might also say, We perceive a very striking agreement between what went before and what has come after. The resemblance which we admit, instead of proving that God did not send Jesus of Nazareth, proves to us that God *also* sent prophets before Him, to teach the people to look for Him. We can contend that such preparation is more worthy of God, more in harmony with all God's ways, than the absence of it would have been.

Our answer will have to be determined by the consideration of what Jesus has actually demonstrated Himself to be. If we believe Him to be truly the Son of the Living God, then, as I have urged, it is both interesting and instructive to dwell on the gradual preparations made for His appearing. Such a contemplation commends to us the whole order and method of God's Revelation, and tends to strengthen our faith in His actual dealings with men.

But there was not such an entire conformity as I have said was conceivable between the popular expectations of the time and the facts of our Lord appearing. Putting aside the intimations contained in the prophetical books of the Canon, we discern in the prevailing notions concerning the Messiah, an unmistakeably superficial, worldly, and carnal stamp, when compared with the character of Christ as described in the Gospels. The counterfeit Messiahs, who were really the product of the popular expectation, answered faithfully enough to their origin. They gathered multitudes about them, made themselves as great as they could, and raised insurrections against the Roman power. How are we to explain the mystery that Jesus of Nazareth, whilst calling Himself the Son of Man and professing to fulfil to the utmost the Messianic prophecies, took pains to subordinate Himself, refused to accept the offered adhesion of great men and of multitudes, chose deliberately the part of One who humbled himself and suffered, and altogether declined to head or take part in an insurrection? How,—except on the supposition that Jesus was a far more Divine Person than the People were able to imagine? And can we confess him to have been peculiarly Divine, and not believe Him to have been what He declared Himself to be?

II.

THE PREACHING OF THE KINGDOM OF HEAVEN.

St. Mark i. 14, 15.

"*Now after that John was put in prison, Jesus came into Galilee, preaching the Gospel of the kingdom of God, and saying, The time is fulfilled, and the kingdom of God is at hand: repent ye, and believe the Gospel.*"

I spoke, last Sunday morning, of that preparation for the coming of Christ which was to be discerned in the previous history of the Jewish people. This preparation consisted mainly in the Jewish expectation of a Messiah,—an expectation which, in different forms and degrees, characterized the whole history of the seed of Abraham. I shewed that the expectation of a Messiah was peculiarly strong in the age in which our Lord appeared, so strong as to give birth to false Christs, who sought to meet the Messianic hopes of the people, and that Jesus appropriated to Himself some of the most definite terms in which this expectation clothed itself. I mentioned that by some historical inquirers the ideas and hopes which were prevalent in that age are considered sufficient of themselves to account for the life of Jesus, and all that has been associated with that life; and I urged that the way to meet such theories is not to forget or underrate the Messianic longings which preceded the appearing of Jesus Christ, but to inquire whether the character and the words and the works of Christ support most strongly the belief that He was the mere product of those longings, or the belief that He came down from heaven to satisfy them with a higher fulfilment than they ever dreamt of.

I now propose, in two sermons, to touch upon the leading historical characteristics of our Lord's appearing, and, in a fourth, to speak of that establishment of His Kingdom, to which the discourses and the writings of the New Testament so distinctly point.

The appearing of Jesus Christ may naturally be divided, I think, into two parts, and the first of these will be our subject this morning.

Looking at the earlier part of our Lord's life and ministry, we perceive that His prominent work,—that which He professed to do, and which He occupied Himself in doing,—was *the manifesting of the Kingdom of Heaven.*

If we were dealing with the personal life or biography of Jesus Christ, we should begin, as two of the Gospels do, with His birth. But when we are considering how His life enters into the history of the time, it is more natural to begin with the mission of John the Baptist. It is thus that the narratives of St. Mark and St. John begin. St. Mark says that "the beginning of the Gospel of Jesus Christ, the Son of God . . . was John baptizing in the wilderness,

C

and preaching the baptism of repentance for the remission of sins." St. John says, "There was a man sent from God, whose name was John. He came to **bear witness** of that Eternal Word who became flesh and dwelt among us." **In** the other two Gospels the narratives of the birth and infancy of Jesus are introductions prefixed to the Gospel history, the his**tory** itself beginning in St. Matthew thus: "In those **days came** John the Baptist, preaching in the wilderness of Judea, and saying, Repent ye, for the Kingdom of Heaven is **at** hand;" in St. Luke thus, "Now in the fifteenth year of **the** reign of Tiberius Cæsar... the word of God came unto John, the son of Zacharias, in the wilderness; and he came into all the country about Jordan, preaching the baptism of repentance for the remission of sins."

John the Baptist, then, presented himself before his countrymen with an announcement. Speaking as one who had received his information from heaven, he said to them, "The Kingdom of God, or the Kingdom of Heaven, is at hand." The kingdom of which **he** spoke had been plainly mentioned in the book of Daniel. In the interpretation of Nebuchadnezzar's dream (ii. 44.), we have these words: "In the days of these kings shall the God of heaven set up a kingdom which shall never be destroyed: and the kingdom shall **not be** left **to** other people, but it shall break in pieces **and** consume all these kingdoms, and it shall stand **for** ever." And again (vii. 13.), "I saw in the night visions; and, behold, one like the Son of Man came with **the clouds of** heaven, and came **to** the

Ancient of Days, and they brought him near before Him. And there was given Him dominion and glory, and a kingdom, that all people, nations, and languages, should serve Him; His dominion is an everlasting dominion, which shall not pass away, and His kingdom that which shall not be destroyed." The name, therefore, of a heavenly kingdom was not new to the Jews. It suggested to them both the old glories of their race, when they had Jehovah Himself and no other for their king, and also the hopes which their more recent prophets had stirred up concerning the future. The kingdom which they had been taught to look for—so John, the son of Zacharias assured them—was at hand. He bade them prepare for it; and the preparation which he enjoined upon them was that of repentance and of receiving a baptism of forgiveness at his hands. If they would behold the kingdom and enter into it as its subjects, they must put away their sins and receive God's forgiveness.

This was the peculiar preaching of John the Baptist. It seems probable, from what we read in St. John's Gospel, that the Baptist spoke to the people of high spiritual truths, and especially that he bore witness to them of the heavenly light which had always been shining into their hearts; but this testimony was not peculiar to him. The special calling which distinguished him from other prophets was that of a herald of the Messianic kingdom. By him, a representative of the old prophetical order, a message was spread throughout Judea, that a kingdom of God, in which another than he was to rule, was about to be manifested.

And as John was the herald of the new kingdom, so it was he by whom Jesus of Nazareth was first personally introduced to his fellow-countrymen. It was part of the Divine method in the incarnation of the Son of God, that the Redeemer should not bring an attestation of Himself to men in a blaze of glory and power, which should prove Him to have come from heaven; but that He should Himself come to the prophet who was baptizing the people in Jordan in the name of the new kingdom, and should there be marked out by him to his followers as the Person in whom the coming of the kingdom was to be fulfilled. The human form in which the Divine glory was tabernacled was not to be thrust upon the people abruptly, as superhuman; they were to learn gradually to recognise the Godhead shining through the perfect humanity. For a while, the Kingdom of Heaven was to be the object presented to the minds of the people, rather than the Person of the Son of God. In accordance with this method, when Jesus Himself after His baptism began to speak to the people, He continued to make the same announcement which the Baptist had made. He, too, proclaimed, "The time is fulfilled, and the Kingdom of God is at hand; repent ye, and believe the Gospel." This kingdom was the subject of the good news which Jesus announced. He kept *Himself*, if we may say so, subordinate to *the Kingdom*. He was anointed, he said, to proclaim the good news of the Kingdom.

To most minds there is some indefiniteness and obscurity in the phrase *The Kingdom of Heaven*. It is very common to say that this phrase in the New Testament means several different things. The most proper meaning for it, people have thought, is that of a place of future bliss; but it is really never used in this sense. It is much truer to say, as it is often said, that it means the Church; but we see that we could not always substitute *the Church* for the Kingdom of Heaven in the Gospels, without introducing confusion. No other word, in fact, would do so well as "the Kingdom of Heaven," or would represent precisely that idea which is understood by a kingdom. The Jew, perhaps, who heard the words of the Baptist and of Jesus, was less troubled than we are to define to himself the meaning of the Kingdom of Heaven. It brought to his mind the government of Israel by the Lord God. An ordinary Jew, when told that the Kingdom of Heaven was at hand, would probably expect that the rule of the Romans, and all other secular dominion, was to cease at once in Palestine, and that, manifested through the Messiah, the will of Jehovah was to be their law and guide.

A difference between John the Baptist and our Lord, in their character of prophets of the Kingdom of Heaven, soon began to manifest itself. We are expressly told that John did no miracle. Jesus, on the contrary, no sooner began to proclaim the Kingdom of Heaven, than He began also to do acts of deliverance and blessing. St. Matthew, in his fourth chapter, thus sums up the works which Jesus did in the beginning of His ministry. "And Jesus went about all Galilee, teaching in their synagogues, and preaching the Gospel of the Kingdom, and healing all manner of sickness and all manner of disease among the people. And his fame went throughout all Syria; and they brought unto him all sick people that were taken with divers diseases and torments, and those which were possessed with devils, and those which were lunatic, and those which had the palsy; and he healed them." In the life of Jesus, the declaring of the Kingdom of Heaven is always thus connected with the healing of diseases. The people were intended to see the powers of the Kingdom actually exercised in these acts of emancipation done upon the bodies and spirits of men. "If I," said Jesus, "with the finger of God cast out devils, no doubt the Kingdom of God is come upon you." One of the early acts of the public ministry of Jesus was to choose twelve disciples to be specially associated with Himself. To them, we are told, "he gave power against unclean spirits, to cast them out, and to heal all manner of sickness and all manner of disease." Those twelve Jesus sent forth, giving them this commission. "Go not into the way of the Gentiles, and into any city of the Samaritans enter ye not; but go rather to the lost sheep of the house of Israel. And as ye go, preach, saying, *The Kingdom of Heaven is at hand.* Heal the sick, cleanse the lepers, raise the dead, cast out devils: freely ye have received, freely give."

These were the chosen signs employed at that stage of our Lord's Advent to prove that the Kingdom of Heaven was indeed preparing to establish itself upon the earth. When John the Baptist, lying disheartened in the prison into which Herod had cast him, longed for some assurance direct from Him to whom he had borne witness, and sent two of His disciples to ask him, "Art thou he that should come, or do we look for another? Jesus answered, and said unto them, Go and show John again those things which ye do hear and see: The blind receive their sight, the lame walk, the lepers are cleansed, and the deaf hear, the dead are raised up, and the poor have the Gospel preached unto them. And blessed is he, whosoever shall not be offended in me." These last words, "Blessed is he, whosoever shall not find a stumbling-block in me," refer to what was then, and became increasingly, a great difficulty to the Jews in the ministry of Jesus, that He, personally, was a poor and lowly man, whose family were known to them, and that He had not come down from heaven in any such way as they supposed the Messiah might come to inaugurate the Kingdom of Heaven.

No doubt the working of miracles compensated in a great degree, so long as they were exhibited freely before the eyes of the people, for the humble station of Jesus of Nazareth; and if He had chosen, He could soon have hidden all the obscurity of His origin in the glory of supernatural achievements. But it was not the design of Jesus to magnify Himself. As we have seen, He wrought the miracles, not so much—at least in the earlier part of His ministry—to prove what *He* could do, as to show that the Kingdom of Heaven was coming down. And He wrought His mighty works sparingly, confining them in the main to acts of healing, although the people craved some more theatrical exercises of His power, and often refusing to work miracles at all when He saw that they were tending to produce an undesirable effect. For we cannot too often observe that Jesus did not seek to gain adherents to Himself, through the display of His supernatural powers. At times, the people were convinced that He was truly the long-looked-for Messiah, and they were ready to follow Him with the devotion of their lives and to make Him their king. But Jesus would not have this kind of support. He pointed from Himself upwards. A belief that stopped in His Person was not what He desired. His purpose was to kindle, through what He did and said, a belief in the invisible kingdom, and in His Father in heaven whose that kingdom was.

As those works of healing which we have been considering were the representative actions of our Lord during His Galilean ministry, so there was a typical class of discourses representing what He taught. These are the Parables. At one time this method of teaching was so exclusively used by Jesus, that the Evangelist not only says He taught the multitudes in parables, but that without a parable He did not speak to them. Now, speaking generally, we might say with sufficient accuracy that the parables of our Lord have *one* subject, viz. the Kingdom of Heaven. You remember how large a proportion of the parables begin with a phrase which expressly defines them as illustrations of the Kingdom of Heaven. "The Kingdom of Heaven is like unto a grain of mustard-seed, is like unto treasure hid in a field, is like unto leaven which a woman took." In the pattern parable, that of the Sower, the word, which is represented by the seed, is called the word of the Kingdom; and our Lord's first reference in this parable was to that word, the proclamation of the Kingdom of Heaven, which He was Himself sowing on the various spiritual soils around Him. When the disciples asked their Master why He taught in parables, His answer was, that to them it was given to know the mysteries of the Kingdom of Heaven, but to the multitudes those mysteries, the mysteries of the same invisible kingdom, must be clothed in parables.

When we inquire what were the characteristics of the kingdom which our Lord sought chiefly to set forth in His teaching, we find that a great part of what He said had reference to the *spirituality* which was the essential nature of His kingdom. In this He was correcting with heavenly wisdom the carnal notions and expectations of His countrymen. On the one hand, it was impossible to entertain too exalted ideas of the kingdom which Jesus was come to establish on the earth. It was in very truth the kingdom of the Eternal God, the Ruler of all things and all men; it was the kingdom of Him who gave nature its laws, and controlled its processes; it was the kingdom of the Father who called all men His children: it was destined to triumph over all that opposed itself to its march. The Galilean prophet of the kingdom spoke with authority when He proclaimed it. But, on the other hand, the sphere of the kingdom was not the visible world; its force was not in external things; its glory was not in riches or temporal dominion; the high places in it were not for those who would exalt themselves and press down their fellows. It was a kingdom of the unseen world, in which thought and will and the affections are the true realities; a kingdom of the spirit; a kingdom in which the supreme power and honour belonged to love and service. In order that such a kingdom might become known and real amongst men, it was necessary that it should come unattended by pomp and worldly greatness; that it should choose the lowliest elements for its outward symbols and its nascent organization; that He, in whom the kingdom was to be established, should prove His claim to it by voluntary humility and sacrifice. Jesus made it clear to those who had thoughts of joining themselves to the kingdom which He announced, that they could only become subjects of it by spiritual illumination, and by the submission of the whole inward life to the principle of service and sacrifice.

Who must not feel that the kingdom which presented itself in this character could be no mere product of the fermenting imaginations of a fanatical people, but must indeed have come to them from heaven? It is not a sign of earthly origin, that the kingdom which Jesus proclaimed was an answer to Jewish aspirations;—that, whilst it answered those aspirations, it also humbled, baffled, and purified them, is a sure sign of its heavenly origin. It is not difficult to understand what a constant struggle our Lord's testimony as to the nature of His kingdom had to maintain against the instincts and wishes of all who surrounded Him. It was not only the simple rustic multitudes of Galilee who thought that a king was a king, and that if their fellow-townsman was indeed the bringer of deliverance to Israel, He must take up His sceptre, and put on His crown, and surround Himself with supporters, and wage war against the legions of Rome. It was not only a highly-instructed Nicodemus, who, when he flattered himself that he detected signs of a real divine power working by the hands of the Galilean peasant, and offered his secret support to the carrying out of the scheme of the kingdom, required to be taught that the kingdom asked not for secret support and patronage, but for the submission of the inward man to a Divine cleansing from sin, and to the vital energy of the Divine Spirit. The very disciples of Jesus, those who had from the beginning taken Him at His word, whose desire was not to patronize Him but to follow Him, were continually lapsing into carnal notions about the kingdom, and indulging ambition for themselves and for their Master, which He as continually suppressed. On one memorable occasion our Lord had been presenting to His disciples the true glories of His kingdom, declaring how heaven and earth were united in Him, and upon Him a Church should be built up against which the gates of hell should not prevail, and promising to Peter, as the representative confessor, the keys by which the Kingdom of Heaven was to be opened to mankind. And then, without having in Himself any consciousness of contradiction, He spoke of the sufferings and humiliation through which he was about to pass. The very apostle who had made the confession and had received the benediction could not bear to think of his Master as thus condescending to suffer, and exclaimed, " Be it far from thee, Lord, this shall not be unto thee." But Jesus sternly answered, " Get thee behind me, Satan : thou art an offence unto me : for thou savourest not the things that be of God, but those that be of men." Those " things of men," how natural they are to the human heart, how difficult it was for the twelve great princes of the Kingdom of Heaven to accept such an exaltation as consorted with the true kingly honour of their Lord ! How they must have grieved Him when they strove amongst themselves, and came to Him asking, Who is the greatest in the Kingdom of Heaven ? And what a heavenly answer was that which He gave them, when he called a little child unto Him, and set him in the midst of them and said, " Verily I say unto you, except ye be converted, and become as little children, ye shall not enter into the Kingdom of Heaven. Whosoever, therefore, shall humble himself, as this little child, the same is greatest in the Kingdom of Heaven." More than once Jesus used this beautiful illustration of the lowliness which was the very ground of His kingdom. When His disciples would have protected Him from being troubled by those who brought Him little children to bless, He was much displeased, and said to them, "Suffer the little children to come to me, and forbid them not; for of such is the Kingdom of God. Verily I say unto you, whosoever shall not receive the Kingdom of God as a little child, he shall not enter therein." His treatment of the poor and afflicted, and even of those sinners who had not had advantages, and were despised by the more righteous, gave similar testimony to the character of His kingdom. It was a hard kingdom for the rich and proud to enter into: it was for the lowly and meek. And, therefore, the Lord of the kingdom shewed forth in a wonderful manner His own lowliness and meekness, consenting to become as a servant, bearing hardships and sorrows, and always proving the truth of those words, "I am meek and lowly in heart," with which he invited the weary and heavy-laden to come to Him.

I have endeavoured this morning to confine our attention to the earlier and what may be called the Galilean portion of our Lord's life, which seems to be distinguished by some marked characteristics from that which followed. During this earlier period I think we may regard Jesus as veiling His own person and nature much more than he did afterwards. He was seeking to awaken the hearts and to open the eyes of his countrymen to the reality and to the genuine characteristics of that heavenly kingdom which they had learned to expect. He did this previously to bringing out distinctly His own relation to the Father as the only-begotten Son of God. The earlier aspects of the Kingdom of Christ and of God are more external than those which are afterwards presented to us. But the simpler teaching remains always precious and indispensable to us. It is most needful to ourselves, at this present time, to remember that the Son of God came to establish a heavenly kingdom, and to make us citizens and subjects in it; that the question which the Gospel puts to us is not whether we will become adherents and supporters of a certain Master, but whether, casting off our carnal pride, disregarding the fashions of the world and the opinions of men, asking God our Father to cleanse us with His loving mercy from all that has defiled us, humbling ourselves to be enlightened and moved by the Spirit of God and of our brethren, we will thus, like little children, enter into a kingdom which only the Spirit can make visible to us. It is well for us to meditate upon the claims which the invisible kingdom puts forth over all that is visible, to remember how Christ illustrated the powers of His kingdom by expelling disease and all the disorders which afflict humanity, and what wonderful relations of analogy and kinship are shown by His parables to exist between the laws of the spiritual kingdom and the laws of the natural kingdom. It is well to be reminded of what sort our ambition must be, if we would be followers of them who followed Christ, to know that we must seek to excel in humility; that, as the Master was amongst His disciples as a waiting servant, so of the disciples he that will be the greatest must strive to be the most sincere and hearty in self-sacrifice. There are rewards in that kingdom which Jesus of Nazareth has received from the Father, and no one who serves will fail of his reward; but these rewards, which in themselves are spiritual and partake of God's nature, are given with exact justice to those who forget and deny themselves the most, and who therefore are the least covetous of personal and solitary distinctions. Let us pray that this heavenly kingdom, with its laws and its treasures, may be revealed in living reality to our eyes, and that knowing it we may honour and love it. God grant that we may be purged of earthly vanities, of selfish ambition, of indolent greediness; so that we may be true disciples of the meek and lowly Jesus, and may with Him inherit the kingdom prepared from the foundation of the world.

III.

THE UNFOLDING OF THE FILIAL GLORY.

St. John xx. 31.

"*These are written,* that ye might believe that Jesus is the Christ, the Son of God."

With a view of considering the life of Christ as a whole, according to the account of it preserved in the sacred writings, I have adopted a division of the history into two parts, which has been very generally recognised, and which helps us much in an endeavour to appreciate the significance of that life. Last Sunday, we were occupied with the first of these two parts, or periods. Let me remind you of its distinguishing characteristics, before going on to speak of the second.

Our Lord's public ministry, or the historical part of His life, begins with His receiving baptism from John. He then took up the proclamation of the Baptist, and made it His own. John the Baptist had founded a call to repentance upon the announcement of the near approach of the Kingdom of God. Jesus repeated precisely the same announcement.

He gave the people to understand that John and He were both heralds of the same heavenly revelation. But He also made it manifest that in Him the kingdom was coming nearer than during John's time. He began to do wonderful works of healing and deliverance, as express signs of the living powers of the kingdom. He gathered about Him followers, from whom He selected the symbolical number of twelve, giving them commissions to act with power in the name of the kingdom. He laboured in word and act, making use of every kind of illustration, to lead both His chosen disciples and the multitudes around Him into some apprehension of the nature— especially of the spiritual nature—of the heavenly kingdom. Whilst, in the course of His ministry, His own personality came out inevitably into prominence, it seemed to be the desire of Jesus to direct the thoughts of His hearers to the kingdom, rather than to draw them upon Himself.

That part of the life and ministry of Jesus which is distinguished by this aim, is further marked by having *Galilee* almost exclusively for its scene. We are to think of our Lord as living chiefly on the shores of the Sea of Galilee; sometimes in the populous villages or towns which surrounded it; sometimes on its waters with the fishermen who gained their living from it; sometimes up in the hills which rose from its banks. The population with which Jesus had to do in Galilee was comparatively rustic and simple. The life in Galilee forms the principal subject of the first three Gospels, which hardly speak of our Lord's doings in Judea or at Jerusalem, until the week of His Passion.

The earlier portion, then, of the public life of Christ has these marks. Its *place* was Galilee. Its *companions* were fishermen, and country people. Its *record* is in the Gospels of St. Matthew, St. Mark, and St. Luke. The *work* of Christ was to bear witness to the Kingdom of Heaven; and He did this by means of direct announcements, of acts of healing, and of illustrative parables. To this period belongs the organization of the company of the Twelve Apostles.

In contrast with these marks, we have the following characteristics of the second period of our Lord's life. It was spent chiefly at Jerusalem. Jesus came much into contact with educated Jews of the higher class. The record of this time is in the Gospel of St. John. Whilst Jesus does not fail to speak of the Kingdom of Heaven, the direct purpose of His words and actions is to unfold His glory as the Son of God. This filial glory, we are given to understand, was manifested not only by words and acts, but in a far higher manner and degree by the sufferings of Jesus, and by His subsequent exaltation.

The Kingdom of Heaven, declared in the Life of Christ, was our subject last Sunday. The unfolding of the Filial Glory of Christ is our subject this morning.

Let us first observe, that the declaration of the Divine Sonship was not altogether absent from the earlier work of Jesus Christ, any more than the declaration of the Kingdom of Heaven was altogether absent from His later work. We must not draw our line of distinction too sharply. The remarkable narrative of St. Peter's confession shows us that Jesus was teaching His intimate friends to recognise what He did not as yet desire to proclaim everywhere amongst the people. We read it in Matt. xvi. Jesus asked His disciples, "Whom do men say that I, the Son of Man, am?"—the name by which he distinguished Himself being that of the Son of Man. They said, "Some say that thou art John the Baptist; some, Elias; and others Jeremias, or one of the prophets." These names had all of them reference to the bringing in of the Kingdom of Heaven. Jesus then asked His disciples, "But whom say ye that I am? And Simon Peter answered, and said, Thou art the Christ, the Son of the living God." On which confession Jesus put His memorable seal, saying, "Blessed art thou, Simon Bar-jona; for flesh and blood hath not revealed it unto thee, but my Father which is in heaven." And immediately after this we read, "Then charged he his disciples that they should tell no man that he was Jesus the Christ." Until the name of the Father had become better known, it would seem that a mere "flesh and blood" declaration of Jesus as the Son of God would not have been a genuine revelation to the people. There is a remarkable chapter in St. John, the sixth, in which Jesus speaks expressly of the mystery of His relation to the Father; and this discourse is said to have been spoken at Capernaum in Galilee. But there are some indications that the words were addressed to a special audience of educated **Jews: and** we also learn that this discourse **had the** effect **of** alienating from Him many of His **followers, to** whom **it was** "hard" and unintelligible. **So much so,** that Jesus said to the twelve, "Will ye also **go away?"** Then Simon Peter is again the great confessor, **and** answers, "Lord, to whom shall we go? **Thou hast the** words **of** eternal life. And we believe and are sure that thou art that Christ, the **Son of the** living God."

When we follow **our** Lord to Jerusalem, we observe, **even in** the first three Gospels, much more of what might be called self-assertion. But this is most strongly brought out in St. John's Gospel. To those who regard Jesus **of** Nazareth as a mere man, the greatest and best of men, there is something strange and repelling in the manner in which He is represented as making *Himself* the subject of His discourses, as well as in the lofty pretensions which He puts forth. **If** Jesus Christ was simply one of the heroes of mankind, and if the Gospels contain anything like a true account of Him, it is impossible to acquit Him—the words are painful, but it is well they should **be** spoken—of **a** degree of arrogance, self-delusion, and egotism, of which no other good or great man has been guilty. It is true that our Lord **asserts** confidently that He does not speak "*of Himself.*" But this does not mean "*concerning*" Himself. **It** means "from," or "out of," Himself. Jesus declares that **His words** do not spring from His own **mind as** their ultimate source: they are the words **of** God in heaven. Jesus makes, without ceasing, the loftiest and most astonishing statements concerning Himself: and he adds force to these statements by claiming for them an authority and a nature absolutely Divine.

But any one who studies with reverence the language of the Lord Jesus concerning Himself, must be struck by the unique combination and harmony of lowliness and self-assertion which it exhibits. He is the Son of God, and He will speak in His true character: but He does not seek His own glory, but His Father's. He is the perfectly submissive, perfectly loving, perfectly unselfish, Son of the Eternal Father. This is the key, and the only key, to the paradoxes of St. John's Gospel. No nature could be more lofty than that of Christ, no character more lowly. And, *therefore*, we may say, throughout all His words and acts, He is invariably sympathizing and brotherly with men. He never separates them from Himself, or Himself from them: He never treats with scorn any except those who are themselves proud and scornful.

It was the task of our Lord at Jerusalem to declare the Father, and Himself as the way to the Father, whether the Jews would hear or whether they would forbear. And the pride of the Jews, their confidence in their religion or their enlightenment, made it necessary that the testimony of Jesus should be antagonistic and combative, delivered more frequently, perhaps, in rebukes than in benedictions. The great miracles which He wrought at Jerusalem, still healing and life-giving acts of themselves, provoked the anger, instead of drawing out the reverence, of the Pharisees. It is a characteristic of St. John's Gospel that it records in detail a few important miracles, which were charged with great doctrinal significance, and which had special results in the history. All these were designed to reveal the filial glory of Christ. One of them, the feeding of the five thousand, belongs to Galilee. Three took place at Jerusalem. The first, the healing of the impotent man at the pool of Bethesda, offended the Jews because the man was bidden to take up his bed and walk, although it was the Sabbath-day. To the complaints of the Jews Jesus answered, "My Father worketh hitherto, and I work. Therefore," we are told, "the Jews sought the more to kill him, because he not only had broken the Sabbath, but said also that God was his Father, making himself equal with God. Then answered Jesus and said unto them, Verily, verily, I say unto you, The Son can do nothing of himself, but what he seeth the Father do: for what things soever he doeth, these also doeth the Son likewise." And these words were the beginning of a profound discourse upon the nature of the Son, and upon the work which the Father had committed to Him. The second of the three miracles, is the restoring to sight of the man who had been blind from his birth. This also was done upon the Sabbath-day, and proved in the eyes of the Pharisees that Jesus was no keeper of the Sabbath. To the poor man himself, Jesus said, after the gift had been bestowed upon him, "Dost thou believe on the Son of God?"—on me, who am the Son of God? The man answered, "Lord, I believe," and worshipped Him. The Pharisees Jesus upbraided with an incurable spiritual blindness, and proceeded to denounce them as false shepherds, hirelings who cared for themselves and betrayed the flock. He Himself, He said, was the true Shepherd, proving His right of ownership over the sheep by sharing their life and their dangers, and by laying down His life in their behalf. "I am the good shepherd, and know my sheep, and am known of mine, as the Father knoweth me, and I know the Father." And again Jesus went on to speak of His relation to His Father on the one side, and of His relation to men on the other side. When He came to the words, "I and my Father are one," the Jews took up stones to stone Him as a blasphemer. Jesus, remonstrating with them, asked, "Say ye of him whom the Father hath sanctified, and sent into the world, Thou blasphemest; because I said, I am the Son of God? If I do not the works of my Father, believe me not. But if I do, though ye believe not me, believe the works; that ye may know, and believe, that the Father is in me, and I in him." Therefore the Jews sought again to take Him. The third miracle is that great one of raising Lazarus from the dead. This miracle was introduced by Jesus with the intimation, "This sickness is not unto death, but for the glory of God, that the *Son of God* might be glorified thereby." Declaring Himself to be the Resurrection and the Life, He drew from Martha the confession, "I believe that thou art the Christ, the Son of God, which should come into the world." Before bidding Lazarus come forth from the tomb, He lifted up His eyes and said, "Father, I thank thee that thou hast heard me. And I knew that thou hearest me always; but because of the people which stand by I said it, that they may believe that thou hast sent me."

Thus uniformly did Jesus seek to make known through His acts and words the true Divine glory, the common glory of the Father and of the Son. This glory could not penetrate or soften the hardened hearts of the Jews, who had not the word of the Father abiding in them, and who did not know the Father any more than they knew the Son. But even the enmity of those who had rejected the true Father, and had given themselves as children to the spirit of falsehood and hatred, was made to minister to the full revelation of the filial glory. All through His life Jesus had been showing that the Divine glory was not asserted by lording it over men, but by sympathizing with them and serving them. But towards the close of it, He began to call the attention of the disciples to the power that lay in voluntary humiliation and suffering for the revealing of His true glory. You remember the incident of the washing of the disciples' feet, and the moral significance which Jesus connected with it. This act St. John refers expressly to the conscious knowledge of Jesus that the Father had given all things into His hands, and that He was come from God and went to God. *Because* He knew this, therefore He would humble Himself to be the menial servant of His disciples. The discourses of the night before the crucifixion disclose to us the mind of Jesus possessed by thoughts of His unity with the Father, of His unity with His brethren, and of the glory which the Cross would reflect in the eyes of men both on the Father and Himself. When the traitor went out to do the deed for which the devil entered into him, Jesus said, "Now is the Son of Man glorified, and God is glorified in Him." He rejoiced in the thought that He was about to prove to the world how He loved the Father. He said to His disciples, "I am the way, the truth, and the life: no man cometh unto the Father, but by me. If ye had known me, ye should have known my Father also: and from henceforth ye know him and have seen him." He bade them expect the coming of a Spirit, to be sent from the Father and the Son, who should open their eyes to invisible things: and then, He said, "If a man love me, he will keep my words; and my Father will love him and we will come unto him, and make our abode with him." The heavenly sacredness and beauty of our Lord's prayer to His Father in St. John xvii. depend on its being the utterance of the perfect filial heart moved by the nearness of an extreme trial. "Father," He said, "the hour is come; glorify thy Son, that thy Son also may glorify thee." For His disciples, and for all them also who should believe on Him through their word, Jesus prayed "that they all may be one; as thou, Father, art in me, and I in thee, that they also may be one in us." What a depth of love, and of unity in love, is disclosed to us in this prayer! What an incomprehensible unity of the Son with the Father! What a unity, hardly more comprehensible, of the Son with His brethren!

The narrative of our Lord's Passion shows us how truly His sacrifice was an offering of Himself through the Spirit to the Father. "Father, if it be possible," was the cry of His agony, "take this cup from me: nevertheless, not my will, but thine, be done." When He was arraigned before Pilate, and the Roman judge could find no fault in Him, the Jews said, "We have a law, and by our law he ought to die, because he made himself the Son of God." Of the few sayings of Christ on the cross, one was, "Father, forgive them, for they know not what they do;" and the last, "Father, into thy hands I commend my spirit." The Roman officer, who stood on duty by the cross, and was a witness of the spirit in which Jesus suffered, could not but confess, "Truly this was the Son of God."

On several occasions, according to St. John's reports, Jesus had spoken of a "lifting up," or raising on high, of Himself, in which the Jews were to be the agents. "As Moses lifted up the serpent in the wilderness, even so must the Son of Man be lifted up." "When ye have lifted up the Son of Man, then shall ye know that I am he, and that I do nothing of myself; but as my Father hath taught me, I speak these things. And he that sent me is with me: the Father hath not left me alone: for I do always those things that please Him." This passage is remarkable as showing that it was a part of the exaltation to which Jesus looked forward, that men should know, not that He was some great one in Himself, but that He *did nothing* of Himself; that His whole being was in joyful submission to the Father. Again, "I, if I be lifted up from the earth, will draw all men unto me." There is some obvious uncertainty as to the meaning of this expression *lifting up*, or raising on high; and St. John adds here expressly, "This he said, signifying what death he should die." We infer that there was some reference in the word lifting up, to that raising of the body which was involved in the cruel punishment of the cross. But it can scarcely be doubted that there is also an idea of personal exaltation expressed in the word,—" When I am raised on high, I will draw all men unto me." His Cross would be the means of setting Him on high for the faith and worship of mankind. Christ crucified would be to men the power of God, and the wisdom of God. But this exaltation could not have been accomplished by the Death of the Cross alone, if it had not been followed by the Resurrection. It is with the Resurrection that we most commonly associate the ideas and the language of exaltation. And it appears that Jesus Himself regarded His Death, His Resurrection, and His Ascension, as one continuous action, which He described by the term, "going to the Father." These events cannot be separated from one another in the faith of a Christian —Christ crucified implies Christ risen; Christ risen implies Christ crucified.

That raising of Christ from the dead, which put a

seal and a crown upon His great sacrifice, is expressly interpreted as a glorifying of the sonship of Christ. St. Paul speaks of the Gospel of God " Concerning his Son Jesus Christ, who was declared *to be the Son of God* with power, according to the Spirit of holiness, by the resurrection from the dead." And the Resurrection was a step to the Ascension, of which Jesus Himself thus spoke, when He withdrew Himself from the touch of Mary Magdalene—"Touch me not, for I am not yet ascended to my Father: but go to my brethren, and say unto them, I ascend unto my Father and your Father, and to my God and your God." Ever since His departure from the world, the Son of Man has been beheld by the faith of Christians sitting at the Father's right hand, claiming in His own person for the family of man a share in the perfected glory of Divine Sonship.

With the descent of the Spirit, indeed, on the day of Pentecost, He Himself came to be present with His disciples. In the Spirit, to be with the Father was not to be absent from men. The bestowal of the Spirit was a glorifying of the Son in the manifestation of that twofold unity which was in the thoughts of Jesus on the night before His death— the unity with the Father on one side, the unity with the human disciples on the other. The gift of the Spirit depended absolutely on the revelation that had been made of the filial glory of Jesus. The Spirit proceeded from the Father and the Son to knit men in the Son, and therefore in the quality of children, to the Father. The word of the Apostles, when filled with the new inspiration, was this—"The God of our fathers hath glorified his Son Jesus." "Because ye are sons," said St. Paul, "God hath sent forth the Spirit of his Son into your hearts, crying Abba, Father."

The coming down of the Spirit, then, was the practical and effectual witness to men, that our Lord's interpretation of His own nature and work, and of the meaning of His death and rising again, was the true one—that He had been declaring realities of heaven and earth, when He testified, "I am the Son of God, whom the Eternal Father hath sent into the world. I am come to reveal the Father, and to make myself through death and sacrifice the living Mediator between God and men, the bond of a Divine and human family."

This is the one leading word of Jesus Christ in that more important part of His earthly history, which was transacted in the Holy City, under the shadow of His Father's house. We must not underrate the significance of the earlier Galilean period, when our Lord discoursed of the Kingdom of Heaven to admiring multitudes, and blessed them with His works of healing and words of encouragement. This period is kept for a longer proportionate time before our eyes as we read the Gospel narratives. But as the worth of John the Baptist's work was in its being preparatory to that of Christ, so we may believe that the chief value of the preaching of the Kingdom of Heaven was, that it prepared the way for the knowing of the Son of God in His spiritual relations to the

Father, **and** to men. All the Gospels, and not St. John's only, are written that **"we may believe** that Jesus is the Christ, the Son of God, and that be**lieving we may** have life in his name."

For a few moments, **in** conclusion, let us fix our thoughts on the distinguishing qualities of this Divine Sonship of Jesus.

1. When Jesus named Himself the Son of God before the religious Jews, the only interpretation they could put upon His words was, that He was setting Himself up as a **rival** God, "making himself equal with God." It is interesting and instructive to observe how Jesus passes by the word *equal*, in order that He may expound and dwell upon His perfect *filial unity* with His Father. He entirely disavows the equality in the sense in which the Jews meant it; and so St. Paul says of Him, that He did not think *equality with God* a thing to be grasped at. **It** was impossible to imagine a more complete subordination than that of the Son of God to the Father. Mark once more those wonderful sayings of Jesus: "Verily, verily, I say unto you, the Son can **do** nothing of himself, but what **he** seeth the Father do." What language could more explicitly repudiate any indepen**dent** equality of the Son with the Father? But then **our** Lord adds the assertion, "What things soever the Father doeth, these also doeth the Son likewise." Such **a relation** as this might not unnaturally be expressed by the term equality. But if we follow our blessed **Lord's** own teaching, we shall make *sonship*, **souship in its most** perfect idea—eternal sonship,

the key to what He was and is at the side of the Father. Jesus did not shrink from saying that it was the Father's purpose, that "all men should honour the Son, even as they honour the Father."

2. We may mark separately, then, that the sonship of Jesus was not only not incompatible with submission, but its only possible manifestation was through submission. At every point and period of His life, it was the glory of Jesus of Nazareth to be perfectly obedient to the Father. This obedience, rooted in the will and in love, is what distinguished Jesus amongst men. His mighty works might have been done by other men. Similar, apparently equal, works were done by Peter and Paul. But no mortal man has approached the Lord Jesus in the perfection of His submission to the will of the Father.

3. This submission to the will of the Father was, in another form, the seeking of the Father's glory. Jesus laid this down—the seeking of the Father's glory—as the absolute principle of all human life, true in fact for Himself, true in idea for His human brethren. No man can be *true*, He said, if he seeks his own glory. Such a disposition disturbs his moral equilibrium, puts him out of harmony with reality. He was to be believed and to be trusted, He said, because He perfectly sought His Father's glory, and made it His meat and drink to do His Father's will. The Son, who was wholly a Son, whose entire nature was comprised in sonship, must, He taught, have this feeling towards the Heavenly Father, must devote Himself absolutely to the revealing of the Father's

glory. Accordingly it was the purpose of Christ, in all displaying of Himself, to make the Father known, **to** lead men to Him, to glorify the name of the Father **in heaven.**

4. Lastly, **it** belonged to the very essence of the sonship of Jesus to claim men as His brethren, and **to** make them true sons of God. "To those who **re**ceived him, to them gave he power to become the sons of God." It was not only *My* Father, but **My** Father *and yours*—your Father who is in Heaven. Never, as I have said, did Christ separate Himself from His human brothers. He is not ashamed to call them brethren. Because the brethren are partakers of His flesh and blood, He also Himself took part of the **same.** His own highest glory, His sonship, He was ready and anxious freely to impart to men. "That they all **may** be one; as thou, Father, art in me, and I in thee, that they also may be one in us: that the world may believe that thou hast sent me. And the glory which thou gavest me I have given them; that they may be one, even as we are one: I in them, and thou in me, that they may **be** made perfect in one, and that the world may know that thou hast sent me, and hast loved them, as thou hast loved me."

My brethren, as we contemplate the glory of sonship **in** our Master and Head, must we not exclaim in awe and wonder, "Behold, what manner of love the Father hath bestowed upon us that we **should be** called the sons of God!" Behold the **Father exalts us** with the Son of His love! He has given us in Him **the** forgiveness of sins, has reconciled us to Himself, has made us sit together with Christ at His own right hand in the heavenly world! What an unspeakable privilege! What need must we not feel of the power of the Spirit working in us, that we may know our heavenly calling, and be enabled to walk worthily of it!

IV.

THE KINGDOM OF THE SON OF MAN ESTABLISHED.

St. Luke xxi. 29—32.

"And he spake to them a parable: Behold the fig-tree, and all the trees; when they now shoot forth, ye see and know of your own selves that summer is now nigh at hand. So likewise ye, when ye see these things come to pass, know ye that the kingdom of God is nigh at hand. Verily I say unto you, This generation shall not pass away till all be fulfilled."

In endeavouring to realize some of the broad aspects which the Coming of Christ into the world presents to our view when regarded as an event in history, I called your attention first to that general expectation of a Messiah, and of a Messianic Kingdom, which pervaded the Jewish mind. Such a kingdom floated before the eyes of every Jewish prophet; some of the prophets express more definitely than others the aspirations of which it was the object. In the Book of Daniel we have a record of visions which distinctly declare the Messiah, and point to the establishment of His kingdom. In the age preceding that of our Lord, there were Jewish books not included in the sacred canon, of which the Book of Enoch is the most conspicuous example, in which the same language as that of the Book of Daniel is applied to the coming Messiah, and in which other expressions occur which afterwards appear again in some of the New Testament writings. The sum of these prophetic indications, which had taken such hold of the Jewish mind, was that a Divine Kingdom, a Kingdom of Heaven, was about to spring out of the Jewish history, and to manifest itself upon the earth. When John the Baptist appeared as our Lord's forerunner, his proclamation was, "Repent ye; for the kingdom of heaven is at hand." Jesus Himself, after His baptism by John, made the same announcement. His Gospel, or good news, was that the Kingdom of Heaven was near. And He went on, as I have reminded you, to give illustrations, in word and act, of the nature of this kingdom. His miracles were signs of it: His parables were figures of it. His moral and spiritual teaching was directed to the awakening of the conscience to the perception of the invisible realities which belong to the heavenly kingdom. After a while, Jesus began to speak of Himself more plainly as the Son of God, declaring that He was come to reveal the Father through the manifestation of Himself, and to bring men into unity and fellowship with the Father. The Sufferings and Death and Resurrection of Christ were means of manifesting the glory of the Father and of the Son. The Holy Spirit came from the Father and the Son to be the inward life and illumination of those who believed in Christ. So it was fully shown that the kingdom which Christ came to introduce was a fatherly kingdom, a divine family, a spiritual commonwealth.

As soon as we begin to see that the kingdom which **is thus** associated with the Coming of Christ is the sovereignty of the Father in heaven, and that to enter into it is to become spiritually a child of God, we perceive that this kingdom cannot be a matter of time and place, but must be eternal in the heavens. Properly speaking, the Kingdom of Heaven existed before it came. It did not come into being like an earthly dynasty or constitution. Its coming consists in manifestation rather than in construction or creation. But taking the words of the prophecies, and those of John the Baptist and of our Lord, **in a** real and simple sense, can **we** say of the kingdom which they announced to be *near*, that it ever *arrived*, and was established? Is there any time or event with which we may rightly connect such an establishing of the Kingdom of Heaven? The answer to this question is what I propose to consider this morning. In other words, we are to look for the historical issue and result of the Incarnation of the Son of God.

The kingdom **of** which the prophets spoke was **the** Kingdom of the Messiah. Our Lord taught plainly that the kingdom which He announced was *His* kingdom. The Father, He said, had given all things into His hands. This being so, it might have been supposed that the establishment of the kingdom **would** date from *the appearance of the Messiah*. When **Christ** began His public acts, then, it would seem natural to say, the Kingdom of Christ was inaugurated. But this is not the Bible language. Again, if we are not to speak of the Kingdom of Christ as established whilst He is yet subjecting Himself to the authority of His enemies, and suffering at their hands, it might certainly seem reasonable to speak of the kingdom as established by *the Ascension*, when the Son of God, having risen from the dead, went up to sit at His Father's right hand. But, although there is so much truth in this view that language expressing it may be rightly used, and occurs in Scripture, we do not find that the coming of the kingdom is absolutely identified with the Ascension. All through the New Testament, or at least through much the greater part of it, we find that the hope and expectation of the believers in Christ are directed to a crisis not yet arrived, but not far distant. There is to be, after the Ascension, and after the Day of Pentecost, *a Coming of the Son of Man*. The Son of Man is to come in His glory, and with this Coming the full idea of the new kingdom is associated.

The great prophecies of the Coming of the Son of Man are to be found in those most remarkable discourses which our Lord delivered in the week of His Passion, and which are reported at such length by St. Matthew, St. Mark, and St. Luke. They are very direct and unmistakeable predictions. They turn upon the Temple—that sacred edifice which Jesus honoured as the true House of His Father. What a glorious building this is! remarked some of the disciples of Jesus: how rich and precious are the materials of which it is composed! Look at them, and mark them, replied Jesus: "Verily I say unto you, there shall **not be** left here one stone upon another, that shall not be thrown down." This destruction of the Temple the disciples knew and felt to be a matter of awful significance. After that solemn prediction had been spoken, the disciples came to Jesus privately, saying, "Tell us, when shall these things be? And what shall be the sign of thy coming, and of the end of the world?" They had had some reason to connect the destruction of the Temple with the Coming or Appearing of their Master, and this with the end of **the world.** It should be observed, however, that the expression, *the end of the world*, is a rather ambiguous rendering of the original, which means, more strictly, the conclusion of the age. It implies the winding-up of a period in the world's history, the closing of one of God's dispensations. It was in answer to that question that our Lord delivered His prophecy. **It** relates professedly to the time of the *destruction of the Temple* at Jerusalem, which should also be the time of the *Lord's Appearing*, and **of the** winding-up **of the** dispensation **or** world of which the Temple was the visible centre.

Jesus declined to give His disciples a chronological **answer.** He would not—it would seem he could not—tell them in what year, in the reign of what Cæsar, during the term of what pro-consul, those things were to take place. But He desires to fix the **attention of** His disciples earnestly upon the signs which were to usher in His coming at the end of the age. He proceeds to enumerate those signs. There should be false Christs, who would deceive many. Wars and rumours of wars should prevail; famines, pestilences, earthquakes, should afflict the nations. The believers in Christ would be exposed to settled and steady persecution. Lawlessness would abound; love and faith would grow cold. The good news of the kingdom should be everywhere published as a witness to all nations. Then the end should come; and it should begin with an idolatrous profanation of the sanctuary of the Temple. This profanation would be accompanied with dreadful afflictions in Judea and Jerusalem, with unprecedented tribulations. Jerusalem would be compassed with armies. "There shall be great distress in the land," said Jesus, "and wrath upon this people. And they shall fall by the edge of the sword, and shall be led away captive into all nations: and Jerusalem shall be trodden down of the Gentiles, until the times of the Gentiles be fulfilled." This destruction and desolation falling upon the chosen people, was to be the chief outward mark of the Divine and heavenly movements which were winding up the old time and bringing in the new. The prevailing misery would cause many to receive eagerly the announcement of a Messiah here and a Messiah there, in the desert or in the secret chamber; but it was an appointed token that men were no longer to look for a Messiah *here* or *there*—that there was one Messiah for the world, the Son of Man in heaven. The Son of Man would come in the clouds of heaven with power and great glory. And His elect, instead of being a chosen race in a single land, should **be** gathered from the four winds, from one end of **heaven to** the other. **To** this Coming of the Son of **Man** the disciples were to look forward with watchfulness and faith. Jesus gave His hearers the most solemn assurances that it should take place in their own generation. Though they were not to know the date of it beforehand, the signs which he had given would be unmistakeable tokens of its near approach. "When the fig-tree and other trees shoot forth, ye see and know of your own selves that summer is now nigh at hand. So likewise ye, when ye see these things come to pass, know ye that the kingdom of God is nigh at hand. Verily I say unto you, This generation shall not pass away, till all be fulfilled. Heaven and earth shall pass away: but my words shall not pass away."

The discourse thus reported was spoken before the death of Christ. After His Resurrection, we are told at the beginning of the Acts, the subject of His conversations with His disciples was still the Kingdom of God—" being seen of them forty days, and speaking **of** the things pertaining to the kingdom of God." The disciples, not remembering what they had been told **of** the signs that would precede the establishment of the kingdom, asked their Master, "Lord, wilt thou at this time restore again the kingdom to Israel?" To which Jesus replied to the same effect as He had spoken before—"It is not for you to know the times or the seasons, which the Father hath put in his own power."

The little community of believers in Christ, therefore,

was started with this expectation fixed in the hearts of its leaders—an expectation of a most important crisis, called the Coming of the Son of Man, which was to occur they knew not when, but within the lifetime of that generation, and which was to be heralded by those signs which Christ had distinctly described.

And that this expectation was not allowed to die out in the minds of the Apostles and first Christians, we have abundant evidence in all that remains to us of their discourses or writings preceding the destruction of Jerusalem. Our difficulty is, that the language used in reference to the Coming of the Son of Man, the Lord Jesus Christ, appears to us too strong. But it is as definite in the writings of the Apostles as in the discourses of Christ. Let us take one or two examples of it.

The earliest Apostolic writings of which we can at all fix the date are, the Epistles to the Thessalonians, the first of St. Paul's Epistles. Of these two letters the Appearing of the Lord Jesus Christ is the key-note. St. Paul reminds the Christians of Thessalonica, that when he preached the Gospel amongst them, they had turned to God from idols, "to worship the living and true God, and to wait for His Son from heaven, whom he raised from the dead, even Jesus, who delivers us," he adds, "from the coming wrath." To this coming wrath, of which there were already signs in the air visible to the prescient eye, he refers again, when he speaks of the Jews as filling up the measure of their sins, "for the wrath has overtaken them at last," or finally.

We might naturally expect that the prospect of great convulsions, and of such a mysterious event as the Coming of the Son of God, would disturb the tranquillity of the Thessalonians, and unsettle them in their common interests and occupations.

This we find to have been the case, and therefore St. Paul reminds them that they who were already living in the light ought to wait quietly for that wider diffusion of it which was the highest mark of the day of the Lord. To believers in Christ, He was already so present, that His coming could not to them be a total change of state. "Ye, brethren, are not in darkness that the day of the Lord should overtake you as a thief. Ye are all the children of the light and the children of the day: we are not of the night, nor of darkness." "Let us who are of the day, be sober." This is a very important passage, as illustrative of the nature of the Apostolic expectations of the Day of the Lord.

Shortly after the writing of this first letter, St. Paul wrote again to the Church of Thessalonica, and again spoke of the Day of Christ, and the Coming of the Lord Jesus Christ. He bade them not look for it immediately. The signs which were to usher it in were not yet visible. And, speaking of what must precede the expected day, St. Paul delivered a remarkable and difficult prediction, the substance of which is, that there would be a falling away, and a manifesting of evil in some conspicuous person or form, before the coming of those judgments in which the glory and kingdom of the Lord Jesus were to be declared.

But all that he spoke of belonged to his own generation. "Already," he says in his prophecy, "the mystery of iniquity is working." The clouds of heaven in which the Son of Man was to come were already brooding upon the earth. They spoke in solemn voices to the believers in Christ, bidding them be steady, watchful, persevering, and patient.

The other example to which I shall refer is one of the latest of the Epistles, that to the Hebrews. Both the authorship and the date of this epistle are uncertain. But its spiritual characteristics are plain. It is written to Jewish Christians—to men who believed both in Moses and in Jesus. It speaks of a certain doubtfulness and despondency which were weakening the faith of such men, and which found issue to some extent in open apostasy. The design of the letter was to exhort them to constancy, and to prepare them for an impending crisis which was about to sweep away the Jewish institutions, by showing them that all those institutions had been pointing to Christ, and were fulfilled in Him. The Jewish institutions had not been annulled by the birth or public ministry of Christ, nor, it is important to observe, by His Ascension or the Coming of the Holy Ghost: but they were to cease entirely in that establishment of the Kingdom of Christ which was just imminent. The writer speaks of that age as the last days. He contrasts that which was growing old and ready to vanish away, with the new covenant which was taking its place. And in one magnificent passage he puts behind himself and his fellow-believers the institutions which were embodied in the Law of the **visible and** palpable mountain of the desert, and unfolds the glories of the New Dispensation under which they were henceforth to live. "**Ye** are come unto **Mount** Zion, and unto the city of the living **God, the** heavenly Jerusalem, and to an innumerable company of angels, to the general assembly and Church of the first-born, which are written in heaven, **and to** God, the judge of all, and to the spirits of just men made perfect, and to Jesus, the mediator of the new covenant, and to the blood of sprinkling, which speaketh better things than that of Abel." Thus were the early Christians taught, that the kingdom whose appearing they were to look for was not a carnal one, depending on visible institutions, but that its very characteristic was, that being invisible and spiritual, having its seat in the heavens, it was to be recognised as the real, actual kingdom of which men and their communities were to be the subjects.

There is one book of the New Testament which is of the highest importance for the complete discussion of this subject, but to which I shall only just allude this morning, on account of the uncertainty of its **date.** I mean the Revelation of **St.** John the Divine. Tradition, and the opinion of the larger number of critics, are in favour of this book having been written, **and its** visions seen, *after* the destruction of Jerusalem; whilst internal evidence and the harmony **of Scripture** seem to me to argue almost irresistibly in favour of its having been written two or three years before that crisis. In either case, we have the following very remarkable fact before us. By far the larger proportion of the writings of the New Testament belong to the twenty years preceding the destruction of Jerusalem. The history in the Acts comes up within a few years of that event. The pastoral Epistles come yet nearer; the Epistle to the Hebrews, the Epistle of St. Jude, and the second of St. Peter, belong to the same ten years, if not also the Apocalypse. But all these writings stop short, the voice of the New Testament is silent, at a point some two or three years before the crisis with which, throughout the sacred writings, the Coming of the Son of Man is associated. For the history of that series of events we are entirely dependent upon secular writers, such as the Jewish writer Josephus, and the historians of the Roman empire. If our notions of what is desirable and to be expected had regulated the Divine Providence in the matter of sacred writings, I cannot but think we should have had some canonical account and interpretation of that epoch of history to which almost all the sacred writings point as a great fulfilment of Divine purpose.

As it is, I think we may see that the silence of Scripture, the absence of Apostolic letters and other sacred writings, harmonizes well with the gloom and misery and despondency which mark our Lord's picture of the crisis of His coming. And we are taught by this circumstance not to despise secular history. The historical narratives of the years to which the destruction of Jerusalem belongs, although they do not unfold the Divine mystery which was then working, yet record faithfully and instructively those outward phenomena which our Lord said should attend the invisible heavenly movements. The works of Josephus and Tacitus are always felt to be a remarkable commentary upon our Lord's great prophecy.

The silence of Scripture, of which I am speaking, is the more remarkable because it was not final. Long after the destruction of Jerusalem, some twenty years or more, the latest books of the New Testament canon appeared, the Epistles and the Gospel of St. John. These books do not tell us that the prophecies of Jesus, and of His appearing, had been fulfilled: they do not directly show us how the Christians of that age read the events that accompanied the sweeping away of the Jewish nation and polity. We may wish that this intimation had been given to us; but we must reconcile ourselves to its absence. But it is to be noted, that in these books the prophecies and aspirations which appear in every other book of the New Testament are absent. And at the end of the Gospel there is a very significant passage. Jesus said of the beloved disciple, in answer to a question of Peter's, "If I will that he tarry till I come, what is that to thee? Follow thou me. Then," we are told, "went this saying abroad among the brethren, that that disciple should not *die:* yet Jesus said not unto him, He shall not die: but if I will that he tarry *till I come*, what is that to thee." There seems to be in these words an intimation that mistaken views about the Coming of the Lord had been current amongst the believers, and that if the saying of Jesus were understood in its right sense, it had even already been fulfilled; that the life of the beloved disciple had been prolonged past the great crisis, and that, by the will of the Master, he had tarried till He came.

I can speak but very briefly of the conclusions to which we seem to be brought.

1. Let me say first, that in studying the Advent of Christ as an historical event, it is indispensable that we should take up a Jewish position, and retain it until, by the very force of the Divine Dispensation, we are removed from it to a universal human position. Christ was foretold by Jewish prophecy; His incarnation was the fulfilment of the whole train of Jewish history. When He came He appeared as a Jew, born under the Law, and He lived to the end as a Jew. His first followers were Jews; the first faith in Jesus Christ was, that in Him the God of Abraham, Isaac, and Jacob, had fulfilled the promises made to the fathers. By degrees the fold is widened; Gentiles are admitted without first becoming Jews; the significance of the title The *Son of Man* dawns upon the believing mind. But not the less, the final establishment of the new Kingdom of Heaven as not Jewish, but human, is a tremendous event to Jews. And that this should come about in Divine wrath; that the chosen people should reject their own Messiah, and therefore be themselves rejected, with such agonies as came upon the Jewish people, and an utter rooting up of temple and priesthood and polity, was a fearful and a horrible thing. We must try to realize these feelings, when we read the Jewish

. Apocalyptic language, in which the Coming of the Son of Man is described.

2. On the other hand, whilst we do justice to that side of the coming of Christ which looks *backward*, we must endeavour also to do justice to that side of it which looks forward. It was, in simple historical fact, by the vanishing away of the Jewish institutions that the kingdom under which we are born and live was established for the world. Jerusalem was a Divinely-instituted local centre. Till it was destroyed, it did not cease to have that character. But thenceforward, the Kingdom of God has had no local centre. It is but a profane dream which has sought to substitute Rome for Jerusalem. The Church of Christ has no centre except in heaven, no Head except the Son of Man, who is in heaven. His throne is the seat of authority, the point of convergence for all men. At the Coming of Christ in the first century, it was declared that He was exalted in order that to His name every knee should bow, **of** things in heaven, of things in earth, and things under the earth, and that every tongue should confess that He is Lord, to the glory of God the Father; that great multitudes which no man can number, of all nations and kindreds and people and tongues, should stand before the throne and before the Lamb.

Of this universal heavenly kingdom—a kingdom **not *of*** this world, but yet *for* this world—the Incar**nation of** the Son **of** God has made us, with our fellow-men, inheritors. He came that we might all **be** made one family in **Him**; that through Him and

His Cross one grand universal Reconciliation should be accomplished. It pleased the Father that in Him should all fulness dwell; and having made peace by the blood of His Cross, by Him to reconcile all things unto Himself, by Him, whether things in earth or things in heaven. He came, on the one hand, that the truth of God and of His promises might be fulfilled, and, on the other hand, that the Gentiles might be taught to bless God for His mercy. He came to crown the special dispensations of God, by bringing in a universal covenant of fatherhood and sonship, of spiritual communion and unity between God and His children.

There may be much in the past to make us wonder and despond; there may be much mystery yet hanging over the future. But when the things of earth, past, present, and future, confuse and distress us, let it be ours, my brethren, as Christians to look up to heaven. It is there, in heaven, that we have our kingdom and our citizenship. It is by the revelations of heaven that we must live, and not by the appearances of earth. May God grant us such a belief in the kingdom which cannot be moved, as may help us to understand the mighty changes in the past, and prepare us for those which yet await us in the future.

V.

THE POWER OF THE DIVINE INFANCY.

St. John i. 18.

"No man hath seen God at any time; the only begotten Son, which is in the bosom of the Father, he hath declared him."

It was one of the most frequent declarations of our Blessed Lord concerning Himself, that He came down from heaven. The Father had sent Him into the world, He said: He was come down to earth from heaven. In a certain sense, this language appeared to the Jews very appropriate to the nature and office of the Messiah, and to the proclaiming of the Kingdom of Heaven. If they had seen the clouds above their heads parting asunder, and the form of the Son of Man emerging from them and descending upon the earth, they would have been ready, they thought, to admit the Divine pretensions of One so coming. It is true that such an apparition would not have been in harmony with the traditions which spoke of Christ being born at Bethlehem, of the seed of David. But the craving of the Jews for the miraculous was so strong, that a great wonder like a bodily descent from heaven might well have induced them to forget those traditions. They would have readily promised their faith in response to such a portent. And in entertaining thoughts of this kind the Jews are very like men of other countries and other generations—indeed, like all men in their more careless and ignorant and carnal moods. But Christ did not thus descend from the firmament; and the people were, therefore, astonished at His language. "The Jews then murmured at him," we read, "because he said, I am the bread which came down from heaven. And they said, Is not this Jesus, the son of Joseph, whose father and mother we know? how is it then that he saith, I came down from heaven?"

According to what is stated and implied in the Gospel narrative, the Galilean neighbours of Jesus knew Him at first only as a fellow-countryman, belonging to a respectable family of Nazareth. The name of Jesus was not a sacred one, any more than that of Simon or John. It was pronounced without the slightest awe. The bearer of it had grown up from infancy at Nazareth, and the whole family, Joseph and Mary, Jesus Himself and His brethren, were well known to their neighbours. This being the case, His countrymen murmured amongst themselves, "How can he say that he came down from heaven?"

Jesus did not mean that, in the outward and material sense in which His words were taken, He had come down from heaven. The heaven of which He spoke was not the blue space above the clouds. Heaven was the name for the Father's home and presence, the bosom of the Father. To say that He **was** come from heaven, was the same thing as to say that He was sent from the Father. Jesus intended to announce that He, the Galilean whom the people of Nazareth knew, was not merely the man whom they beheld before them, but had heavenly relations with the Invisible Father; that His existence did not begin on the earth, but had its home with the Father; that He knew the Father, as only the **Son** of God could know Him, and that He was revealing the Father to men.

It was not easy to explain such things to the people. "How shall ye believe," He asked, "if I tell you of heavenly things?" But Jesus uttered many sayings which might serve as avenues through which the true heavenly light might reach the hearts of **men. And** above all things, He repeated without ceasing the Father's name, using it with authority, and making men feel that He who thus spoke must be in a position and have **a** right so to speak of the Father.

The relation of Jesus to the Father was to be learnt, if we **are** to trust the Gospels and the preaching **of** the Apostles, from **what He** spoke and did and suffered **and was** as a grown man, and scarcely in **any** degree from **the** circumstances **of** His birth. **Jesus** Himself, so far as we know, in His public **preaching** and His controversies, never referred back **to His** birth. When the Apostles proclaimed Him **after** His ascension, they spoke of Him as having been sealed and glorified by the Father through the resurrection from the dead; as having shown the Divinity that was in Him by the works He had done and the words of eternal life which He had spoken. But it became a question of intense interest to the believers in Christ, How did this Revealer of the Father come into the world? He was seen and known by His disciples as the Word made flesh dwelling amongst men, full of grace and truth, manifesting a glory as of the only begotten Son of the Eternal Father; but how did the Word become flesh? And the answer given by the mother of Jesus and by His friends to this question, was, that He had been born of Mary at Bethlehem, in the natural helplessness of a human infant, and that He had grown up with her through childhood and boyhood to the age at which He was baptized by John and began Himself to proclaim the Kingdom of Heaven.

There has always been something of strangeness in the thought that the Son of God, He who said of Himself that He was in heaven whilst He was upon the earth, that the Father was in Him and He was in the Father, should have ever been clothed with the flesh of an infant and have lain upon the breast of a human mother. This wonder is so great, that all the accompaniments of the birth and childhood of Jesus sink into comparative insignificance by its side. If the Son of God were to be born at all, it seems to make little difference, in respect of wonderfulness, whether He was born in the stable of a country inn, or in the chamber of the most sumptuous palace. But in other respects it is a most important part of the Divine plan, that the Son of God should be born in such lowly circumstances, and that **the** first persons to pay Him honour should **be a** company of poor shepherds. The whole story of the Nativity of Christ seems very different from what men would have pictured to themselves in their own imaginations. How many there are who would say to themselves that such an entrance into the world, through the portals of birth and childhood, is but a poor introduction **for** the Son of God, compared with the descent of a full-grown kingly form from amongst the clouds of heaven!

So men might foolishly dream. But God's wisdom is justified by those who will allow themselves to be guided into true knowledge. The still small voice is more powerful and more divine than the great and strong wind rending the mountains and breaking in pieces the rocks, than the earthquake or the fire. Practically, whatever the love of the marvellous may have suggested in the way of derogation, the birth and infancy of the Son of God have exerted a mighty influence upon **the** hearts of men. **If** it were permitted to us to trace the workings **of** Christian faith throughout the history of the Church, how much of the truest and tenderest belief, how much of the most encouraging hope, how much of the most human and brotherly love, might be traced to the contemplation of the Babe of Bethlehem! Think, my friends, of what the joy of Christmas has been in all **ages.** Just as that act of our Lord, when He placed **a** little child in the midst of His followers, and bade them honour and cherish the childlike spirit, must have softened and humbled the hearts which had grown hard under the influence of worldly cares and ambition—so God seems to have placed the only begotten Son as a little child in the midst of the memories of mankind, in order that proud men may unlearn their worldly pride in the contemplation of this wonderful sight; that women may feel the sympathy of God penetrating their inmost souls, and that humanity may praise God in lowly and fearful exultation for the glory thus put upon it. Much of the very gentlest and holiest sentiment by which the world has ever been blessed, has been drawn forth by the memories and associations of Christmas. Glance for a moment over the Christmas-keeping now going on throughout Christendom. Everywhere it is marred and weakened by much unbelief; in many places it is degraded by a tawdry and silly superstition; too often there is so much coarse sensuality blended with Christmas mirth, that one is almost tempted to say that God's blessing is turned into a devil's curse. But notwithstanding all this, on this very day the seed of that Nativity at Bethlehem is bearing branches throughout all lands, adorned with the loveliest flowers and most precious fruits. The celebration of the birth of Jesus Christ has still the power to unlock the holy joy, the tender sympathies, the gracious charity, of countless thousands. The thought of Mary of Nazareth rejoicing in her Divine babe, of the Divine babe depending in natural helplessness upon the human mother, still proves itself akin and infectious to the best emotions, to the emotions which lie deeper than the arguments of reason or the calculations of prudence.

And surely heaven comes closer to earth, the Divine and the human coalesce more perfectly, through the human birth **of** the Son **of** God, than would be possible in any other way which our imaginations can conceive. What theories of human perfection, what **inferences** from the progress **of** civilization, could give us the strength and comfort we may find in the fact, that the Son of God consented to become altogether and from the beginning *a man?* Did He not, in this way, most powerfully and touchingly reveal the Father to us, by claiming human nature in its entirety for sonship to God? It is not only an elect spirit here and there which can claim the right, in virtue of its special endowments or special graces, to address God **as a** Father: the infant Jesus, the Divine Son of God, claims every human infant **as** His brother. The sonship of Christ is a more glorious inheritance for our children than all the achievements and hopes of humanity, regarded as apart from God. Because the children were partakers of flesh and blood, their Elder Brother, who was in the bosom of the Father, **did** not abhor the Virgin's womb, **but** Himself also likewise took part in the same, subjecting Himself, for the sake of a more perfect and consummate glory, to **the** limitations of human existence, and, whilst thus coming near to us, enabling us to come near to **God.**

As I said, it is Jesus the grown **man,** the master

of disciples, who mainly reveals the Father to us, and through whom we are to come to the Father. Christ crucified and risen, rather than the babe in the Virgin's arms, is He whom we confess as our Saviour. But it wonderfully extends and completes the revelation of the Father, that the Son should have given Himself to us as a brother in infancy and childhood no less than in manhood. It is not only that the fellowship of Christ with us is thus spread over a wider range, but that that fellowship is made at the same time deeper and more natural, rooted in a more entire identification of the existence of the Son of Man with that of every human brother. Thus it is that God uses the weak things of the earth to confound the mighty, and gives the victory and dominion to meekness.

May God teach us on this day to feel in our hearts that power which He has caused to reside for ever in the feeble form of the infant Jesus—the power to subdue our pride, the power to soften our affections, the power to kindle our faith and our hope.

Let us learn the lesson which Christ was so desirous to teach, that in all human life and at all ages, the childlike element is that which is pleasing to God. Not the capacity of the trained intellect, not the matured force of human powers, is that which is most enduring and most acceptable in God's sight; but trust and hope and love, these are the Divine elements that lie at the basis of humanity; these are what our Maker and Father chiefly desires to cultivate in us all; these are what will endure when all that is transient passes away. It is in the nature of **the little child** to trust and to hope and to love. Let us pray that we may all, with ever-growing insight, **be** kept continually in these same graces.

Let us also allow that tender, fatherly love of God, which is revealed in the Incarnation of Jesus Christ, to carry its due influence into our hearts. The disci**ples** of Jesus would have repelled little children and those that brought them, thinking of those little ones **as** too insignificant for a great Teacher and Prophet **to** care for. But He, in whom the Father was visible, rebuked them **and** said, Suffer the little children to come unto me, and forbid them not: and He took them up in His arms and blessed them. Surely in the event which we celebrate this day, we may behold **a** similar gesture of the eternal God taking up all simple and helpless human beings in His arms, and hear the benediction which puts His own Divine love upon them. When the Infinite God condescends, there is no alloy of stiffness or exclusiveness in His condescension; He condescends utterly—to the simplest needs and sympathies of those whom He has created in His own image. How can we sufficiently adore the love of Him who gave His own Son to be born of a woman at Bethlehem?

And, lastly, let us consider the glory that has thus been put upon human nature.

When theorising philosophers seek to make out a case for humanity, and to magnify what man has done and **will** do, what he is and will be, they are compelled **to** look lightly **over** the evidences of human sin and unreasonableness and misery, and to use all possible methods of observation and argument, to shut out from their calculations this terrible element. If they deal unflinchingly with human evil, their estimate of the glory and hope of humanity must be proportionately lowered. But it is not so with those who derive their faith in humanity from the revelation of that fellowship which God has established with it in His Son. It is not our part to shut our eyes to any of the signs of human perverseness and suffering. We are not compelled to evade the fearful tokens of oppression and hardness, of sensuality and vileness, of stupidity and wilful ignorance, which the history of mankind and its present condition exhibit in such sad abundance. The revelation of perfect humanity in Jesus Christ has undoubtedly a tendency to put a darker shade on human sin. We are led to think more seriously of it, to confess it more earnestly as not misfortune only, but guilt. It is well for us to know and admit how culpably men have gone astray from God. And we may do so without in the least abandoning our hope for the future of men and of humanity, without lowering by one degree our sense of the true glory of our race. For that glory does not depend on the achievements of any person or community, upon any heights or average of moral excellence which have hitherto been reached. It depends on the fact that we have a Father on the throne of heaven, a Brother at God's right hand, a Spirit who is not a result of civilization, but is the Divine mover of all good. This evil which we behold about us, of which we are conscious in ourselves, it is as real as it is deplorable. But God sent His own Son, let us heartily believe, to be our Saviour from it. In Him we behold the champion of the good in our behalf. Under Him we are called to serve, with the fullest faith in the inheritance of humanity, against all the wickedness and evil-doing that remains in the world. We are the heirs of all the ages, and this may seem a proud position; sometimes we may think the pride of this consciousness too inflating. But we have a much higher pride—the pride of knowing that the Son of God took our nature upon Him, and has for ever identified our destinies with His own.

I say, then, dear brethren, let us look on human nature in the light which the Incarnation throws upon it. Let us behold ourselves and other men as made God's children by adoption and grace. Let this view quicken our fellow-feeling, our sense of responsibility to our brethren, our desire to be helpful to those amongst whom we find ourselves placed. It is a glorious tradition of Christendom, that the season at which we celebrate the Saviour's birth should be marked by a special thoughtfulness as to the healing of all quarrels, as to the self-denial and kindness which may be shown in ministering to the wants of those who are in suffering or in need. This tradition, like the widening circles on a lake, has spread so as to embrace many who do not trouble themselves as to its origin or its centre. But we know why we ought to show ourselves at this season tolerant, forbearing, gentle, and kind. We are brought into the presence of the heavenly Father bestowing His own unspeakable gift upon our race. We are remembering the Sacrifice of which the Divine Nature has proved itself capable—the sacrifice which has disclosed the fountain from which all Divine bounty flows. Each new Christmas says, with Divine authority, to our hearts, Freely ye have received, freely give. Do not forget or despise the weak, the helpless, or the ignorant. Allow no temper or remembrance which tends to break the bond of family love established for mankind. Learn to look upon human nature as itself sacred, and upon all wrong and impurity as profaning that which God has claimed for His own.

VI.

THE TWO COVENANTS.

HEBREWS XII. 24.

" Ye are come . . . to Jesus the mediator of the New Covenant."

THERE are Christians to whom the word Covenant is distasteful, and who think that it belongs to a circle of ideas from which Christianity has set us free. It seems to them to represent a **narrow** Jewish notion, out of harmony with those wide views **of** God which Christians are taught to entertain. This rejection of the word covenant may be due to **two** causes. The word covenant may be taken to mean a *contract* or *bargain*, and **in** this sense it would certainly be our duty to reject it. **Such a** use of the word covenant would imply that God and man are **two** independent parties, making a conditional agreement with one another. **No** doubt covenants between **man** and man have this character. We bargain with **one** another, saying, On condition that you will do **this,** I will do **that. If** the one party fails to fulfil **his share of** the engagement, the other party is discharged from fulfilling *his* share. The relations between God and man, have been sometimes represented as having the nature of a contract, and some wholesome exhortations may have been founded on such an account of them. But it is true that the whole teaching of the New Testament presents the relations of God and man not under the form of a contract, but as being those of free spontaneous grace on God's part, and of thankful acceptance and submission on man's part. The word covenant, however, ought not, even in the Old Testament, to be understood as meaning a contract. It represents a bond between God and man, not formed by two contracting parties entering into conditional engagements, but created wholly by promises and goodness on God's part towards men. In such a sense the word covenant may still be available to describe a bond existing between God and us. But there is also a feeling opposed to the use of this word, which is not to be met by a mere explanation. There is a tendency existing, a most powerful and penetrating tendency, to regard all religions as the natural speculations of men about God, and the Christian religion as simply the highest and purest of those speculations. Now, it is the gravest possible question for us, Are we, in our religion, guessing about God, or has God been revealing Himself to us? The word covenant distinctly affirms that God has been revealing Himself to us, and that He maintains a connexion with us. If on this account the idea of a covenant is by some rejected or evaded as unreasonable, it is also precisely on this account that we ought, if possible, to preserve and to cherish it.

Reflections on what is involved in the term "the new covenant," appear to me particularly suitable at the present moment, and at the beginning of the new year. There is nothing in the circumstances of the day more interesting or important to us, as a Christian congregation and members of the Church of England, than that agitation which is still going on as to the grounds and assurance of our faith. The form taken by this agitation is chiefly that of discussions as to the nature and authority of Holy Scripture,—a subject which must always have a profound interest for any Christian community, but which has been disproportionately exciting and disturbing in consequence of the tradition which has so widely established itself, that the Christian Faith has nothing else to rest upon, except the infallible certainty of whatever is contained in the Bible. At the Reformation in the sixteenth century, the Bible, which had been so neglected and so pushed out of its place by unscriptural beliefs and practices as to have become almost an unknown book, was brought down from the shelves of the learned and put into the hands of the common people, to be not only the guide of private devotion and morality, but the test and criterion of all Church doctrine. Since that age, the Bible has been often proclaimed as itself the ground and evidence of all true belief. It has not been too highly valued—that is impossible, so long as it is taken for what it professes to be—but it has been made a kind of Divinity, which Protestants were required to fall down and worship. It has been separated too much from history and from the permanent continuous life of the Church of Christ and from the Providence and Inspiration continually watching over and sustaining the Church. And it happens, therefore, that the free critical inquiries of the present day, as to the origin and nature of the sacred books, have given a greater shock to the faith of many Christians than they ought to have had the power to do, even if those inquiries were more destructive than they are likely to be.

But what has the authority of the Bible to do with the idea of a covenant? Why this: that when we open the Bible, to see what it is, we find it to consist of two distinct volumes, each of which is made up of many books, and each of these volumes is called by the name of *a covenant*. The older and larger volume is the collection of the writings or books of the Old Covenant; the other contains the books of the New Covenant. It has to be regretted that the word Testament has come into use instead of Covenant; but the meaning intended by it is the same. We have two sacred volumes; one of these is about the Old Covenant, and the other is about the New Covenant. These titles represent the nature of the contents as accurately as any other books are described by their titles.

The books which we prize, then, and about the nature and authority of which there is so much controversy, are written records relating to an old covenant and to a new covenant, between God and men. And the primary question which the study of the Scriptures ought to raise is this: Is the thing which gives them their title *real* or not? Was there in reality, in former days, a covenant between God and one race of men? Is there now a covenant, established according to the account given in the books of the New Covenant, between God and mankind? These covenants, you will understand, were not *created* by the books which tell us about them, any more than the British Constitution was created by the Commentaries of Blackstone, any more than the actual history of England is created by a library of works on English history. The question of the inspiration of the Scriptures may be distinguished from the question of the reality and nature of those dealings of God with men which are described by the name of Covenants; and, when we have made this distinction, we perceive that the character of *the writings* must be quite secondary to the character of *God's dispensations* which the writings record. It is quite conceivable that the Old and the New Covenants should have existed in all their force as God's methods of connecting mankind with Himself, without having sacred books to expound them, without what is technically called a *canon* of Holy Scripture. It is conceivable that God should have chosen and guided Israel without causing particular prophecies, particular histories, to be set apart and preserved; that He should have sent His Son into the world to be born and to live and to die and to be raised again, without causing a certain number of narratives and letters to be put together under one title in the course of the second century. The speaking of God to men through His chosen saints in the older time, His speaking to men afterwards in the Person of His Son, are the facts of supreme importance; the *records* of this speaking are only means of expressing it more safely and completely to succeeding generations. It is instructive to reflect upon this fact, that whereas to us the New Testament or Covenant is the more sacred part of the sacred Book, to the Christians of St. Paul's time there was no such thing as a New Testament.

This distinction between the covenant itself and the written books which relate to it, is one which we should endeavour to fix clearly in our minds. Practically, I admit, we cannot sever the connexion which must always exist in our minds, say between the actual Life of Christ and the Four Gospels; but it may be important to remember that *Christ lived* before any Gospel was written or designed. For our faith is due to the Living Christ, and not to the books which enable us to know Him; and when we see this, any doubts which may be thrown on particular passages of Scripture will not be regarded by us as affecting the grounds of our faith. In short, the sacred writings are means to an end, that end being the knowledge of God and of His fellowship with men; and as they are not the only means to that end, so we are not justified in assuming beforehand, however important and precious they are, that they are absolutely without a flaw.

Let me illustrate what I wish to convey, as follows: Suppose a missionary to go amongst the heathen to preach the Gospel of Christ. He might begin, as St. Paul did when *he* preached Christ to the heathen, **without** mentioning sacred books at all. He might speak of Christ the **Son of** God, and commend the main truths concerning Him, say in the form of a Creed, **to** those who had not heard of Him. He might **do** this with so much power **of** the Spirit as to produce conviction **in** the hearts of some, and these he might baptize as Christians, in the name **of** the Father and of the Son and of the Holy Ghost. He might go thus far, if he thought it wise and desirable, without telling the converts of the existence of the New Testament. And then he might begin to inform them that there were certain books professing to be written, and believed to be really written, by contemporaries of the Lord Jesus, giving detailed accounts of things which He did and said and went through. **With** what delight would the new Christians hear of these books! **Of** what unspeakable value would such books be to them in confirming and expanding and deepening their faith! With what growing reverence and trust would they **be** read, being such books **as** they are! But these supposed believers would never dream of their faith in Christ depending upon **the solution of** any question that might be started **relating to** the criticism of these sacred writings.

As we grow **up,** generation after generation, the **great** presumptive evidences of our **faith** are such as these: the belief **of** our parents and of our country, the existence of the Church and of Christendom, the continuous **traditions of** history from the Apostolic age to the present, the wonderful qualities of the Scriptures, the beauty and sanctity of our inherited prayers and hymns and of all good Christian books. All these are arguments which tell with immense force upon our minds. Then come the more moving and convincing reasons which we find in our inward sense of the reality of what we believe, in the harmonies we observe between one truth and another, in the spiritual influences which affect us, in our practical discoveries of the will of God. By degrees we learn to verify and prove to ourselves, in many undefinable ways, the truth of what we are taught; we unlearn, perhaps, some things which will not bear the light which God Himself seems to be sending into our souls. And just in proportion as that which professes to be a revelation of God commends itself to our deepest and purest insight, in that proportion it will gain a hold over us and conquer us, and be really and altogether believed.

Now the aspect of divine revelation which the titles of our sacred books present to us, and which we find continually offered to us in those books themselves, is that of a covenant, or of close mutual relations which God has established between Himself and us.

There is an Old Covenant and a New Covenant.

The Old Covenant was that which was expressly made by Jehovah between Himself and Abraham and his seed. It was a union between God and one family chosen out of the rest of mankind. For a long time this covenant had no written records, or at least none that have survived in a separate and independent form. But, after a while, various books of the Hebrew nation grew together into a sacred and authorized collection, which was understood to be illustrative of the national covenant. In the first of these, the Book of Genesis, we read of the institution of the covenant; how God called out Abram, gave him the new name of Abraham, and promised to be the God of his seed after him. "I will be a God unto thee, and to thy seed after thee." One of God's promises to Abraham was, that he would give the land of Canaan to his seed; another, that in his seed all the nations of the earth should be blessed. The substance of the covenant was contained in the words, "I will be their God, and they shall be my people."

As a seal of this covenant, God appropriated the sign of circumcision. Every descendant of Abraham was to be circumcised; this circumcision was to remind him that he belonged to a family which was in covenant with the Lord God. At this season we are commemorating the fact that the child born of Mary was circumcised on the eighth day after His birth, and I think we can hardly ascribe any higher significance to this act, than by seeing in it a homage to the reality of the covenant. If an ordinary Israelite had not been circumcised—or, rather, had not brought his child to be circumcised—he would have been guilty of disbelieving or despising the covenant which Jehovah had made with His race. And so if Jesus had not been circumcised, not only would he have been separating Himself from His brethren, but the ancient covenant would have lost its most glorious testimony.

All the history of Abraham and of his posterity is a series of illustrations of God's faithfulness to the covenant which He had made. He caused a son to be born to Abraham and Sarah in their old age, expressly as a child of promise and in reward of faith. He made the seed of Abraham to multiply till they became a great nation. In the course of time He put them in possession of the land which He had promised to Abraham. At the same time, He gave them laws and a constitution, that they might be an organized people, having Jehovah for their God. A priesthood and a system of worship was established, in order that the people might have spiritual approach to Him. Kings were given, to reign in Jehovah's name; prophets rose up, to give special utterance to His will and to declare His purposes. Whenever the people confessed Jehovah as God and consented to be His people, then they found glory and blessedness, and prospered in strength and unity. When they broke the covenant, and followed other gods, they became disunited, weak, and corrupt, and were given over to conquerors to be chastised. The covenant was the abiding basis of all God's dealings with the chosen people; it furnished also a permanent law and principle for the public and private life of the people themselves.

The promise of the Abrahamic covenant found its highest fulfilment when God gave His Son to be born of the seed of Abraham and David, and to be the blessing of all the nations of the earth. It found this fulfilment; and then, as a special covenant, it expired. The coming of Jesus Christ was the signal for the passing away of all that was exclusive in the Divine dealings with men. Hints had been given through the prophets of a **new** covenant, which should be more glorious than the old. As the Old Covenant began visibly to pass away, in the extinction of those institutions which had been its appointed signs; in the destruction **of** the Temple, Jehovah's house; **in the** trampling under foot of Jerusalem, the holy city; **and** in the cessation of the sacrifices through which **the** sacred people had access to their God—the glory **of** the New Covenant began to shine out more distinctly to the eyes **of** the believers in Christ. Then it was seen and declared that the New Covenant was founded upon better promises, that its bond was stamped by a holier seal, that its blessings had a wider scope, that the fellowship with God which it bestowed was nobler, more intimate, and more spiritual.

The New Covenant was not expressed in words, but in the person of Jesus Christ, the Son of God. He was *the living Word* of the Father, in whom the Father's mind was known **and** heard, in whom the Father's new **and** better promises were plainly written out. We have **in the** Lord Jesus Christ an eternal pledge and bond **and** means of union with the invisible God. In sending His only-begotten Son to take our nature upon Him, **to** be born, to live, and to die, as a man, **and** then **to be raised** again and exalted by the glory of **the Father, God** not only said more expressively than any words could say **it**—Ye who share the flesh and blood which my Son has worn shall be my sons and daughters—but He showed us in *what kind* of sonship we were to be united with Him, what fatherly love would flow down from Him upon us, with what filial feelings we might look up to Him, what a holy spirit would bind the heart of God to man, and the hearts of men to God. Jesus, the Son of God, is the living Mediator of the New Covenant, in whom God has declared Himself to us, in whom we have access to God.

I do not know that any term will do better than the old Jewish word *covenant* to express the reality and the binding force of the fellowship with God which has been given us in Christ. And the sense of this is a power upon our hearts which we cannot afford to lose. We learn how decidedly it was God's will that we should regard ourselves as brought into covenant with Him, from His appointment of an ordinance which replaces the old national rite of circumcision, and seals us as partakers of His promises. Our baptism stamps us severally as members of Christ, brought through Him into filial and spiritual fellowship with God. And our common Church life, our public prayers and praises and our holy communion, are witnesses that we should not confine the sense of the covenant-relation each to himself in secret, but that we should regard one another as partners in the same fellowship, knowing no man after the flesh merely, but accounting of all as *in Christ*, under the law of a spiritual creation, God's redeemed children.

Do we want to enter fully into the meaning of this

heavenly covenant? The Scriptures of the New Covenant are intended to teach us about it. Their first principle and highest office is to relate to us the manifestation of the Son of God in our flesh; to present to us Jesus of Nazareth, speaking, acting, suffering, and glorified, as the Son of the living God. All the covenant may be studied in Him. But these writings go on to exhibit to us a society of men called out to bear witness of the covenant, and to be bound together by voluntary public ties in the name of Christ, as men for His sake reconciled to the Father. This society, the Church of Christ, is set before us as the permanent external form of the fellowship of mankind with God. We have much, therefore, recorded for us, especially in the letters of the Apostles, which throws light upon the nature, the calling, the duties, the dangers, the glorious rights and hopes of the Church of Christ. All these helps, blessed be God, are richly supplied us in the books of the New Covenant. Let us prize them, and let us use them. Let us seek through their means to know our calling better, and to act up to it more loyally and faithfully.

And, on this first Sunday of a New Year, dear brethren, I would commend to you a pious recollection of what God has done and provided for us in His Covenant, as a fit preparation for what is before us. Times pass away, and with them the generations of flesh and blood. Privately, we may have other anniversaries which touch us more closely—birthdays, wedding-days, even days of death, serving as marks of time, as milestones on our earthly road. But, as a community, bound together by common interests which we all know and recognise, it is at the end of each year that we publicly take account of the lapse of time, and say to ourselves, Thus much of our life, of our history, we put behind us; we stand between the past and the future—the awful past and the awful future; for the past we are, in our measure and degree, responsible; over the future— mysterious thought!—we have some power. What are we, that such responsibilities should be entrusted to us? What are we, that we should be called upon to work in this great world, to reduce some disorder to harmony, to diffuse some light into surrounding darkness, to carry on the mighty designs of the Maker, to bring forth some small results which He will accept as *fruit* according to our kind? What are we? Children of dust; creatures of frail flesh and blood; subjects of impulse and custom; weakened, all of us, and stained, by conscious sin. True, but not all this *only*. It is not as sinful mortal creatures that we are called to gird ourselves to the performance of duty, and to aim at doing good and being good. We are sons and daughters of the Divine covenant, which stands sure while seasons revolve and times change. God in heaven has reconciled us to Himself, and redeemed us out of the kingdom and from the power of darkness, and has set us as children of light in His own kingdom of righteousness and love. This is the character in which we are called upon to forget that which is behind, and to press forward to that which is before, to attempt tasks for which **our** mortal weakness **is** plainly incapable, to cherish hopes **which nothing on** earth could inspire.

Let us, therefore, take courage; and while **we repent of the** sins and shortcomings of the past, let us go forward in hope. **He to** whom **we** pray is not a new God. He is the Ancient of Days, the Rock of Ages, the God in whom our fathers hoped, a faithful and covenant-keeping God; let us have faith in **Him,** that He will be our God, and the God of our children, for ever.

VII.

JESUS IN THE MIDST OF THE DOCTORS.

ST. LUKE II. 46.

"*It came to pass, that after three days they found him in the temple, sitting in the midst of the doctors, both hearing them, and asking them questions.*"

It is a very natural curiosity which would prompt us to ask questions about our Lord's boyhood. In an early age of the Church, attempts were made to gratify this curiosity by the invention of fabulous stories. Some of these narratives have come down to us: there is one in particular, called the "Gospel of the Infancy," which gives many anecdotes relating to the childhood of Jesus. These stories are for the most part extremely trivial and unworthy; and the only use of them is to serve as a contrast to the authentic Gospels. They show the kind of product to which the imaginative instincts of those ages would give birth—especially the sort of miracles which would be popularly attributed to a Divine Son of Man. If the Gospels were a mythology, they would be something very different from what they actually are. They might probably have contained more incidents belonging to our Lord's boyhoood;

but there would have been nothing in them so simple, so noble, so instructive, as the occurrence which St. Luke has recorded—the single fact which breaks the long interval between the infancy and the baptism of Jesus.

The first remark which I would offer upon the whole purport of this narrative of Christ amongst the doctors is this: that its significance turns very mainly upon our Lord's *age* at the time of this visit. It is the opening of a special epoch in the life of Jesus, that of boyhood or youth, which is here presented to us.

This aspect of the narrative becomes clearer when we see it illustrated by a fact which commentators have been able to supply from the history of Jewish customs. It appears that the twelfth year was a marked point in the life of a Jewish youth. He was then called by a title which means "Son of the Law." Thenceforward he began to bear a part in the various duties prescribed by the Law. Without pressing the analogy too closely, we might compare this time of life amongst the Jews with that of Confirmation or the First Communion in the Christian Church.

Now, one of the regular duties of pious Jews was to go up to Jerusalem to worship at the great festivals. For women, it was prescribed, not by the Law of Moses, but by the tradition of doctors of the Law, that they should go up once in the year only. Accordingly, we read that the parents of Jesus, Joseph and His mother, went to Jerusalem every year at the Feast of the Passover. Whilst He was still under the age of twelve, they went up in all probability without Him; but when He was twelve years old, they took Him with them.

It is most likely that this was the *first visit* of Jesus to Jerusalem and the Temple. It could not have been usual to take young children upon so considerable a journey as that from Nazareth to Jerusalem; and the first occasion of seeing the Holy City—when combined with the first performance of one of the most solemn religious duties of his nation—must have been in a high degree exciting and awakening to any Jewish boy.

It is under these circumstances, then, that we are to consider our Lord as separating Himself from His parents, and staying behind them when they left Jerusalem. Do not endeavour first or chiefly to think of Jesus as *unlike* any other Jewish boy. We ought to think of Him, rather, as at each point of His life the pattern and ideal of other human beings. And He was not only the Son of Man, but He was also, it is to be remembered, born under the Law. He was the true Israelite, as well as the perfection of humanity. He must therefore have been filled, up to the measure of a child, with reverence and loyalty towards the institutions and the history of His nation. From a child, He must have known the Holy Scriptures, and must have learnt how God had been manifesting Himself to the fathers, and guiding them ever onwards by the light of the Great Promise. He must have heard His elders speak of the city which God had chosen to place His name there; and of the Temple which was God's tabernacle, the sign of His dwelling amongst His people; and of the sacrifices which were continually smoking upon the altars; and of the priests who were appointed in behalf of the people in things pertaining to God; and of the learned scribes and lawyers, the rabbis or masters, whose profession it was to copy and to expound the sacred books. Year by year He had watched, with growing interest and yearnings, the departure of His parents as they went up loyally and devoutly to take part, according to the Law, in the great National Festival, chanting, perhaps, the words, certainly feeling the aspirations, of the 122d Psalm: "I was glad when they said unto me, We will go into the house of the Lord. Our feet shall stand in thy gates, O Jerusalem. Jerusalem is built as a city that is at unity in itself. For thither the tribes go up, even the tribes of the Lord, to testify unto Israel, to give thanks unto the name of the Lord. For there is the seat of judgment, even the seat of the house of David. O pray for the peace of Jerusalem; they shall prosper that love thee. Peace be within thy walls, and plenteousness within thy palaces. For my brethren and companions' sakes, I will wish thee prosperity: yea, because of the house of the Lord our God, I will seek to do thee good."

And now, having reached the appointed age, Jesus also was come up as an Israelite and worshipper, and beheld with His eyes the things of which He had heard with His ears. There was much at Jerusalem that would disappoint and shock Him when He came to be familiar with it; but, perhaps, at first the objects which had been present to His youthful imagination absorbed His attention; and He could not sufficiently gaze upon the buildings and the persons which bore witness of the Law and of the worship of Jehovah.

We can never approach the subject of the actual consciousness of the Lord Jesus Christ—what He thought and felt—without a sense of ignorance and perplexity. We are often tempted to dismiss it entirely from our minds, and to be not only silent, but uninquiring about it. But this can hardly be right. If we are to *consider*, as the Apostle bids us, Jesus Christ, our Representative and Leader, we must think of His *mind*. With what reverence and caution we must do this, we should all be ready to acknowledge. But the danger does not lie, I think it may be said, in ascribing to our Lord the most truly natural consciousness under any circumstances, even though in so doing we necessarily assume limitations which appear to deny His Divine nature. Such limitations are involved in the very fact of the Incarnation; and we do not in the least escape from them by merely attempting to make Christ a superhuman person. And we are faithfully following the Evangelist, who tells us that Jesus *grew* in *wisdom* and stature, and in favour with God and man, if we take this growth for granted, and assume that the mind of Jesus really opened by degrees to take in the facts of the Divine dispensation under which He **was** made in the likeness of our mortal flesh.

Let us, therefore, suppose, as **we** surely may without introducing vain conjectures, that the youthful Jesus was so intensely interested and occupied by what He **saw** and took part in at Jerusalem, that He hardly thought of the departure **of** His Galilean neighbours for Nazareth. He is drawn to the Tem**ple,** and to the schools of the rabbis, held in outer chambers of the Temple; for this sacred edifice was not like a Church, consisting of one large open area, but like some **of** our other public buildings, with many chambers and courts. In one of these chambers rabbis were teaching the Law, in that lively manner of questioning and answering which was the habit of the time, and which has always been usual in the East. Jesus joined the circle, and took part in the discussion of the subject. He heard the doctors deliver their interpretations and opinions, and asked them questions. And all that heard Him, we are told, were astonished **at** His understanding and answers.

It has been often, perhaps most commonly, supposed, that the usual parts of teacher and learner were inverted in the case of our Lord and these doctors, and that the young boy was seen giving instruction to mature and learned men. There is some foundation for this belief. For although there **is no** reason whatever to suppose that our Lord appeared as a teacher **at** that **early** age, or that His questions were put with any purpose but that of gaining information, there is no doubt that the learned teachers were themselves learning a new and awakening lesson. Nor is it, indeed, a rare thing for the instructor to learn from the pupil. Many a pedant, trained in the maxims and traditions of a school, would learn more by familiar intercourse with an open-hearted and inquiring child than his books could teach him. A fresh, wondering, eager human mind is suggestive of many thoughts which may throw light upon the subjects of human inquiry. Some such effect, proceeding from the perfect innocence and humility and godliness of the boy Jesus, was probably made upon the rabbis. They were awed, we may believe, by the simplicity of the Divine youth, and startled by the intelligence of His answers and inquiries. But it is better not to suppose that there was any departure, in the conduct of Jesus, from the modesty which is the divinest ornament of the young.

Meanwhile, the parents of Jesus had lost Him for three days. The first day of their journey they thought He was in some other part of the company, and did not seek Him anxiously till nightfall. Then they sought Him amongst their kinsfolk and acquaintance; and not finding Him, returned to Jerusalem. There they looked for Him in the public places, and at last found Him in the Temple, sitting in the midst of the doctors. When they saw Him thus calmly engaged, their feelings of tenderness and joy were mixed with surprise. "My son," exclaimed the mother's heart of Mary, "why hast thou **thus** dealt with us? Behold, thy father **and** I have sought thee sorrowing." The answer of Jesus was that which **is** rendered in our version, "How is it that ye sought me? Wist **ye** not that I must be about my Father's business?"

It seems to be doubtful whether the last words of this answer **are** quite correctly rendered. Jesus does **not** say exactly, "I must be *about my Father's business*," in the sense "I must be doing that which my Father has commissioned Me to do;" but "I must be in my Father's house, or occupied in my Father's things." "Did you not know that I must be at my Father's?" "Did you not know that my Father's affairs must interest Me?"

It is more natural that Jesus should say this, than that He should speak distinctly of His mission from the Father. The rendering of our Bible gives some countenance to the mistake that Jesus was professedly instructing the doctors, and in that way was doing His Father's business. But if He was in the Temple, partly that He might *be in* the Temple, as God's chosen house, partly that He might learn about the recorded doings and laws of God from the professed teachers of them, then He was truly "at His Father's," **or** "engaged in the things of His Father."

How much was in the mind of Jesus when He spoke these words, we cannot venture to pronounce. Whether we think of the Son of Man in His youth, or of any other boy wearing the same flesh and blood, would it not be always impossible to pronounce how definitely and clearly, under what precise limits, a new and higher consciousness is making itself felt? It is in the very nature of growing thoughts to be indeterminate, to have something of the character of hints and anticipations of what is coming. The analysis of any man's thoughts and feelings is far beyond the power of human science; still more, we might perhaps say, the analysis of a *youth's* thoughts and feelings is impossible to us, let us have all the information about him which we can ask for.

Therefore, let us not endeavour to determine *how far*, when Jesus spoke of the house or the things of "His Father," He had realized the knowledge which that name, my Father, afterwards expressed when He uttered it. The teaching of the sacred history would guide us thus far—that it would lead us to attribute to our Lord at that time, *not* the thoughts of the grown man, but those suited to boyhood. But as I have said, if we cannot analyse the thoughts of any boy, still less may we find it in our power to analyse those of the Divine Boy.

Every Jewish child, we may remember, was taught to call God his Father, and to honour the Temple and the Law as sacred to his Father. And Jesus, we may further observe, is suggesting something which He thinks ought not to be quite strange to His parents, when He says, Did you not know, that I must be interested in the things of my Father? We might therefore be safe, perhaps, in concluding, that, with the knowledge of His mission from the Father yet undeveloped, waiting indeed for His baptism by

John to call it forth, the mind of Jesus expressed in His answer to His parents, was what the perfect Jewish Boy, fulfilling exactly according to the Divine will the conditions of Jewish youth, might be expected to disclose.

To proceed now to the observations by which we might connect this revelation of the Divine youth of our Saviour with ourselves, I should say that our interest in it would be primarily associated with *a similar age* in common human life. In reading something that tells us concerning Jesus as a youth, we think first of youth and boyhood amongst ourselves.

We perceive, then, that that which is most characteristic in this time of life is hallowed by having been manifested in our Head and Lord. I speak here of the independent energies, the spirit of inquiry, which will naturally mark the schoolboy age, the period, say, from twelve to eighteen years. It is not without interest that we observe the characteristics of this age thus recognised. It is not always agreeable to parents to find that childhood is ending. The anxiety which will, and which should, contemplate the change from infancy to youth, is sometimes mixed too much with fear and regret. It is true that infancy is an image of the Divine, and is brooded over by heavenly care and love. It is true that reasonable manhood has its pattern and leader in the Son of God, and that the service of its mind and its deeds is acceptable to God in Heaven. But it is also true that the transition state, in which energies may seem irregular, in which curiosity may seem wandering, in which you can neither recognise the passive simplicity of the child nor the settled independence of the man, is in like manner God's creation, has in like manner a Divine ideal, and may seek in like manner Divine approbation. The eager spirit of the boy, the forgetfulness—may one say?—of earlier associations, the keen interest in learning about the things ennobled by history and cared for by grown men, these have their example in the Lord Jesus Christ, when He left His parents and let them seek Him for three days sorrowing.

And let me call your attention here to another characteristic, not only of the youth of Jesus, but of all human youth; I mean the special *seriousness* which belongs to the dawning of a higher consciousness upon a young mind, and to the first awakening of an interest in real life and history. A wise parent or teacher will not be ignorant of this seriousness, which is one of the most beautiful of God's inspirations; no one but a profane person would crush it or blight it. Happy those young persons in whom it is cherished and responded to by the tone of those about them; who are led from their earliest thoughts to honour all that is good and noble and godlike; in whom the fresh admiration of what is high and aspiring finds a congenial atmosphere in which to breathe. Do not forget this law in human nature. Do not make light of what may seem the premature seriousness of the young. Think of Jesus Christ, when He had become a Son of the Law and was the companion of His parents in their going up to Jerusalem, with what absorbing eagerness His young mind was drawn to the study of the sacred things **which** were the inheritance of His race, how deeply **He** felt that He must be concerned in the things of His Father in Heaven.

And let us learn this, also, from the narrative before us. We have assumed, not without sure grounds for it, that our Lord's mind had been fed with a knowledge of the glories of His nation, and of the great things which God had done for it. It was the **mind thus** nurtured which burst forth **in** the school of the rabbis. We may almost imagine our Lord to have answered His parents' expostulation more fully thus: ' You have told me for many years of this city and its glory; you have made me learn about David and Solomon, about Moses and the giving of the Law, about Isaiah and the Captivity, and the return from that bondage, and about the splendour and piety of the restored Temple; did you not know that these things would be irresistible in their attraction **to** Me? Did you not know that amongst these signs and witnesses of my Heavenly Father I must linger and ask questions?' Brethren, let us see here our own obligation to present similar **food to the** minds of our children. Let them have **the** power of saying, with ourselves, " O God, we have heard with our ears, and our fathers have declared unto us, the noble works that Thou didst in their days, and in the old time before them." Let our children be taught, not only by the help of the Scriptures what God did eighteen centuries ago, but by the help of history what He has been doing since for the Church universal, and especially for our own nation and for His Church in these realms. Then shall we not rejoice if we see them grappling with any sort of curiosity, even with irregular and wilful impulses, with the questions that are sure to arise in their minds; if we see them longing to solve the mystery of good and evil, to separate rashly the admirable from the contemptible, to take sides eagerly with what they honour most in the past and in the present?

But, again: it is a true principle that nothing in human life that is really good and divine ought to be thrown away as useless. The good of childhood ought to remain in the grown-up person; if it seem to be lost, it must come back. Similarly the good of boyhood ought to remain in the grown man. That spirit of hope and wonder and inquiry ought not to go out in mere extinction. The more it lives and burns under the quieter outside of manhood the better for the man and for his neighbours. Let us claim the example of Jesus, therefore, as a warrant for the uncovering of our doubts, instead of the crushing of them; for the *hope* of finding out truth instead of despair; for the conviction that God wishes us to be occupied in His mysteries, and to ask questions about Him, even if those who surround us are not able to give them satisfactory answers. Nowhere in the Scriptures, in the teaching of our Saviour or His Apostles, do we find any warning against honest and hopeful inquiry, any advice to rest in what is told us through despair of obtaining any better knowledge. The Bible teaches us, rather, that God Himself awakens our doubts in order that He may meet them in His own way; that only those who seek shall find; and that the blessedness in store for every man without exception is that which is at the same time the glory of the most inspired minds, the actual knowledge of the Father and of the Son in the fellowship of the uniting Spirit.

But whilst we may profitably learn this lesson, another remains, equally good both for boyhood and manhood. Jesus went home with His parents, was subject to them, grew in wisdom as in age, and in favour not with God only, but also with men; and for some eighteen years was content to be in obscurity, working with His own hands, restraining, it may be, the prophesyings of His coming destiny within His own spirit, a young man with other men. What a witness to us all of the blessedness and authority of the family affections, of domestic government, of social well-doing? Will it not be well for the young amongst us, if they will make the example of Jesus their guide? Let them not stifle the workings of their youthful energies, of their youthful desire to know as well as to do. Let them believe that God has been with their fathers and that He is **still** with them, and that He would have them trust in Him as their teacher and helper. Let them be persuaded that there is a Heavenly Teacher above all earthly teachers, who uses earthly teachers as His instruments. Let them rejoice in hope, in speculation, in the former and the future glory of their people and of their race. But let them remember, also, the commandment which associates the honour of parents with the continuance of national prosperity. Let them cherish a spirit of respect towards their parents at the same time that they look beyond their parents' rule. Do they begin to discover imperfections in their parents, signs of want of wisdom, want of self-control, want of that purity and simplicity of life which would make them good guides to their children? Let them remember how the sinless Boy and Youth was subject to parents of like passions with ourselves, and led a domestic life which won Him the favour of men as well as of God.

And let us all remember how the order of family life has been consecrated by the submission of our Lord Jesus Christ. We find this order existing as a fact, a part of nature itself. But we are tempted at times—some of us much more strongly than others—to rebel against it, to dislike its discipline, to profane its sanctities, to complain of the vexations which are often associated with it. At such times it may help us to be reminded of the plain family of Nazareth, in which the Saviour of the world spent His childhood and youth. It may make us feel what worth there is in the Divine institutions to which we are born, even when, through our faults and the faults of others, they do not work smoothly. It may teach us to make the best and not the worst of things; to think less of our happiness and more of our duty. So shall we be in the way to inherit the highest blessings — the blessings which are grounded in reverence towards God, in piety towards parents, in **the conquest** of self. It will contribute in part to **the attainment of** a perfect fellowship with the Son of God, if we learn to conform with sweetness and cheerfulness to the obligations of domestic life; and to be made like unto Him is our highest glory and reward.

VIII.

THE MIRACLE OF CANA.

St. John ii. 11.

"This beginning of miracles did Jesus in Cana of Galilee, and manifested forth his glory."

THE life of our Lord, after His baptism, was full of those works which are for the most part called "signs" by the Evangelists, but which are commonly spoken of by us as "miracles." I said, "after His baptism," because we have good reason to believe that, until Jesus was thus commissioned and began to proclaim the Kingdom of Heaven, He wrought no such works. The mighty works which our Lord wrought most frequently, and by which He was best known, were those of healing. But He occasionally did other wonderful works; and this work done at Cana, which St. John appears to relate as the very first of His miracles, and to which, on this account, a peculiar interest attaches, was not an act of healing. It was by turning water into wine for the use of a marriage festival that Jesus began that exercise of a more than human power, which was one mode of the manifestation of His Divine glory.

THE MIRACLE OF CANA.

St. John's narrative gives to this sign a marked place in the personal history of our Lord.

Jesus had already gathered a few disciples round Him. Their acceptance of Him as the Messiah had depended primarily upon the testimony of John the Baptist. Whilst announcing the Kingdom of Heaven, John had spoken of one whose forerunner he was, in whose person the kingdom was to be manifested. When Jesus of Nazareth came to him, John knew Him, and pointed Him out to some, at least, of his followers. Two of these, of whom Andrew was one and John the son of Zebedee in all probability the other, heard their master say of Jesus, "Behold the Lamb of God!" This brought His two first disciples to Jesus. Some others joined them, and immediately attached themselves, as a small band of personal followers, to the Prophet of Nazareth. It was the witness of John, combined with the personal authority of Jesus—and not any display of supernatural power—which won these first adherents.

But it was not long before a remarkable sign was given them, by which their first faith was rewarded and confirmed. In a village or small town of Galilee, probably not far from Nazareth, a marriage took place, which was celebrated, according to custom, with a feast. We are not told who the bridegroom and the bride were; but it may be inferred that they were connected either as relations or friends with the family of Jesus. His mother was one of the guests at the marriage, and both Jesus and his followers were also invited. The supply of wine began to fail, and the mother of Jesus was in some way made aware of it. St. John thinks it important to record what took place between the mother and her Son. She said to Him, "They have no wine. Jesus answered, Woman, what have I to do with thee? my hour is not yet come. Then His mother said to the servants, Whatsoever He saith to you, do it." And almost immediately the sign was wrought.

What is here said about the mother of Jesus is evidently intended by the Evangelist to be carefully noticed. The story of the miracle might have been told without any mention of Mary. Those words of Jesus which sound strange in our ears had a real strangeness, and were exceptional and significant. Attempts have been made to show that the language of the original does not express the rebuff which strikes us in the exclamation, " Woman, what have I to do with thee? my hour is not yet come:" and certainly the original is free from that discourtesy which there would be to us in addressing any one as Woman. But there seems to be no doubt that Jesus was expressly and even peremptorily rejecting the interference of His mother. It is well to remember that the Evangelist who records an occurrence which cannot be said to be flattering to the mother of our Lord, is he who heard, amidst the extreme agonies of the Cross, the words, "Woman, behold thy son," "Behold thy mother," and who took Mary thenceforth to his own home. Indeed it is probable that it is from Mary herself that St. John learned what took place at Cana between her and her Son.

Now, in considering the repulse thus given to Mary, we must recall what St. Luke tells us, that Jesus grew **up at** Nazareth subject to His parents. We cannot be sure, but it seems not unlikely that His quiet life under the parental roof had continued up to the time of our Lord's going to John. Day by day, and year by year, we may suppose, Jesus continued to discharge the duties laid upon Him, paying honour and reverence both to Joseph and Mary as to parents. **If** so, it was most natural that Mary should have continued to exercise a kind of gentle motherly authority over her Son. She may have learnt to think of Him **as of** one always ready to carry out her wishes, always anxious to consult her pleasure. She knew Him only as her loving Son. When she became aware, indeed, of what had taken place at the baptism, and of the exalted character publicly recognised in Jesus **by** the Baptist, and of the adhesion of the disciples to Him as a Master, she must have been profoundly interested and excited. Memories which had perhaps almost gone to sleep in her heart, must have been awakened into wondering life. She may well have looked for striking demonstrations of power, for overwhelming displays of glory, from Him who was now proclaimed as the Messiah. But, at the same time, she would not have been the true woman she was, unless she had longed, perhaps unconsciously, to retain her motherly influence over her Son, and had felt something of a personal pride in the expectation of His mighty achievements.

Jesus, however, **was** not to go forth amongst **men**

as the Son of Mary. His Baptism had sealed Him as the Son of the Eternal Father. In the name of that Father He was to speak and to work. Not only inwardly, but also outwardly in the sight of men, He was to be devoted to the doing of His Father's will. This it was necessary that Mary should understand. She was now not to look upon her Son as moved and guided by her. He was to be to her, as to others, the Revealer of His Father in heaven. We may rejoice to believe that, in the after-time, this change did not quench or impair the love between our Lord and His mother. But it is possible to see, nevertheless, that the change could hardly occur without some violence being done to the old motherly feeling of Mary. Once for all, she learnt what she had to learn at that marriage feast at Cana. That her feelings, even then, were not deeply wounded, we infer from her saying immediately to the servants, "Whatsoever he saith unto you, do it."

The remark which called forth the rebuff, "They have no wine," cannot have been without purpose. Whether Mary distinctly contemplated some such act as that which our Lord afterwards performed, we cannot positively say. But that some hint, distinct or vague, was implied in the observation "They have no wine," is certain from what Jesus says in answer to it. His words have no meaning unless we suppose that His mother was moving Him to do something extraordinary. We may expand her remark thus: "They have no wine: is not this a favourable opportunity of showing thy power?" If a motion of this kind were to be accepted by Jesus from any one on earth, it would have been from His mother. But with reference to such manifestations of His heavenly glory, He had nothing to do with any one on earth, nothing even with her whom He loved best. His hour was not come when she made a suggestion to Him. He was waiting on the moving will of the Father in heaven.

The saying, "My hour is not yet come," is not without difficulty, and it has been variously interpreted. There can have been, at the most, but a short interval of time between the moment when Jesus spoke those words, and the moment when He wrought the miracle. It has been asked, therefore, what Jesus meant by His hour; and some have thought that He meant here, as elsewhere, His hour of suffering and humiliation. But I am inclined to think that our Lord, though using time-language, is not speaking so much of time, as of motive: that He says to His mother, "Your desire is not the proper occasion for my doing a mighty work; I await a higher impulse; till *that* moves me, my time for working is not come."

But, from whatever cause, Mary retained her expectation. She still felt that, though not at her bidding, her Son was going to manifest His power. What gave rise to this presentiment, we cannot say. Perhaps Mary, with womanly sympathy, was concerned for the credit of her friend the host, and trusted instinctively to the same sympathy in the heart of her Son. She would **not** have been wrong in giving Him credit even for so humble a sympathy as with a host and his party at an entertainment at which the supplies were failing. No human fellow-feeling was foreign to the heart of Jesus. However that might be, the presentiment was so strong and lively, that Mary gave vent to it by preparing the servants to do whatever Jesus might bid them.

The servants soon received the anticipated direction. Certain waterpots, of which St. John realized both the size and the position when the whole scene came back vividly to his mind, were standing near. Jesus said to the servants, Fill these waterpots with water. They filled them to the brim, and then Jesus bade them draw off some of the water into wine-jars, and present it to the governor or chairman of the feast. The water was found to have become—probably in the smaller vessels only—good wine. St. John remembered that it was genuine good wine, because the chairman of the feast had remarked specially how good it was.

This, then, was the beginning of the signs and wonders which Jesus wrought so abundantly. St. John's comment upon it is, that "He manifested forth his glory," and that "his disciples believed on him." He had done an act which transcended human power. Suddenly, and without any visible processes, He had changed water into wine. An act so marvellous must have naturally produced a great impression upon the minds of the disciples. And it was for the disciples especially, as it would appear, that this miracle was wrought. Nothing is said of any effect which it produced upon the guests generally. The miracle was done "as it were in secret." The servants who drew the water knew of it, but the guests were allowed to drink the wine as if it were from the bridegroom's stores. "Thou hast kept the good wine until now." But the disciples and Mary, who already believed in Jesus, when the sign was made known to them, believed in Him the more. This is quite in harmony with the subsequent exercise by our Lord of His superhuman power. He never made a miraculous work the ground of faith in Him. He desired first to touch the conscience, the heart, the will; and when He had already drawn out some degree of trust, He would then do mighty works, which would enable those who believed in Him to understand more thoroughly *who* He was, and to confide in Him more implicitly.

If, then, any keen-eyed critic were to examine the proofs of this miracle, taken as St. John has related it, and were to come to the conclusion that, so far as we are enabled to judge, there was nothing in it which might not have been accomplished by easy jugglery; that there was no such searching inspection of the whole process of it as the scientific men of our day would apply—say to some spiritualist miracle; that, therefore, this narrative is a very insufficient basis upon which to build supernatural pretensions;—it would be reasonable at once to admit that this is so. The conduct of Jesus in the working of miracles was not that of one making supernatural claims, and submitting them to the rigid investigation of the incredulous. To have acted in such a spirit and manner, would have been to discard His own method, and to adopt a quite different one. The Evangelists tell us, that when the people were disbelieving, Jesus could do no mighty works *because of their unbelief*. In the case of a suspected impostor, such conduct would of course increase our suspicion against him. "Those only are convinced," we should say, "who are prepared beforehand to be convinced." But we may also say the same thing of our Blessed Lord, accepting all the inferences from it. For it is plain to those who look carefully into the Gospels, that the Lord Jesus did not present Himself to men as a miracle-worker desiring to have His pretensions investigated. He spoke with authority to their hearts and consciences. If they were not ready, as spiritual beings, to recognise His authority over their spirits, but professed themselves willing to recognise Him on the condition of His demonstrating His power by miracles, then he used to *refuse* the miracles; for He positively disapproved of this kind of faith. It was not that which He desired. It was likely to interfere injuriously with the true faith— the faith which looked up through Him to the Eternal Father in heaven.

Look again at the illustration which the narrative we have been considering affords us of our Lord's method. He was made known in some way to John the Baptist—not by any supernatural act which He did, but by some sign which John inwardly recognised. The Baptist had so far gained the confidence of some of his followers, that his testimony had great weight with them. When he pointed out Jesus as the **Lamb of** God, two of them were so far persuaded as to go to Jesus and talk with Him. His conversation impressed them still more. What they heard and saw convinced them that **He** was *true*, and that He came from the Father in heaven. Jesus made them His disciples, and they followed Him. Then, after **a** short time, Jesus performed a work which did not, indeed, court concealment, which was done simply and openly, but without courting attention or inquiry, and which certainly would not of itself have satisfied any sagacious critic. But it was suitable and sufficient for its end. It manifested His glory to those who were prepared to see it. It gave Him a position in the eyes of the disciples, and of His mother, which He desired to occupy, and which it was important for them that He should occupy. It taught them to look upon Him as one wielding the powers of nature, exercising a real heavenly authority over the things of earth.

Now, which character is the more worthy of the Son of God—that of one who speaks **with** authority to the minds of men, and claims a spiritual faith and obedience, or that of one who should present him**self** to men **as a** miracle-worker, submitting himself to **their** scientific judgment upon his supernatural pretensions? I cannot conceive **of** any hesitation in answering this question. The way of Jesus was evidently more lofty, more Divine, more efficacious, than the other way, which some, both friends and foes, would wish to thrust upon Him. And we, now in this day, must take Him as He is shown to us in the Gospels, and not according to our notions of desirable or necessary evidence. We must consider, with our hearts open and humble, whether Jesus of Nazareth is true, and a speaker of truth, or not ; whether His character, and words, and acts, are those of one really sent from God, or those of a mythical hero or inflated enthusiast.

And when we have believed in Jesus Christ, His miracles will do for us the work which they did for the first disciples. They will manifest His glory, so that our faith may become deeper and more adoring. Every miracle of Christ is *instructive*, and charged with some testimony as to the nature and will of God. So it is with this, the beginning of the signs of the Lord Jesus, the miracle of the Cana marriage. Let us glance at some of its special lessons.

1. A festive party wanted wine. The scenery of the story is perfectly simple, and we ought to take it in all its simplicity. Men and women in a country village were eating and drinking together, in celebration of a domestic rejoicing, not to excess, but heartily. Whether it were through the poverty of the host, or that the party was larger than he had expected, the supply of wine ran short. Jesus, who had just been sealed as the beloved and perfectly-acceptable Son of the Heavenly Father, comes to the help of the entertainment, and provides wine, which the guests drink and enjoy. Who must not recognise in such an act a benediction pronounced upon simple social enjoyment? You know that the

tendency of *religion*, as mere religion, has always been to call enjoyment evil, and to put a ban upon the things which minister to enjoyment. Self-denial for the sake of doing the Father's will, has been turned into a refusal of the good things which God has created, as if they had a curse upon them. But what has such religion to say in the face of this act of Jesus? We know that our Lord did not seek to please Himself. His meat and drink were to do the Father's will. He drank the cup of voluntary sorrow to the dregs. He is the one perfect example of devotion and self-sacrifice. And yet the very first sign that He gave when on earth, of His command over the powers of nature, was an encouragement of homely festivities which depended in part on eating and drinking! What a sanction is thus given to those instincts that prompt men to social enjoyment! What a protest, at the same time, against that excess which would turn what God has blessed into a deadly and degrading curse!

But what was the occasion of the festivity which the Son of God thus honoured? It was the marriage of some unknown and unhonoured couple—a country wedding. The first miracle has cast its lustre upon a common wedding. Jesus and His disciples, at the very beginning of His ministry, went as willing guests, invited by the bridegroom, to this ceremony. And when they were there, Jesus lent His divine power to promote the comfort and pleasure of the entertainment. You remember again, that religion, in all countries, has made it a virtue to abstain from marriage. "Forbidding to marry" said St. Paul—a warning strangely disregarded even in the Christian Church — of *false* teachers. But the Lord has honoured marriage; He has adorned and beautified this holy estate with His presence and first miracle in Cana of Galilee. The example which He set was followed by His Apostles, who have upheld marriage as a sacred Divinely-appointed ordinance, and as the type of a heavenly mystery.

It is a truth concerning all Christ's miracles, as it is concerning this of Cana in Galilee, that their tendency is not to disparage and throw into the shade common things by their display of extraordinary powers, but, on the contrary, expressly to impart to common everyday matters a special and heavenly glory. Why did Christ do an extraordinary thing at Cana?—That he might honour an everyday marriage, an everyday festivity, and so the whole class of marriages and festivities which they represent. The acts of healing which the Lord delighted to do were signs that all healing energies are under His sanction and protection. Even the physical element in the miracles, whilst it is a departure from the ordinary course of nature, is yet rather with nature than against it. The most devout students of this miracle of the creation of wine, and of the parallel acts of the creation of bread, have been wont to see in them the more conspicuous manifestations of the one Divine power which everywhere produces out of various ingredients the wine and the food of common life. It is God who gives the sap to the vine, who changes the juice of the grape into wine. **It is** God who prepares the grain, and teaches man to make it into bread. The commonest things are as much God's doing as the rarest; and one of the most precious offices of our Lord's miracles is to **open our eyes to the** wonders that are always about us, and to teach us to see in them, not **a** dead course of things, but **the** hand of a Father in Heaven.

And who will say that we do not need to be thus awakened? There is an immense power in regularity and uniformity to deaden the sense of life and will. What takes place always seems to us too easily as if it took place of itself. We are apt to turn the garment which should disclose to us the very form of God into a veil by which He is hidden from us. Let us use the works of Christ in faith **as a** help against this tendency. Let us reflect that if there is a Creator, those things precisely which are most necessary are the most important manifestations of His will. The great laws of external nature are the signs of His hand. Still more, the ordinances of human life and society which seem most **natural are** also the most divine. Marriage is a law of nature **for** mankind;—true, a most necessary and most useful law: but *therefore*, it has the clearest mark of Divine will and appointment upon it. The efforts of human energy to contend against disease are most instinctive, and their results commend themselves in the highest degree for their utility. *Therefore*, they **have the** very guidance and pressure of the Divine **hand upon** them. And so of all things.

Christ did not come into the world to tell men that God had nothing to do with the visible external world. What He said to men, by His words, and by His acts, was rather this: "The whole world is the work of my Father's hands. Your bodies, and the outward things with which they are in relation, belong to Him, as well as your souls. It is He who makes the sun to shine and the rain to descend, and without Him no sparrow falls to the ground. I am come to reconcile all things to my Father, things in heaven and things in earth. I am come to make you spiritually children of my Father, that you may use outward things and bless God for them, without becoming subject to them. It is the Father's will that in time the lower part of Creation, being purged from evil, should share in the glorious liberty of God's children. The more your eyes are spiritually opened, to know me and Him that sent me, the more clearly will you discern in all things that surround you the light of the Father's glory and the tokens of the Father's love."

IX.

THE TEACHING OF JESUS NOT HIS, BUT HIS FATHER'S.

St. John vii. 16—18.

"Jesus answered them, and said, My doctrine is not mine, but his that sent me. If any man will do his will, he shall know of the doctrine, whether it be of God, or whether I speak of myself. He that speaketh of himself seeketh his own glory; but he that seeketh his glory that sent him, the same is true, and no unrighteousness is in him."

THERE are two statements which our Lord makes here, upon which it may be well to fix our attention separately.

1. The first is, that His teaching did not originate in Himself, but came from His Father. His teaching was His, so far as anything could be His; but nothing that He was, or that He said or did, originated ultimately in Himself; all was from His Father.

2. The second statement is, that in His teaching, the motive, or the spirit by which He was animated, was the desire of His Father's glory. This, also, was the universal principle of His nature, and of all that He did. He came to seek not His own glory, but His Father's.

Now, our Lord makes the latter fact the test and

proof of the former. If He had sought His own glory, He might have been supposed to be speaking from Himself, without inspiration from above. But inasmuch as He did not seek His own glory, but the Father's, it was a legitimate conclusion that His teaching was inspired by the Father. This, at least, was a legitimate conclusion to the spiritual sense, if it was not demonstrative to the logical faculty. Those whose minds were set upon doing the Father's will would perceive, Jesus said, that His teaching came from the Father.

Our Lord's appeal, therefore, here as in other places, is to the following effect: "Judge of me, whether I am seeking the Father's glory or not. If I am not, my teaching has no claim upon your belief. But if I am, if the whole character of my life and of my words declares that I am not seeking my own, but my Father's honour; then you must accept my teaching as from God: you yourselves, in proportion as you also are seeking the Father's honour, will know that what I say is from above, and is true."

You will observe that we have here an example of a different kind of argument from that formal one based on miracles, which falls so naturally into schemes of Christian evidences. The argument from miracles runs as follows:—Christ taught certain doctrines, and also wrought miracles. The miracles prove that He was more than man, and therefore that His doctrine was either from above or from below. It could not, from its nature, be from the Evil One; therefore it is from God. The force of this argument rests so ostentatiously upon the evidence in favour of the miracles, that where this evidence **is not** convincing, the argument has no weight. But apart from this precarious character, the argument does not seem to be in itself best suited to **the** kind of teaching which our Lord wished to communicate. The heart and the conscience do not easily yield to the signs of external power. Even, therefore, when Jesus Himself was living before the eyes **of** men, we find Him using other arguments, to say the least, besides that from extraordinary works. If He had chosen this kind of appeal, nothing was easier to Him, we might say, than to go on working conspicuous miracles till the convictions of men could resist no longer. But in truth He preferred **to** make His appeal to the spirit that was in His hearers. **He** desired to open a way between the hearts of men and the Father who had sent Him. Mighty works might have some power to do this, as revealing the nature and purpose of God; but as evidences of supernatural authority, they could have little effect upon the heart.

If that was the case when our Lord was acting visibly in the world, it is reasonable to believe that it must be so in a tenfold or hundredfold degree now, when we can only read the account of the miracles in ancient records, and cannot see them with our own eyes. Such appeals as those in our text must be the **arguments** most suitable both to our circumstances **and to the** nature **of** the conclusion to be arrived at. **It may still** be said in our day, If any man's will **be**

to do the will of the Father in Heaven, he will know whether Jesus spoke as one sent from God, or whether His teaching grew out of His own thoughts and fancies. Devotion to the will of the heavenly Father is still a power to discern the highest kind of truth, the truth concerning God.

It is a disadvantage in our translation that the word "doctrine" has been used for *teaching*. We ought to bear in mind that wherever in the Bible the word doctrine is used, it is exactly equivalent to teaching. "My doctrine" is "my teaching." "They were astonished at his doctrine" means "they were astonished at his teaching." The reason for making this observation is, that we have come to understand by the word doctrine, something of the nature of a formal theological proposition; whereas one of the most remarkable features of our Lord's teaching is the absence of such propositions. When our Lord's teaching, or doctrine, is mentioned, the manner, the tone, the spirit of it is intended, as much as the particular statements contained in it.

Let us consider a little more particularly what the nature of our Lord's teaching was. We may describe it as the natural language of *the Son of God*. It is St. John especially who enables us to attach so much significance to this title of "the Son of God." He gives us this name as the *key* to interpret all the mysteries of the life of Christ. "Son of God" is not merely *one* of the titles which might be given to Jesus Christ. His Sonship is the very essence of His inmost nature, the governing principle of His whole existence. It is not only as man, in the flesh, that He **is Son of** God. His Divine nature is determined by this relation to the Father. He is nothing else but the Son of God—nothing that is not included in, or caused by, this Sonship.

It follows from this fact, that when our Lord took our flesh and dwelt among us, He was wholly devoted to the Father's will. Devotion to that will was not merely *one* principle or law or obligation **of** His life; it was the root of His whole being. He never had an object that was not included in His Father's will and glory. **It was** His perfection, not to have been drawn away by any temptation for a moment from devotion to His Father's will. He was the perfect Son, living in dependence upon the Father to whom He was bound in the closest spiritual unity, rendering up every act as a sacrifice to the Father.

This does not imply that it was not the object of our Lord's coming to redeem and to save mankind. He came for this purpose because it was the Father's will that mankind should be saved. And He saw how closely the salvation of man was associated with the Father's honour. For, that men should **be** saved, meant that they should be brought to the knowledge and worship of the Father. And therefore the work of Christ, in the redemption of mankind, was essentially the work of the *Son* of God. The highest and most precious teaching which He could convey to men, was that which would lead them to know the Father. The teaching of Jesus **was, in** fact, a bearing witness of the Father.

And this is the account which He Himself delights to give of His teaching. He calls it a testimony, a bearing witness or record. He names the Father, declares His will, shews in action His purpose and feeling towards men, endeavours to awaken in the human heart its natural consciousness of the Father in heaven. And hence proceeded the *authority* which astonished the people in the teaching of Christ. Whereas the scribes and lawyers were arguing and defining, Jesus spoke as one sent from heaven of what He knew. He had a right to bear witness concerning the Father, because He was from eternity in the Father's bosom. He knew what was in men, because He knew them as children of His own Father; He knew that their truest and best feeling was that of children towards the invisible God.

The teaching of Jesus, therefore, was in all senses *personal*, rather than, according to our use of the word, *doctrinal*. He spoke, *as* the Son of God, to men, concerning His Father and theirs. All His teaching was essentially Divine and human; it was living and fruitful, not a system of abstractions. It was strongly marked by the paradox, that He who was thus living out of Himself, who spoke by the Father's inspiration and with a view to the Father's glory, not from Himself or for His own sake, yet spoke with great emphasis *concerning Himself*. He spoke of Himself, because it was through Him that men were to know the Father; because He, in His filial and brotherly perfectness, was the bond and way between men and the Father. He could say therefore, without in the least violating the criterion He had Himself laid down, "*I* am the light of the world; he that followeth me shall not walk in darkness, but shall have the light of life." The Pharisees, hearing such assertions, thought they had caught Him in a contradiction. They said, "Thou bearest record of thyself: thy record is not true." But Jesus replied, "Though I bear record of myself, yet my record is true: for I know whence I came and whither I go; but ye cannot tell whence I come, and whither I go." Jesus, knowing His Father, could speak of Himself as the Son. Not to declare Himself to men, would have been to rob the Father of His honour. And thus we have the contrast, otherwise so utterly inexplicable, between the lowly self-devoting nature of Jesus and the wonderful claims He makes for Himself; between the faith which He Himself places, without reserve, in the Father, and the faith which He exhorts men to place in *Him*. To such apparent contradictions the true Sonship of Jesus Christ is the only key. If we do not regard Him as the true Divine Son of the Father, we shall not be able to reconcile the many apparent discrepancies which appear on the surface of the Gospels.

We say, then, it was the aim of Jesus, as a teacher, to make His Father known to men, and that therefore His teaching was authoritative, personal, and varied. Whatever might serve, in the way of illustration, to bring home the invisible realities of the Father's kingdom and nature to the minds of His hearers, was freely and powerfully used by Jesus in

His discourses. He used parables from the operations of nature, parables from the ways and customs of men. He spoke kindly; He spoke severely. He encouraged the humble and desponding; He rebuked the proud and self-confident and hard-hearted. But in all the variety of His teaching He sought as His ultimate end, to give glory to His Father, and to make Him better known in His justice and mercy to men; and this fact, He says in our text, was the best proof that His teaching was absolutely true; that though it came through His mouth, it was not His, but the Father's that had sent Him.

And now let us consider what Jesus says as to the recognition by men of the truth of His teaching. "If any man will do his will, he shall know of the doctrine, whether it be of God." Our Lord does not mean to say that every one who honestly tries to do God's will, shall be taught whether any particular doctrine is true or not. That is an application of our Lord's saying, which must be hesitatingly and guardedly made. What our Lord says is this: "Devotion to the will and glory of the Father is the moral basis of truth. I am speaking from God, because I altogether seek the Father's glory. Those of you who care for the Father's will, can discern whether I am true or not."

It was a great question for the Jews, whether Jesus should be received as a true speaker, or denounced and rejected as an impostor. Some believed in Him, others disbelieved Him: what made the difference?

It happened, our Lord says, according as men cared, **or** did not care, for the Father.

The Pharisees, on the whole, rejected Jesus. Why did they reject Him? It was not through want of a proper attention to His miracles. They are never reproached for **not** scrutinizing and testing the supernatural character of His mighty works. The reason **of** their unbelief is several times plainly given. See, for example, the latter part of St. John, chap. v. Our Lord had been speaking of the testimonies borne to Him. There was that of John the Baptist. There was the witness borne by His own works. There was the direct witness borne by the Father speaking to the hearts of men. "Ye have not his word, the voice of the Father, abiding in you," says Jesus to the Pharisees: "for whom he hath sent, him ye believe not. . . . I know you, that ye have not the love of God in you. I am come in my Father's name, and ye receive me not: if another shall come in his own name, him ye will receive. How can ye believe, which receive honour one of another, and seek not the honour that cometh from the only God?" And again in chap. viii. verse 42, Jesus said unto them, "If God were your Father, ye would love me; for I proceeded forth and came from God: neither came I of myself, but he sent me. Why do ye not understand my speech? Even because ye cannot hear my word. . . . Because I tell you the truth, ye believe me not. Which of you convinceth me of sin? And if I say the truth, why do ye not believe me? He **that is** of God, heareth God's words: ye therefore hear them not, because ye are not of God." And in another place, St. John tells us that even among the chief rulers many believed on Jesus; "but because of the Pharisees they did not confess him, lest they should be put out of the synagogue; for they loved the praise of men more than the praise of God."

Here, then, is the reverse of what our Lord says in the text. Those who cared *not* to do the will of the Father in heaven, or to promote His honour, or to win His approbation, could not recognise Jesus as having come from the Father; they could not perceive the Divine truth of His teaching. Not having their ears open to the spiritual silent voices of the Father, they knew not and believed not the words of Jesus. Not loving the Father, they had no instinct of recognition for the Son.

Those on the other hand, who *did* receive Jesus and believe in His teaching, who said with Simon Peter, "Thou art the Christ, the Son of the living God," proved by this faith *that they had some fellowship with the Father*. The Sonship of Jesus was not revealed to them by flesh and blood, nor by the mere signs of supernatural power: it was revealed to them by the Father in heaven. "Blessed art thou, Simon Bar-jona; for flesh and blood hath not revealed to thee my nature as the Son of the living God, but my Father which is in heaven." This was true in measure of every one who confessed and followed Jesus. The Father had drawn him; no one could come to Jesus unless the Father drew him. Some voice from the heavenly home of the Father must have reached the soul of every man who understood Jesus. Some spiritual message, declaring the Eternal righteousness and love, must have rendered itself audible to him. Then the words of Christ made a harmony with this spiritual voice, and commended themselves to the man's heart. He said, he could not help saying, Truly this is the Son of God: He has come from the Father above; He speaks the words of the Father.

Contrast in this light the Pharisee and the publican who went up into the Temple to pray. These may serve as types **of** those who rejected and believed in Jesus respectively. What knowledge of the Father had the Pharisee? What desire to serve the Father's glory? What care to receive praise from the Father? What power to say, in the spirit of a child, Our Father who art in heaven? He was religious, it is true: he came to the Temple to pray: he fasted and gave tithes. But he was filled with a sense of his own excellence, and with a desire to be regarded and envied by his neighbours. He despised the poor publican whom he saw humbling himself in genuine prayer. Suppose this Pharisee, on issuing from the Temple, had come upon Jesus, and heard the parable of the Prodigal Son, would it have been reasonable for him to say, This teacher has plainly come from **the God** whom I have been worshipping? Jesus had, in truth, *not* come from the God whom the Pharisee had **been** worshipping. For that God, so far as the Pharisee thought of any God at all, was not the God of Abraham and Isaac and Jacob, the deliverer, the just God and the merciful, but a god made after the imaginations of his own heart, proud, arbitrary, partial, rewarding his favourites. But think of the publican. He dared not lift up even his eyes to heaven, but smote upon his breast, saying, "God be merciful to me a sinner!" That poor sinner had some knowledge of the true Father in heaven, of Him who was too pure to behold iniquity, but who delighted to forgive and to cleanse. He felt himself to be sinful in the eyes of such a Being; but he knew Him to be merciful: and therefore in all simplicity and self-abasement and trust, he cried, "God be merciful to me a sinner!" Would not this publican's heart have leapt up in sympathy and reverence, if *he* had heard Jesus of Nazareth speaking in his Father's name? Could he have helped believing in Him? Do we not see in what is recorded of the actual followers of Jesus, of the simple fishermen, of the sinful but repentant women, of the despised publicans, examples of persons who thus believed in the Son of God because He represented a Father who had already made Himself partly known to them?

In seeking to derive a lesson from our text for ourselves, we must not think of any particular doctrine, and of the means by which we may ascertain its soundness or unsoundness. We must think rather of faith in Jesus as the true Son of God, and of the helps and hindrances to that faith. What our Lord declared to be the law or reason of faith in His teaching whilst He was visible on the earth must be no less true now. Every age of the Church has indeed been adding illustrations without number of its truth. That heart of man which has no knowledge of the Heavenly Father cannot receive Christ. The heart which inwardly honours the Father must recognise Christ.

There may seem to us to be some exceptions to this law; but they are only apparent. In the sight of God this principle must be absolute and universal. The unity between the Father and the Son is so close, that, as Jesus Himself testified, to honour the Father is to honour the Son; to honour the Son is to honour the Father.

The state of mind which in the New Testament is put in opposition to the love and worship of the Father is what we describe as *worldliness*. "If any man love the world," said St. John, "the love of the Father is not in him." Let a man live for this world—that is to say, for the praise of men, for riches, for rank and station. To live for these objects is inevitably to place *himself* foremost to himself—to become selfish. He cannot give himself up to the service of God; he cannot cherish a spirit of love and reverence. He is sure to separate himself in interest from his fellow-men; he will acquire the habit of thrusting them farther and farther—as persons to whom he is under any obligations—from his thoughts. How, let us ask, will such a man stand towards that great revelation of God which was made in Christ, towards the love which chose the Incarnation as a way of manifesting itself, towards the sympathy which made the cause of miserable sinners the cause of God Himself, towards the sacrifice which completely overcame self and triumphed in surrender? Whatever such a man may profess, the revelation of the Son of God must be really incredible to him. It must seem unreasonable, unaccountable, disagreeable to him. The most godlike thing to him is to be above every one else. How can he believe in a manifestation of God which makes voluntary humiliation the display of Divine glory? He is not training himself to regard his fellow-men as brethren: how can he think of his supreme invisible Lord as taking the most despised of men into the bond and fellowship of brotherhood with himself? "Ye cannot serve God and Mammon," said Jesus. So it is not possible to believe in self, and in the Son of God. It is not possible to cherish a spirit blind and hardened towards all tokens of the Father, and at the same time to recognise the loving words of Jesus as Divine.

Suppose, on the other hand, a heart tender and sensitive to the proofs of Fatherly love which are shed abroad in nature and in life. Suppose a man to believe, with some awe and reverence, that there is a Being above who is altogether just and gracious, who has begotten all men as His children, and who draws their hearts to Himself. Such a man cannot help feeling ashamed of much that he is conscious of in his own habits and feelings, in the bent of his own will. He must be the subject of some struggle between the good and the evil—the good disposition which honours the Father, and the evil which **worships** self. **He** must feel humble before God. **He** must long for deliverance from that which he **knows to** be hostile to God. He must wonder **and** sorrow over the condition of his fellow-men, children of God in heaven, but how ignorant, how fallen! And what will such a man think of Christ? When he hears that the Eternal Father has sent His own Son into the world, to enter into the lost estate of His creatures, to speak heavenly words to them, to bear with all their folly and perverseness and enmity, to die by their hands, in order that He might raise Him from the dead, and mankind with Him from the death of despair and ignorance, and that He might inspire with a new life one family of regenerate children—how will this announcement strike him? Will it seem to him unworthy of God, impossible, incredible? Surely it will seem to him the very opposite. Surely he will say, this Gospel must be true, it must be from God Himself, because it speaks of a love and condescension of which no being except God in heaven is capable. Such love is astonishing, difficult to believe: but then, is not the whole relation between the infinite Being and His human children most mysterious and amazing? If I can think of God as truly my Father, of myself as really His child, is it not reasonable to go on to believe that that Father has sent His Son into the world to claim and restore us, to prove His fellowship with us by suffering with our miseries and by dying our death?

Yes, brethren, we must be drawn to a firmer and a closer faith in Christ, by fixing our thoughts upon all that speaks to us of a fatherly love towards us in Him who made and sustains us, upon all the signs that appear in the midst of our sin and darkness of the high nature bestowed upon us, and the high destinies which beckon us forward. If we choose rather to feed our natures upon the visible things only, and to live by fashion, seeking ease or entertainment or advancement, it will inevitably follow that Christ will become incredible to us. The god of this world, according to St. Paul's powerful declaration, will blind our unbelieving minds so as to prevent the light of the glorious Gospel of Christ, who is the image of God, from shining upon them. Remember this danger, dear brethren, and ask for the true enlightenment. Ask that you may not be conformed to this world, but may be transformed in the spirit of your minds, so that you may prove, by obedience and life, what is the good and acceptable and perfect will of God. To prove and submit to the will of God is the sum of our duty, the beginning of all Christian knowledge and Christian virtue. What, then, is the bent of our wills? Is it towards harmony with the Divine will? Much as we may fail, little as we may be able to carry out our resolution, God demands of us that there should be some movement of our wills towards His righteous and loving will, some sentiment of admiration for goodness, some yearning desire to be made true and pure, and just and kind. He gives us such impulses by His own Spirit. God grant

that we may not resist and quench them. May He preserve us all from the narrowing, hardening, corrupting influences of the common life of which we are partakers; from the petty jealousies which sting and poison so many hearts; from the base desire to keep the general standard low in order that our own unworthiness may be excused; from that magnifying of self which makes us discontented with our lot, and which turns so many events into disappointments; from every cloud which covers our hearts, and shuts out the light of the crucified Saviour, the Son of the Father **in** heaven. The humble, the patient, the kind, the generous, will have their reward. The Father and the Son will come to them and make their abode with them. The Spirit of the Father and **the** Son has been an accepted guest in their hearts, and He will enable them to hear the voices of heaven, **and** to discern with open eyes the rays of the heavenly glory.

X.

WHY JESUS SPOKE IN PARABLES.

St. Luke viii. 10.

"Jesus said, Unto you it is given to know the mysteries of the kingdom of God: but unto others in parables."

ACCORDING to St. Matthew's account, the disciples, after hearing the parable of the Sower, came to Jesus and asked him, "Why speakest thou unto them in parables?" We also are interested in asking a similar question. It is plain, upon the surface of the Gospel records, that Jesus adopted the form of parables, to a very remarkable extent, as the vehicle of His teaching. We are accustomed to use the term "our Lord's parables," as describing what is most peculiar and striking in His discourses, in much the same way as we habitually apply the term miracles to the most peculiar and striking of His acts. It is natural, therefore, that, in considering the character of our Lord's teaching, one of our first questions should be, Why did He speak in parables? The use of external illustrations in various forms is familiar enough in the East, and there are examples in the Old Testament of apologues not very unlike our Lord's parables. But little is to be gained in considering the parables from a comparison of them with any similar modes of speech. They stand by themselves, and have a unique character of their own*. They grew out of the creative mind of Jesus, and justify themselves by their perfect adaptation to the work which He had to do.

It is remarkable that our attention is specially called in the Gospels to this method of teaching by parables, and some account of the purpose and effect of it is given by our Lord Himself, in connexion with what may rightly be called the pattern parable. This parable, that of the Sower, is contained in all the first three Gospels. It is the first of the regular series of the Gospel parables. It is represented as having awakened an inquiry in the minds of the disciples, and it is followed by a formal interpretation given, as a kind of example, by their Master.

1. What our Lord said to the disciples in answer to their question has something of the *paradoxical or* surprising character which so often distinguishes His sayings. **In** St. **Mark** it stands thus (iv. 11) " Unto you it is given **to** know the mystery of the kingdom of God : **but** unto them that are without, all these things **are** done in parables : *that seeing they may see and not perceive;* and hearing they may hear and not understand ; lest at any time they should be converted, and their sins should be forgiven them." In St. Luke viii. 10, the answer is shorter, but expresses the same startling purpose : " Unto you

---

* **M.** Renan says : " Rien dans le judaisme ne lui avait donné le **modèle de** ce genre délicieux. C'est lui qui l'a créé."

it is given to know the mysteries of the kingdom of God: but to others in parables; that seeing they might not see, and hearing they might not understand." In St. Matthew, the answer is reported at greater length, and with a difference which strikes the ear at once: "Because it is given unto you to know the mysteries of the kingdom of heaven, but to them it is not given. For whosoever hath, to him shall be given, and he shall have more abundance: but whosoever hath not, from him shall be taken away even that he hath. Therefore speak I to them in parables: because [*because*] they seeing see not; and hearing, they hear not, neither do they understand. And in them is fulfilled the prophecy of Esaias, which saith, By hearing ye shall hear, and shall not understand; and seeing ye shall see, and shall not perceive: for this people's heart is waxed gross, and their ears are dull of hearing, and their eyes they have closed; lest at any time they should see with their eyes, and hear with their ears, and should understand with their hearts, and should be converted, and I should heal them." The paradoxical part of our Lord's answer is His appearing to say that He spoke in parables *in order that* his meaning might be veiled from his hearers, and that so they might be left in their sins. It is utterly inconceivable that Jesus should have wished the ignorant multitude to remain unawakened and unconverted, or that He should have taken a pleasure in addressing to them words which they were sure not to understand. We are compelled, therefore, to consider what our Lord's intention really was. The variation in St. Matthew from "in order that" to "because" is a kind of indication that we must look at the *things* in order to understand the *words*. If we think a little of what our Lord wished to convey, and what the natural effect of a parable is, we may be able to enter into the explanation which He gave to His disciples.

2. My present subject compels me to repeat once more, that *the Kingdom of Heaven*, or the Kingdom of God, is the great topic of the Gospels. The works that were done by Jesus were signs of the Kingdom of Heaven. The disciples who proclaimed it, were at the same time to heal the sick and cast out devils. And this kingdom, which was announced by a proclamation, and interpreted by mighty works, was also explained by illustrations; and these illustrations were the parables.

The parable of the Sower, as the pattern parable, relates to the Kingdom of God. "To you," says the Saviour, "it is given to know the mysteries of the Kingdom of God; but to others in parables." Mysteries of the Kingdom were illustrated in this, and in the other parables. The *seed* sown, which in St. Mark is called simply "the Word," and in St. Luke, the "Word of God," is in St. Matthew the "Word of *the Kingdom*." Our Lord was speaking, no doubt, of *His own word*, the message or declaration or account of the Kingdom of Heaven, which He was delivering to those who heard Him, and of the various ways in which it was received. We need not, indeed, limit the teaching of this great parable to that country and the few years of our Lord's or of John the Baptist's ministrations; but we shall be following the safest method for arriving at the true and even at the *widest* meaning of the parable, if we take the terms of our Lord's interpretation, first of all, in their strictest sense, and seek to know what He intended the disciples who surrounded Him to understand by them.

Let us say, then, that the express purpose of the parables generally, and of this of the Sower in particular, was to illustrate the invisible principles and processes of the spiritual kingdom—in other words, to convey the mysteries of the Kingdom of Heaven. Unless this had been specially our Lord's work, the use of *parables* would not have been so characteristic of His teaching.

3. Let us now consider what *suitableness* there was in the parables, to make them serve as useful exponents of the Kingdom of Heaven.

In the first place, they testify of a real connexion between God's *invisible* kingdom, and the *outward* provinces of His creation. The miracles of Christ shewed that He in whom the kingdom was established and manifested had power over the ordinary processes of nature; that He could create wine and food, that He could arrest disease and bestow health, that He could even give life to the dead. With somewhat similar effect, the parables, which are drawn from the experience of daily life, from the phenomena of sowing and of vegetable growth, from the business of merchandize and property, from the social and political relations of men, bear witness of a connexion between the spiritual world of which our Lord had to speak, and the outward world, which belongs to the same God.

And this effect of the parables does not consist merely in the fact that our Lord found these illustrations from the visible world available for the setting forth of the invisible things of His spiritual kingdom. He has encouraged, by His example and practice, the *habit* of looking at visible things as signs of the invisible. Any one who realizes the parable of the Sower by looking abroad upon a field and watching how the seed may be snatched away from the trodden wayside by the birds; how it may fall upon a thin layer of earth covering a substratum of stone, and spring up rapidly and without depth; how it may be choked by weeds and thorns; how it may be received into good and deep soil and grow up prosperously, and bear fruit,—and who then uses these various fortunes of the seed as interpreters to his mind of what happens to God's word according to the various dispositions of the hearers to whom it comes,—will find himself insensibly referring the two worlds to the same Divine author: he will reverence the laws of nature the more, whilst at the same time he will gain a fresher and more healthy perception of the realities of the spiritual life. The parables unfortunately lose to our minds much of their proper power, because they are to us words written in a book and not the lively realities of nature and society which they were to their first hearers. Often our Lord's parables were borrowed from what was going on at the moment under the eyes of His hearers. They always brought up to their minds visible practical matters with which they were constantly familiar. It is a rare gift, and especially in an age of books, to make parables naturally and effectively; but we can easily understand, I think, that if we were hearers of a teacher who could borrow illustrations of spiritual things with simplicity and force from the occupations in which we are most interested, those occupations would become more sacred to us, and spiritual things more real, and there would be less of a divorce between the objects of faith and the objects of sight.

But what, in the next place, is the mental effect produced by a parable, as distinct from a spiritual statement in spiritual language? Our Lord refers to this kind of effect, when He says, "To you it is given to know the mysteries of the kingdom of heaven, but to others in parables." The disciples were in a condition to understand without parables; the multitudes were not in such a condition, and to them parables were appropriate.

Every one feels that a simple parable is likely to be taken hold of by the most careless and ignorant and inattentive mind. The Galileans, whom Jesus addressed, were people of narrow knowledge, of uncultivated minds, of dull spiritual perceptions. It is to be presumed that if Jesus had spoken to them only in the terms of morality and religion, they might not have attended to Him, and if they had, they might not have understood Him. But there was something which appealed to every mind in a description of sowing and of its results. Just as they could perceive when a blind man had sight conferred upon him, when a cripple was restored to strength, so they knew what Jesus was talking about, when He began, " Behold, a sower went out to sow his seed."

This, then, we may reckon as a first universal property of a parable—its power to engage the attention of even the dullest minds.

But would the words remain a mere natural description? Would the multitudes go away with the idea that Jesus had been simply telling them what became of the seed scattered by a sower? No: every one of his hearers knew at least so much—that Jesus was meaning something beyond the obvious sense of what He said. We cannot separate the parables from Him who spoke them. He was already known as proclaiming a Kingdom of Heaven, as doing mighty works, as teaching with authority. It was well understood, that when Jesus spoke of the seed and the sower, He was meaning something about the Kingdom of Heaven. His closing appeal, "He that hath ears to hear, let him hear," would only confirm a general impression, that Jesus was conveying in the parable some important truth.

That the multitude in general went away without knowing at the time what the truth was which was wrapped up in the parable, we are compelled to conclude, by the ignorance of the disciples themselves, who did not know how to interpret the parable until their Master explained it to them. But it is important to lay stress upon the limitation "*at the time.*" It very often happens that words do not produce their full effect at the moment when they are heard.

Some, at least, out of the multitude, would remember the words which the remarkable Teacher had spoken. Nothing can be easier for even a child to take hold of than the history of the seed sown upon a varied tract of land :—the seed the same, the reception of it, and the consequent results, so different. The Master had called upon them to lay up these facts in their minds, "He that hath ears to hear, let him hear;" the parable was an important illustration of some mystery of that kingdom which was always being presented to them, a mystery which, as it would seem, it behoved them all to learn. A curiosity would thus be excited in the minds of all those who were at all in earnest about the things of the kingdom. The parable would be talked about; there would be opportunities for inquiring what it meant; and neither Jesus nor His disciples would be unwilling to respond to a real thirsting after knowledge in even the humblest and most ignorant.

I am endeavouring to mark what would be the most natural and obvious effect of the parable, according to the account given us of it, upon the minds of the multitude. It is reasonable to suppose that Jesus intended the parable to produce the effect which it actually did produce. We observe, then, that He, having assumed the character of a teacher sent from heaven, delivered this parable in a highly significant manner; that it was of a nature to interest and to

be remembered by the dullest; that He explained it immediately with precision to His disciples. We may reasonably assume, therefore, that it excited attention and thought and inquiry; and that when the meaning of it was known, it served to *keep* the truth it contained from being scattered and lost, and to lead the minds of many to associate revealed mysteries of the heavenly kingdom with ordinary and visible occurrences.

We might confidently interpret the fortunes of this particular "word," by what the parable itself tells us. It would, no doubt, be snatched away immediately out of the minds of many. By others it would be kept for a time, and be the seed of some little knowledge which would soon die out. Some would take it deeper into their hearts, and the truth of it would struggle for a while with the cares and pleasures of the world, but be choked at last. In the few, it would find a good soil and bring forth fruit abundantly.

In the case of some, therefore, the parable would actually have the effect of *veiling* the spiritual truth it contained. If they were utterly impenetrable, even to the pioneering force of an interesting and easy parable, they would learn nothing from it, and sacred things would have been preserved from being outraged. Pearls would not have been cast before swine. But to such persons, the parable gave, so to speak, the best chance. If this did not find its way into their minds, statements devoid of illustration would fail still more to do so. **The** law which our Lord states so repeatedly, and which is contained in His answer to the disciples on the present occasion, as reported by St. Matthew, was always observed. "To him that hath, shall be given; and from him that hath not, shall be taken that which he hath." Jesus would condescend to the dullest spirit and most careless mind. The least symptom of awakenment was rewarded; light was given according to the opening of the eyes. If the heart was too gross and carnal to receive anything, nothing was received.

The parable, then, we may say, was used to try the sense-bound multitude. No method of bringing home the mysteries of the Kingdom of Heaven more favourable to their state and case could have been employed. Their dulness was the reason of the adoption of it; and it was addressed to them, in order that—*if it came to the worst*, if even this condescending method proved unavailing with them—they might remain as they were before, blind and deaf and stupid, dead in trespasses and sins.

We ought, I think, to imagine our Saviour as saying these words with a kind of bitterness of sorrow and disappointment. He was striving to make known the Kingdom of Heaven to His countrymen: they came out to hear Him in large numbers, moved by curiosity, astonished by the mighty works which He wrought, mechanically impressed by the authority of His manner. That they showed so little spiritual discernment, that they were so hard, so carnal, so untouched by the name of the Father in heaven, must have been intensely painful to the Saviour's heart, and it is only probable that He showed, in the tone of His remarks, the sorrow He was feeling. **We** miss some of the truth and reality of Christ's dealings with His disciples and His opponents, through not attributing to Him *emotion* enough. The paradoxical character of much of His language is obvious enough to all readers; and this form is the natural vesture of intense emotion, partly confessed and partly restrained.

Instead, therefore, of perceiving in what Jesus said of the effect of His parables upon the multitude a cool purpose to baffle them and to leave them in ignorance and sin, and then seeking to justify this by some theory of judicial or penal hardening,—the spirit of which would seem so utterly opposite to the whole course of our Lord's dealing with ignorant multitudes, and to the object for which He came down from heaven, which would represent Him as *breaking* the bruised reed, and *quenching* the smoking flax,—we are rather to understand Him as uttering a bitter sense of disappointment that all that He could do, the most condescending methods which He could employ, would still leave many of them hard and dull, and incapable of understanding the mysteries it so much concerned them to know.

For the mysteries of the Kingdom of Heaven are indeed as unlike as possible to the pretended human mysteries over which men have drawn a veil of secresy, making it a favour to initiate the few into sublime or abstruse theories, with which the multitude had nothing to do. Every mystery of Christ's heavenly kingdom concerns every man. It has to do with the commonest human spiritual life. It is intended to give light to every one's path. The message of God in heaven coming to His creatures, to His children made in His own image, telling them of the love He has for them, of the hopes set before them, of the privileges of serving Him and holding communion with Him; the danger of not listening to this "Word of God," the various conditions of men's hearts, like the unfavourable conditions of soil, which militate against the reception of God's word; the particular causes, in hardness, cowardice, worldliness and vanity, which make the heart unfruitful, and which may be deliberately striven against by the enlightened will; the blessedness of receiving God's word into good ground, into a heart simple and unencumbered with the roots of bitterness and with the rubbish of proud speculations, so that it may bear its due and natural fruit to the glory of God and the good of men; these are the mysteries of the kingdom—and who is there who ought not to be interested in these? What reserve is to be put upon the diffusion of these?

There is not, there could not be, in the practice of the Son of God, the slightest justification for a deliberate withholding of truth from any human being, who could by any means be persuaded to receive it. What inference we are to draw, as to *our* mode of teaching, from our Lord's use of parables, is a very interesting question, and one not to be answered in a moment. There is good reason to conclude that the conditions of the case were altered by the death of the

Saviour, by His resurrection and ascension, and by the coming down of the Holy Ghost. **The** Apostles appear to teach us that the simplest method of appealing to the hearts of all men is the naming and presenting of Jesus Christ and Him crucified. It may be that our Lord's method of teaching was precisely that which was best suited to the time and to the circumstances, but that now, the time and the circumstances being altered, that method of teaching is no longer to be universally imitated. It might therefore be a mistake for a minister of Christ in these days to address even a heathen multitude, much more a Christian congregation, in the manner of parables, as much as our Lord so addressed His hearers.

But we may draw two conclusions safely and with advantage from our Lord's use of parables. (1) We ought to use every means we can, whatever may seem to us in our discretion the most available for the purpose, to bring home spiritual truth to the minds of men. What may be the best means we must ask **the** Spirit of God to teach us. But we ought to have solemnly before our minds the duty of winning the most ignorant and the most hardened to an apprehension of the truth. The Son of God used the simplest and most condescending illustrations to reach, if it were possible, the hearts of Galilean peasants. Let us take care that we do not underrate the duty of commending the truth to every man's conscience in such ways as may appear most expedient and most promising. It is, indeed, a great necessity that we and all men should come to the knowledge of the truth. May God help us to labour towards this end! (2) The second conclusion is, that we should not be indifferent to the apprehension of a real Kingdom of Heaven about us. Sometimes, even when we are thinking and speaking of Jesus Christ and Him crucified, we are in danger of forgetting that we are actually set in a spiritual kingdom, of which He is the Head. We need to be reminded continually of the invisible world, of which our spirits are inhabitants. We may well be grateful to all poets and artists who may aid us by their illustrations to see, in the face of outward things, the tokens of a glory which outward things may either declare to us or conceal from our view. But the study of our Lord's parables will give us the safest and most authoritative help in connecting the phenomena of our daily life with that Kingdom of Heaven, which the Lord Jesus has opened to all believers—a kingdom of which we were made inheritors in our infancy, and to live as citizens of which is our highest duty and privilege.

XI.

THE FEEDING OF THE FIVE THOUSAND.

St. John vi. 5.

"*Whence shall we buy bread, that these may eat?*"

It is instructive to compare together in our minds the position that would be occupied by an extraordinary man, having the power of working miracles, and the position occupied by the Lord of glory, the Divine Son of the all-ruling Father, as he acted amongst men during his sojourn in the flesh upon the earth.

The miracle-working man, according to our supposition, acts **in** a particular place and time, amidst general laws which he has power to suspend on occasion, but which otherwise control the things about him and himself amongst them. In the community to which he belongs, he stands forth as a **person** possessed of astonishing resources, capable of being turned to important account. If he is ambitious, **he** can do more to promote his own interest and glory than all the kings and potentates of the earth. But, according to the universal feeling of mankind, miracle-workers are not selfish in their aims. Receiving their power from heaven, it is their habit to exercise it for the good of others. They work their miracles to help the unfortunate, to guide the ignorant, to terrify the wicked. If you had any access to a worker of miracles, it would be an exciting thing to watch for the exercise of his power, to prevail on him to use it for your benefit or for some purpose in which you are interested, and with this view to try to gain his favour. It would seem a disappointing circumstance that when there are so many good things that might be done by an act of one man's volition, the extraordinary power should be put forth unaccountably and at rare intervals. We might go on to observe, that to be habitually in contact with a worker of miracles would produce the same kind of effect upon a population, in promoting speculation and idleness and deranging quiet, trustful industry, as the establishment of a lottery system. A wise man would pray that his city or country might be preserved from such a dangerous and hurtful distinction as the presence of even a good and saintly miracle-worker.

It would not be difficult to find illustrations of what I am supposing. There is a town in Northern Italy, of which the patron saint bears the distinctive title of the Thaumaturge or miracle-worker. If you were to go into the church of St. Antony the Thaumaturge at Padua, you would see indications of the continuance of that power which is supposed to have been possessed in a remarkable degree by St. Antony when he was alive. His massive tomb, surrounded by representations of the chief miracles of his legendary life, is also hung round with memorials of more recent miracles, such as little pictures illustrating diseases or infirmities which the saint had healed, and crutches no longer required by the lame whom he had enabled to walk. At the same spot you would see numbers of poor people gathering every day, some kneeling, some placing their hands reverently on the tomb, all imploring St. Antony to put forth his thaumaturgic power in their behalf. Whatever we may think of the reality of the actual exercise of such powers, there is no difficulty in imagining a man possessing and using them according to what his worshippers believe of St. Antony. Such miracle-working, supposing it to be real, obviously has two disadvantages about it. (1) It is likely to create disappointment and perplexity at its going just so far as it does and no farther. (2) And the unsettling of the minds of those who set their hopes upon it, is likely to do more harm than the rare and limited exercises of it can do good. But still, we can conceive of a man moved by proper causes in vouchsafing or withholding a miracle, as for example giving a miracle as a kind of prize to the most deserving. And his action relatively to the people about him resembles, though it surpasses, that of one who by exceptional skill or wealth, or any other means, might be able to do occasional acts useful or gratifying to his neighbours.

But when we think of our Saviour and His actions, we think of One who is the Lord of all things, who keeps all the forces of the universe in motion, according to laws of which He is the author, and who cannot therefore be asked to interfere with a course of things apart from Himself, though He may be asked to bring to pass particular ends in particular cases. If we believe the world in general to be under Divine government, the idea of *God* as a miracle-worker, in the sense in which we so conceive of a man, becomes almost absurd. If the laws of nature are *God's* laws, it is no triumph for Him to interfere with them in any way, and to ask Him to do so would imply some reflection upon His all-present wisdom and goodness. It would seriously impair our trust in God, if we thought it likely that He might change His ways in order to confer occasional startling benefits.

Now, when the Lord Jesus came, He came to act in the Father's power and to reveal the Father's nature. He did work miracles or do mighty works. He healed the sick, He fed the hungry, He raised the dead to life. Acts like these might be regarded as the performances of a thaumaturge; they might be wondered at, craved, besought, just like the supposed achievements of St. Antony or any other saint. It was inevitable that wonderful works should by many be so regarded. And yet, seen in this light, miracles are eminently *un*-Divine in their nature, and prejudicial in their operation. They minister, strange as it may seem to say so, to the greediness, the idleness, the gambling dispositions, of men. It was not appointed that there should be no symptoms of such effects in the case of our Lord's miracles. The story of them is most true to life in indicating symptoms of this kind. The fellow-townsmen of Jesus clamorously demanded that He should do miracles for *their* glory and benefit as well as in other cities. The multitudes would have taken Him by force and made Him a king. There was a disposition to make bargains of faith with Jesus: Do so and so, and we will believe. On the other hand, we find Jesus counteracting to the utmost these undesirable influences of His miracles. He does so especially by refusing altogether to work miracles on demand. He protests against the kind of faith which rested upon them. He draws up and absorbs the merely astonishing elements of His miracles into the mightier and more solemn purpose of revealing the will of the Eternal Father.

In no other way, it would seem, could miracles be prevented from being morally pernicious, and detrimental to men's genuine faith in God. But if a miracle was given expressly as a sign of God's will and operations, and if it was capable of being so interpreted, those who could thus receive it might even learn from it to be more quiet and contented, to look with more reverence upon the ordinary ways of God's **providence,** and to crave less for anything miraculous.

This paradoxical character may be traced in the records **of** our Lord's wonderful works. Considered as what they are in themselves, and further regarded, as they ought to be, in the light of our Lord's constant teaching, they tend to promote, not an eager demand for interpositions, but a humble faith in God's fatherly dealings. They come to us as revelations of a real but invisible world which is around us. They serve to open our eyes to wonders more vast and more awful than their own outward phenomena.

Let us now turn our attention to that feeding of the Five thousand which is recorded in all the Gospels. It was susceptible of being regarded merely as an extraordinary thaumaturgic act. It was a special piece of good fortune for that multitude to have the benefit of it. Could it not be repeated? Why should not this Prophet relieve hunger again in the same convenient manner? This was clearly a man to follow, a man whom it would be wise to urge to action by any flattery and honours which could be paid him. Such feelings prevailed largely amongst the partakers of our Lord's bounty. They are so natural and plausible that it is easy for us to realize them in our own minds. But then we remember that He who fed the five thousand professes to feed men every where at all times. The same Jesus who caused the bread to multiply under His hands, had said, "Take no thought for your life, what ye shall eat or what ye shall drink, nor yet for your body, what ye shall put on. Is not the life more than meat, and the body than raiment? Behold the fowls of the air: for they sow not, neither do they reap, nor gather into barns; yet your heavenly Father feedeth them. Are ye not much better than they?" There is nothing thaumaturgic in the feeding thus set forth. We feel that we are raised into a higher atmosphere, to which the wondering and the craving after irregular manifestations of power **and** favour do not properly belong. And if we are to believe in God at all, this is the true atmosphere of our faith. We are intended to live in a constant dependence upon God, in a mind which can say trustfully, "Our Father who art in heaven, give us this day our daily bread. Thou who knowest that we have need of all these things, grant them to us according to thy own knowledge of what we really want for our good and for thy glory."

What relation, then, has such an act as the extraordinary feeding of the five thousand, to the higher truth of God's continual providence? Surely this: that it may, if rightly received, set forth that truth and open men's eyes to it. Our blessed Lord spoke continually, to ears and minds that were very deaf to His words, of the Father in Heaven, their Father and His, who was blessing them and seeking to bless them. He bore witness of the mercy and goodness of the Father towards even the unthankful and the evil. He said that He Himself had been sent, most specially sent in fulfilment of all God's promises, to manifest the Father's love towards them. "Behold," he said, "the works that I do. These bear witness that what I say is true." If the Son of God was to come at all in our flesh, at a given time and place, it is scarcely conceivable that he should *not* do acts out of the ordinary range of human power. But if His works were to bear a genuine and useful testimony to what He was and what He had come to declare, it was necessary that they should fall in, by a natural harmony, with the ordinary ways of Divine dealing. Because Jesus was the Son of God, He could feed five thousand men with five loaves and two fishes. Because He was the Son of God, this act was not an irregular wonder, but it spoke to the imaginations of men of Him who was always the giver of bread, in whom men lived and moved and had their being.

But if this miracle, in its true significance, sets forth the Father as always feeding His children, in what sense are we to think of God as giving us bread? How does God practically feed us?

The answer is, By means of the ordinances of nature and of human society, which are of God, and which He causes to work to good ends. No truly inspired teacher has ever taught men to look upon these as a system of fate or as the fruits of chance and of man's wisdom, or to expect of God help which should not come through His own appointed instruments. It is God who covereth the heavens with clouds and prepareth rain for the earth; and maketh the grass to grow upon the mountains, and herb for the use of men. There is a remarkable piece of instruction on this point contained amongst the prophecies of Isaiah, in the latter verses of chap. xxviii. "Give ye ear, and hear my voice; hearken, and hear my speech. Doth the plowman plow all day to sow? doth he open

and break the clods of his ground? When he hath made plain the face thereof, doth he not cast abroad the fitches and scatter the cummin, and cast in the principal wheat, and the appointed barley, and the **rye, in** their place? For his God doth instruct him to discretion, and doth teach him. For the fitches are not thrashed with **a** thrashing instrument, neither is a cart wheel turned about upon the cummin; but the fitches are beaten out with a staff and the cummin with a rod. Bread corn is bruised; because he will not ever be threshing it, nor break it with the wheel of his cart, nor bruise it with his horsemen. This also cometh forth from the Lord of hosts, which is wonderful in counsel, and excellent **in** working." We may not be able to understand precisely the operations here mentioned; but **we** can see clearly that all the distinctions in agriculture which are learnt from experience are referred by the prophet to the teaching of God. Similarly, the productive operations of all the arts are rightly to be regarded as means by which God feeds the multitudes of His people. Sometimes we should be disposed to call these means general, and sometimes special; but there is no vital distinction between the general and the special. The discovery of new countries; the drawing to them of a population which shall develop their fruitfulness by cultivation; the opening out of productive employments by which men may earn wages and their bread—these acts of God's providence sometimes appear to have an appositeness which we describe by the term special. But the great fact is, that by these and the like methods, the great God, the Creator and Ruler, does feed the generations of His children, as truly and effectually, as wisely and advantageously, as the five thousand were fed by the hands of Jesus in the wilderness.

When we have become accustomed to the contemplation of those universal methods of God's fatherly government of men, and are duly impressed by their vastness, by their complexity, by the closeness with which they come near to the daily life and pursuits and the spiritual experience of every man, we can hardly fail to acquire a distaste, on moral and spiritual grounds—(I am not now speaking of physical grounds)—for the mere thaumaturgic element in miracles. The only miracles which we shall respect will be those that tend to lead men upwards to that which is above the miraculous, to serve as stepping stones from the visible into the invisible. Such a feeling, I believe, is not only warranted, but is actually taught us by the narrative of the mighty works of our Lord wrought by Himself in visible person or through His servants.

And it is remarkable to find how little of that way of regarding miracles which prevailed amongst the multitudes of Galilee and Judea is to be observed amongst the communities of the first Christians. Though miracles were wrought amongst them, they seem to have been very little disturbed by them. The unsettlement which St. Paul so earnestly and practically denounces amongst the Thessalonians, as adverse to quiet, trustful industry, was occasioned, not by miracles being expected to supersede the tedious operations of common labour, but by a mistake as to the coming of the Lord. Miracles were evidently absorbed into the heavenly principles of a life led in the Spirit. Christians were called upon to work industriously, and to make sacrifices to aid one another. "Let him labour, working with his own hands the thing which is good, that he may have to give to him that needeth." St. Paul himself set an example of humble, persevering industry by working with his own Apostolic hands at the trade of tent making. He did not say, How much more useful it would be for me to be sustained miraculously and set free to devote my whole time to prayer and the ministry of the word. And no doubt he believed that the bread which was bought with the money for which the tent cloth was sold, was just as much given him by his Heavenly Father, as if it had been brought to him through the air by a bird from heaven. I can imagine that in the former case there was even more of deep thankfulness and reverence in the Apostle's mind than there would have been in the latter.

After the five thousand had eaten, a remarkable direction was given by Jesus. "Gather up the fragments that remain, that nothing be lost." Acting under this command, the disciples filled twelve baskets full of the fragments. All the Evangelists mention these twelve basketfulls of the fragments. It is usual to explain this direction, as intended to bring vividly before the eyes of the disciples the miraculous increase of the food —more being left over than the distribution had begun with. And some such purpose appears to be implied by words which Jesus afterwards used. When He told the disciples to beware of the leaven of the Pharisees and Sadducees, they reasoned amongst themselves saying, It is because we have taken no bread. But Jesus rebuked the unworthy notion that He was troubling Himself about bodily bread, saying, "O ye of little faith, why reason ye among yourselves, because ye have brought no bread? Do ye not yet understand, neither remember the five loaves of the five thousand, and how many baskets ye took up; neither the seven loaves of the four thousand, and how many baskets ye took up? How is it that ye do not understand, that I spake it not to you concerning bread, that ye should beware of the leaven of the Pharisees and of the Sadducees?" Our Lord evidently refers to the baskets of fragments as conspicuous signs and fruits of the miracle. But His immediate purpose in causing them to be collected is stated in his own words by St. John, "gather up the fragments, *that nothing be lost.*" The command was a warning against *waste.* And how sure it was to be needed by those who had witnessed so astonishing a display of creative power! The disciples of Jesus were likely to entertain disdainful thoughts of the ordinary gifts of God and the ordinary methods of supplying human wants; they were in danger of assuming that for them at least the common processes of nature were suspended. Every such effect of His miracles our Lord studiously combats. He guards them from casting any disparagement upon the ordinary ways of life. These common ways are not to seem flat and tame in the presence of His mighty works; the mighty works are rather to reflect glory and interest upon common laws. In the multiplying of the loaves, Jesus would not have it supposed that He was making a lavish use of supernatural power which resided in Him. He was acting under the Father who gives to men all things richly to enjoy. He gave thanks to the Father before distributing the food. He caused common loaves to grow imperceptibly under His hands, rather than create new food in any sudden or startling manner. And when the multitude were satisfied, He would not have the fragments wasted. Apart from any reasoning about the matter, good food cannot be wasted without a sentiment of *irreverence* towards God's gifts. "Waste not, want not," is a good maxim of prudence and economy. But "Waste **not** that which the Heavenly Father provides for the support of strength to be used in His service," is a maxim of higher obligation, a voice of true practical religion. For once or twice, in order to produce a great and lasting sign, the Son of Man would call into existence bread for which no tiller of the ground had wrought in the sweat of his face; but these rare acts were to be proofs of God's compassion upon a multitude who had followed Jesus out of the reach of food; they were to be links, connecting every day's food with God the giver; and all the remains of the food thus brought into existence were to be made as much of as if they had been obtained by toil and could only be replaced by fresh toil. The teaching of the kingdom was not to introduce disorder into men's lives: its permanent exhortation to men would be, that in quietness they should work and eat their own bread.

Let us now observe, with St. John, the effect actually produced by this miracle.

St. John describes it in the next verses. "Then those men, when they had seen the miracle which Jesus did, said, This is of a truth that Prophet which should come into the world. When Jesus, therefore, perceived that they would come and take him by force to make him a king, he departed again into a mountain himself alone."

We must bear in mind that Jesus had publicly claimed the character which the Galileans were willing to ascribe to Him. He had been declared by John the Baptist to be the Messiah. He had Himself been speaking and working in the Father's name, as the Son whom the Father had sent. The Jews were looking for the appearance of the Messiah as a

Prophet and Prince. The mighty work which they had seen, therefore, only confirmed the surmises which their following Him into the wilderness proved **that** they had previously entertained. If they confessed Him **to be** the Prophet who was to come, and sought to have Him for their king, they were only admitting claims which He had Himself put forward.

But the effect produced on their minds was, nevertheless *not* in the main the right one. It was not that which Jesus desired to produce.

His first act was to *withdraw Himself* both from the multitude and from the little band of His disciples. These He directed to go before Him in a vessel to Capernaum. The multitudes He left on the coast of the lake, retiring under the cover of **the** night to commune with His Father in prayer. How He afterwards taught the multitude we shall consider on a future occasion. But it is interesting to observe, in passing, what the Lord did for the disciples.

We may take it for granted that their minds had been receiving the same impression as that made upon the multitude. It could scarcely be otherwise. What mind of man could resist, without the special grace of God, the vulgar wonderment which it is in the nature of a miracle to produce? Is it not safe to suppose that the disciples were thinking of the advantages which might accrue from being friends **and** followers of such a Master; that they were rejoicing in the thought of the extraordinary impression which *their* Master was making upon the **world?** St. Mark says simply, that their heart was hardened or blinded, without explaining in what their insensibility consisted. But such hardening *must have* been an inability to recognise Jesus in His true nature, as manifesting the glory of the Father, and bringing men spiritually to the Father. It seemed fit to Jesus to leave them for some hours to themselves; and not to themselves only, but to darkness and danger. The wind was against them, the sea rose, and the disciples were distressed and frightened. They, the followers of One who could exercise the Divine power of creating bread, were toiling anxiously in a boat at sea, and afraid of being engulphed. Their high thoughts must have been taken out of them; they must have felt the pressure of common human need and danger. But just when their hearts were thus bruised and softened, they beheld the form of their Master coming towards them, as one walking upon the water. This appearance, had their faith in Him been deep and spiritual, would have comforted them; whatever they might have thought of it, it would have recalled them to trust in God, and to a stout courage. But their vain faith had been crushed out of them, and the true faith was all but extinct too; and when they saw the form of Jesus, they were the more frightened, thinking it was a ghost. But they had now been chastened enough. Jesus presented Himself graciously to them as their Friend and Saviour. "It is I, be not afraid." Then he entered the vessel with them, and they were speedily at the place for which they were bound. The hearts of the disciples, we are specially informed, were awed and humbled by this manifestation. They felt once more that they were in the presence, not of human power magnified to the supernatural, but of a Divine providence and goodness. "They came and worshipped him, saying, Of a truth thou art the Son of God." This was what He desired to teach them, and to make them feel, not that He was a leader exercising supernatural powers, but that He was the Son of God, sent into the world to manifest the Father, and to do His will.

This, therefore, must have been the intended lesson of the sign of the loaves. It was to be, as we afterwards learn, a type of spiritual nourishment; but we may be sure that it was also designed to carry home to the hearts of all who witnessed it, a direct and simple impression. It was a putting-forth of the Father's bountiful hand from behind the veil of His ordinary providence. The Son of God was teaching His hearers of the Father, and the Father's kingdom. He was seeking to lead them to a true spiritual knowledge of the Father. Impelled by many and mixed motives, multitudes followed Him, hanging upon His lips, hearing gladly of the Father. Under the pressure of this enthusiasm, they had forgotten their bodily wants, and were now in danger of fainting with hunger. Then, for their benefit, and in the light of the truths which had been flowing from the teaching of Jesus, the Father put forth by the hand of Jesus an entirely extraordinary manifestation of His creative power. The food which they would have provided for themselves, had they not been following Jesus, was miraculously supplied to them, under solemn and orderly arrangements; and they were called upon to give thanks to the Father for this food. The proper effect of this sign on their hearts, we may confidently say, would have been to make them conscious, in awe and thankfulness, of the presence of the Almighty Maker, the God of their Fathers, and to lead them to see in Jesus of Nazareth, whom they were following and wondering after, the Son of Man in whom the Father revealed His nature and power.

XII.

CHRIST THE BREAD OF LIFE.

St. John vi. 35.

"*Jesus said unto them, I am the bread of life: he that cometh to me shall never hunger; and he that believeth on me shall never thirst.*"

THE feeding of the five thousand men with five loaves and two fishes was made by our Lord the introduction to several discourses, in which He proclaimed *Himself* to be the spiritual food of mankind. Let us go on to consider the first portion of the sayings in which this wonderful truth was set forth.

We have seen that the sign of the loaves failed to produce upon the minds of those who witnessed it the effect which Jesus desired. The multitude were impressed by **the** wonder-working power it exhibited, and thought it would be most advantageous to have one who could do such things as the head of an insurrectionary movement. They were ready to seize **upon** Jesus, and **to** make Him their king. But this **was not** the end which Jesus sought by His mighty **work.** He therefore withdrew Himself from the multitude, and went up into the **hills** to pray. The disciples—that is, the Apostles, with, perhaps, a few others—understood the mind of their Master better than the multitude; but they also were dull to the purpose of the sign. They rose with difficulty out of carnal and worldly apprehensions. Jesus, therefore, seeking to train them specially to a right knowledge of Himself, caused them to encounter peril by sea during the night, exposed their want of faith to their own view by appearing to them as one walking upon the water, and then drew forth in them a spirit of trust and worship by manifesting Himself as a heavenly friend and protector. And so, on the morrow after the miracle, Jesus and His disciples arrived at Capernaum.

We then find that the withdrawing of Himself from the multitude was only temporary, and that Jesus was desirous of leading *them* also into a truer apprehension of what He was come to do. Those who had followed Him across the lake, when they had lost Him through His disappearance after the miracle, returned to Capernaum seeking Him. Having found Him, their first expression was one of wonder, "Rabbi, when camest thou hither?" Jesus answers, not their curiosity, but their eagerness to find Him. He says solemnly to them, "Ye seek me, not because ye saw the miracles, but because ye did eat of the loaves, and were filled." This reproach requires to be carefully considered, as it seems to contradict the fact which the previous narrative exhibits, that the mind of the people was thoroughly impressed by the wonder which Jesus wrought. We might have been inclined to say that the multitude were seeking Jesus *precisely because* of the miracle which they had just witnessed. On referring to the original passage, we find that here, as in many other instances, our translators have substituted the word "miracle" for another word, "*sign*," which they did not see the necessity of distinguishing from "miracle." But, in truth, the distinction may be very important. Our Lord's words are, "Ye seek me, not because ye *saw signs*, but because ye ate of the loaves and were filled." They were quite alive to the *miracle*, that is, to the *marvel*, in what Jesus had done. They had no doubt that the loaves had been multiplied by some superhuman power. They were ready to give any degree of credit to Jesus for the power He had exhibited. But they did not regard the work of Jesus as *a sign*. They were not looking for what was signified in it. They thought of it as a most opportune marvel, and that was all. They were delighted at having had a meal which cost nothing. He who could give them so surprising a benefit was one whom they would eagerly follow.

This carnal mind towards Him and His works is what Jesus rebuked. In whatever He did, He wished to lead the hearts of the people upwards to the Father in heaven, and to the spiritual kingdom which He was come to open to men. His works were signs or tokens, intended to witness of the Father, and of **the** Father's kingdom. He proceeds **to use** the multiplying of the loaves, not as a marvel **which** proved His power, but as a sign through which spiritual realities might be interpreted. By the side of "meat which perishes" He places "meat which endures unto everlasting life." Of this meat, or food, He says, "The Son of Man shall give it to you; for he was sealed by the Father, even God." This is the food for which He exhorts them *to work*.

You observe that Jesus is now beginning to communicate the spiritual reality of which the feeding of the body with food that perishes is a symbol. The multitude were eager for bodily food. Jesus tells them that there is another food, of no perishable nature, sustaining another kind of life which was far more precious, which they ought to seek, and which they might obtain of Him, the Son of Man, because the Divine Father had sealed Him as the giver of it. Let us mark, without dwelling upon them, the ideas thus presented to the minds of the hearers.

The first is that of "*everlasting life*." We have no means of knowing with certainty what sense the hearers of Jesus would give to this term. But it must have raised their thoughts to something above the visible and passing world, something in which they had an interest as immortal beings, something spiritual and heavenly.

The food which would have issue in this eternal life, was to be given by *the Son of Man*. Jesus bids His hearers to look to Himself for a kind of food so much more precious than that which He had supplied to them the day before. He calls Himself the Son of Man, that they may feel their fellowship with Him, and may look to them as the Head of their race.

The living food was to be given by the Son of Man **as the** representative of the Father, God in heaven. The Father had sealed Him for this office. That is, **the** Father had owned Him. The Son of Man was sent by the **Divine** Father, with an express commission and true credentials, to bestow upon men the food of a divine life.

These ideas were simple and clear enough to commend themselves in some degree to the minds of the multitude. The Son of Man who was amongst them, the Heavenly Father who had sent Him, the higher **life** to which he could minister nourishment—these were not mere unintelligible names to the Galileans who followed Jesus. Neither, on the other hand, were they likely to understand completely what Jesus said to them. Very naturally they take hold of the first word of the exhortation. "Work," Jesus had said, **"for** the true food." They ask Him, "What shall we do that we may work the works of God?" They profess a willingness to obey the command addressed to them in God's name, to work God's works. How were they to do it? No doubt they asked honestly, though with no very deep or earnest purpose. Jesus therefore replies plainly, "*This* is the work of God, **that ye** believe on him whom he hath sent." "This is what you have to do. The Father has sent the Son of Man to quicken you with true spiritual nourishment: your business, your task or work, in seeking for yourselves this food, is *to believe* on Him whom God has sent." Thus Jesus led His hearers into the spiritual region, calling them to faith in Himself, and promising them life through this faith. "Believe in me," he said plainly to them.

This is already a direct interpretation, at least in part, of that feeding on the bread of life to which Jesus had invited His hearers. And they partly understood Him. They thought of the old servant of God, who had guided and fed their fathers, of that Moses in whom his countrymen believed, and who had given them strong proofs that he had a commission from God. Jesus was apparently claiming to be the prophet whom the Lawgiver had said their God would raise up unto them, like himself. If they were to hear and believe Him, they must have clear warrant for doing so. They ask, therefore, "What sign shewest thou then, that we may see and believe thee? what dost thou work? Our fathers did eat manna in the desert; as it is written, He gave them bread from heaven to eat." We might have thought that they would have gone back to the sign of the day before, and that that would have sufficed them. They cannot have forgotten it; and the very illustration they adduce, "He gave them bread from heaven to eat," seems to prove that it was in their minds. How, then, are we to account for their asking for a sign? The explanation appears to be, that they had not thought of the multiplication of the loaves as *a sign* at all. They had not connected it with the profession of Jesus that He was come down from heaven, or with the demand that they should believe in Him as one sent from God. There had been a mysterious increase of bread; and this gave them an exalted idea of the character and power of Jesus. But if they were to think of Him as coming directly from God, ought there not to be an appropriate sign; if He gave them food, ought it not to be some unearthly kind? ought it not to descend out of heaven? Such would seem to have been their reflections. They looked for something surpassing that "angels' food" which had descended from heaven for their fathers when they were under the guidance of Moses. A greater than Moses would display a more heavenly power than that which Moses had exhibited.

There is always some uncertainty in supplying the links of thought which are wanted in St. John's narratives or the discourses he has preserved. This is one of the chief difficulties in the interpretation of his Gospel. But we lose a great deal if we disregard the connexion of passages, and consider the sentences as fragmentary and isolated. Generally, a cautious meditation on the words which are recorded will lead us to supply safely the feelings or reflections which have not been recorded.

This is the more necessary, as it was the custom of Jesus to reply rather to what He knew was in the minds of those with whom He was speaking, than to the form of their remarks. So it is in this place. In answer to the inquiry about the sign, which should correspond to or surpass the manna, Jesus says, "Verily, verily, I say unto you, it was not Moses that gave you the bread from heaven; but my Father gives you the true bread from heaven." We can only infer from this answer, that the people had been thinking of Moses as the real worker of the sign, and forgetting Him who used Moses as His instrument. "It is not a question," Jesus seems to say, "of the glory of Moses, or of my glory. Look to Him who dealt with you through Moses. He is my Father, and He has sent me. The bread of God, the greatest gift of God to men, is He who comes down from heaven and gives life to the world." The multitude hearing of this bread, say to Jesus, "Lord, evermore give us this bread." They probably spoke with more wonder and respect than true intelligence or earnestness in their hearts. They did not know what they were asking for. Jesus therefore states more explicitly the truth He is teaching men, in the words, "I am the bread of life: he that cometh to me shall never hunger; and he that believeth on me shall never thirst. But I said unto you, that ye also have seen me, and believe not."

This, then, is our Lord's account of what He means when He says that He is the bread of life. "To come to Him," "to believe on Him," was to eat that food which would sustain the true life in the soul.

Elsewhere and often Jesus invited men to come to Him and to believe in Him; as *e.g.* in those well-known words, "Come unto me, all ye that labour and are heavy laden, and I will give you rest." What is specially brought before us in the chapter we are considering is the truth that there is a spiritual life, the due inheritance of every man, which is nourished by coming to Jesus and believing in Him. Let us endeavour to think what sense this language bore, and **what** illustration it had, when it was first spoken.

Now, our Lord Jesus Christ, we may remember, when He walked upon this earth, wished men in the most literal sense to *come to Him*. After He had **been** sent forth by His baptism upon His ministry, He invited men to hear Him, to wait upon His teaching, to follow Him. Though He did not always court publicity, yet it belonged to His work to be for the most part surrounded by the people. Therefore, when He said Come to me, it might be understood literally. On one occasion, some little children were brought to Him for His blessing. His disciples would have repelled those who brought them; but the Master said, "Suffer the little children to come unto me, and forbid them not. And he took them up in his arms." So He wished their fathers and their mothers to come to Him—not once, but often. Many he would allow to follow Him day after day; **and** in such companionship He rejoiced. Some at least He wished to give **up** their homes and occupations, and to go with Him wherever He went. He **was** glad that the sick should come to Him to be healed, that the ignorant should come to be taught, that the afflicted and heavy-laden should come to be comforted.

Of course, it was possible to go frequently to hear Jesus **and** to company with Him, out of mere curiosity, or from some selfish motive, without any *faith in Him*. But those who went to Him in a simpler and nobler spirit must have *believed in Him*.

They trusted in His power and His will to heal; they confessed the authority with which He taught; they felt His goodness; they saw something of the grace and truth which were revealed in Him. In the disciples, the first rudimentary faith in their Master was gradually strengthened and enlightened. They saw by degrees what He was. They learnt His love, His power, His knowledge. They trusted in Him, believing what He said, and committing themselves to His guidance. The expression, therefore, "to believe in Jesus," had an obvious interpretation in what men were doing every day. There was mystery, indeed, beneath it; but it would not have seemed in itself a mysterious expression; it was one which any man might have used.

If then there were persons actually doing what our Lord spoke of, coming to Him and believing in Him, that which He said was the fruit of such action might be practically tested. If to come to Him and believe on Him was to feed on Him, and if to feed on Him was to be nourished by the bread of eternal life, then that life, supposing it to be of a nature to be manifested, might be looked for in those who came and believed. Were there any effects visible in them, any signs of such a life having been stirred within them? Our Lord's declarations courted this question; and it was not one which could not be answered. The true disciples of Jesus *were* made alive, in varying degrees according to their faith. No doubt the least sympathizing of their neighbours could discern some signs of that quickening, and could trace them to their contact with Jesus. The fishermen of the Galilean lake were not indeed at first all that they became in later years; but it is evident that a brighter and purer and nobler spirit was awakened in them from the first through their knowledge of the Master whom they loved. They had interests and hopes and **joys** such **as** they had not formerly known. **They** were enabled to walk in greater innocence of **life.** They were filled with zeal, and a power of sacrifice. They were raised above petty cares. They had a freer approach to God. They were made more **helpful** to one another and to their neighbours. They were delivered from much cowardice and superstition. They had the light of a worthy love steadily shining **in** their lives. It was a natural and reasonable observation to say of them that they were quickened with a new life. They felt in themselves the impulses and the joys of a new spiritual life; and the fruits of this life were visible to their neighbours.

In this way we can perceive that the profession of Jesus, I am the Bread of Life to those who believe **in Me, had** a practical demonstration which would explain as well as prove **it.** When He spoke of the effect produced by Him on those who came to Him, the people would naturally look to John, to Simon, to Nathaniel, who *had* come to Jesus and believed on Him, that they might see the effect produced. And they would not look in vain. In the hopes, the courage, the aspirations, the calm confidence, the well-directed **energies of** the disciples, the word of **their** Master was realized. And it was not the less realized when the life of these disciples flagged, as it so often did, through want of faith in their Master. To themselves the negative experience would be as convincing as the positive. They might recall, for example, the night just passed which they had spent on the sea. During the earlier part their faith in Jesus was almost dead; and then we may be sure they were miserable, discouraged, cowardly, selfish, ready to blame one another, sinking into mere carnality and death of the soul. How different their state when their faith in their Master as a heavenly Friend was again revived! Along with their faith came an access of peace, love, unity, strength to do or to suffer anything in the common cause, with Him whom they worshipped as the Son of God. And such experience would enable them to understand what Jesus said about faith in Him as satisfying the hunger and thirst of the soul. In the early hours of the night their soul was hungering and thirsting, a gnawing desire for something to satisfy them inwardly was felt by them, as it had been felt by men before, and has been felt by men since. The revealing of their Master's face to them was meat and drink to their souls; they were *satisfied* with it.

I have wished to interpret our Lord's saying in the simplest way in which it was likely to be understood and put to the proof at the time when it was spoken. We have been considering how Jesus proved Himself to be the bread of life to those who sought Him when He was in the flesh, and believed in Him as having come down from heaven. There is a wider and deeper sense of His words, which does not imply any knowledge of His bodily form or presence. There is a coming to Him which is not dependent upon His being seen with the bodily eye, on His being found here or there. Our Lord's own words forbid us to rest content with a mere Galilean interpretation of them. Indeed, the very fact of His being the bread of life to the disciples who surrounded Him, implies in Him a power, a nature, a relation to the human spirit, which could not be bounded by those narrow limits. If Jesus Christ was the bread of life to twelve men, or to one man, it was in Him, as He said, to give life *to the world*. And it is for us the most interesting question in reflecting on these sayings, How has Christ been the life of the world? How is He now the life of men? How is He the life of each one of us? In following such an inquiry we are led of necessity into broad and mysterious views of the relations of the Son of God to mankind universally, to the Church which confesses Him, and to the individual believer.

But, for the present, let me remind you how helpful the consideration of the feelings of the disciples in Galilee may reasonably be to ourselves. The Son of God whom we worship is He who was then manifesting Himself in the flesh. Our understanding and knowledge of Him come to us, and were intended to come to us, through the lineaments drawn on the pages of the Gospel history. No single act which Jesus of Nazareth did, no true effect which He produced upon those about Him, is to be cast aside from our conceptions of the Son of God, or separated from His work as the manifestation of the Divine nature. If we try to think of the Lord Jesus Christ without the genuinely human elements which come out in the Gospel narratives, we do not really make Him more Divine to our hearts, we only make Him less living and real. It is good for us, therefore, in our own endeavours to come to the Son of God and to believe in Him, to remember the simple allegiance of the companions who gave themselves up to Him, and who hung upon the lips from which the words of eternal life proceeded. That early allegiance of followers to a master was afterwards deepened and elevated into more adoring conceptions, into the consciousness of what their Master was to others who had never seen Him as well as to themselves. But they never threw away or lost the feelings of personal love and loyalty which had been the beginning of the life eternal in their souls. The Son of God, who had gone up into heaven that He might fill all things, was to them the Master whom only a few had recognised, but who had given life to those who believed in Him. And it was appointed that the knowledge and faith of the church in all ages should be chiefly nourished by the historical details in which Christ appears as the Head of a little company of followers and friends.

Let us take an interest, then, in remembering that when our heavenly Lord manifested Himself on earth, there were some whose eyes, when they beheld Him, were open to the Divine grace and truth which lived in Him, and who yielded themselves to the power of the grace and of the truth; that there were others, and they the immense majority, who, when they saw Him, yet believed Him not. To the latter He was unable to give life. They remained in the death of their ignorance and darkness. The life of heaven could only reach them through their recognising the glory which shone in Jesus of Nazareth. The others, who saw and believed, received the life intended for them. Jesus, their Master, was as daily bread to the wants and vigour of their souls. The love and the truth which shone from His words and acts, won their growing trust, stirred up in them the unselfish hopes which are salvation to the human spirit, softened their rough hearts into the tenderness and constancy of a true affection, gave them a self-possession and a courage which were strange qualities for uncultured peasants, and endowed them with a power of which the world's history can show no similar examples. Those fishermen of Galilee were instruments in the regeneration of the world. How could they have been thus effectual unless they had themselves been made alive? And to what food was their life due but to that bread from heaven with which their Master daily nourished them?

XIII.

DISCIPLES DRAWN TO JESUS BY THE FATHER.

St. John vi. 44.

" No man can come to me, except the Father which hath sent me draw him."

WE considered, last Sunday, the proclamation of Jesus, "I am the bread of life." We saw that He meant by thus describing Himself, that He sustained the spiritual life of those who came to Him and believed in Him. I endeavoured to show you that this assertion proved itself to be practically true in the experience of His disciples. Those who believed in Him were made alive. In proportion as they trusted Him and allowed Him to be their life, they felt life in themselves, and manifested the fruits of life. They became spiritually stronger, more courageous, more self-possessed, more happy, more loving, more able to do and to suffer as the light which was in them directed. When their faith failed, they sank into weakness and atrophy; they became victims of cowardice, selfishness, and disunion.

Seeking then to be received by those amongst whom He dwelt as the bread of their life, so that many might thus be nourished unto life eternal, Jesus, we observed, was wont to invite men to come to Him. "Believe in me," "Come to me, and I will give you rest," were invitations continually addressed by Him to those who surrounded Him.

But at the same time that He thus urged men, with all grace and tenderness, to come to Him, we have to notice that He was also accustomed to deliver the testimony which I have taken for our subject this morning. He said "No one can come to me unless my Father draw him." These words must have a very important bearing on our Lord's declarations concerning Himself. It was evidently the desire of Jesus, and of His Apostle St. John, that men should connect together, as closely as possible, the truth that they might come to the Son of God and find in Him the support of their spiritual life, and the truth that they could not come to Him unless the Father drew them.

There are certain lights in which the Gospel of St. John would lead us especially to contemplate this latter truth.

1. Let the first of these be, the rejection of our Lord by the religious Jews.

Jesus invariably testified that the reason why the Jews would not acknowledge Him was, because they were alienated from the Father. This is sometimes expressed in the language of our text, "No man can come to me, except the Father which hath sent me draw him;" that is, in words which *might be* taken to mean, that each man who came to Jesus was a passive instrument in the hands of the Father, and that those who did not come were without responsibility, being untouched by that act of the Father through which alone they *could come.* Thus, towards the end of this chapter, verses 64, 65, Jesus says, " But there are some of you that believe not. Therefore said I unto you, that no man can come unto me *except it were given unto him* of my Father." These sayings answer to the true feeling in the human heart, that the very power to respond to God's will must be referred to God Himself. We cannot too absolutely renounce for ourselves, and ascribe to God, all the motions towards Him of which we are conscious. But Jesus was very far from meaning that the drawing of God was arbitrary, and left men without responsibility. Another class of His expressions describing the same fact consists of the sayings in which Jesus speaks of the Jews as *not knowing* the Father, and *not hearing His voice.* Thus, in verses 37, 38, Jesus declares, "The Father himself, which hath sent me, hath borne witness of me. Ye have neither heard his voice at any time, nor seen his shape. And ye have not his word abiding in you; for whom he hath sent, him ye believe not." Here our Lord affirms the presence of a testimony of the Father, a word of God which sought access to the hearts of the Jews, which they would not receive. The Father was speaking to them; if they had listened to His voice, they would have heard Him directing them to Jesus of Nazareth as His Son; but the monitions of the Father could not find entrance into their hearts,

and therefore they did not believe in the Son when **He** came. **We** must understand by this testimony **or** word of the Father, the direct spiritual teaching of which men are never left wholly destitute, and which was promised and given in a clearer form to the Jews. They were refusing the Divine instruction to which their inward souls might have listened. They were shutting out the voice of the Father, which they would have heard had they been His true children.

The eighth chapter contains the most striking assertions of Jesus to this effect. They bring before **our** minds clearly that the one fault in which the Lord summed up the evil dispositions of the Pharisees was ignorance or denial of the Father. In the latter part of that chapter Jesus is reproaching the Pharisees with much severity. "Ye do the deeds of your father," He says, verse 41. They replied, "We be not born of fornication; we have one Father, even God." This boast of theirs explains in part the reproaches **of** Jesus. They *ought* to have known the Father. **He** had been revealing Himself to them, and calling **them** His children. **But** they knew Him in name only. Therefore Jesus said to them, "If God were your Father, ye would love me; for I proceeded forth and came from God; neither came I of myself, **but** he sent me. Why do ye not understand my speech? even because ye cannot hear my word." The "*word*" is the declaration of the Father. If the Jews had been able to admit this into their hearts, they **would** have **been able** to recognise the "speech" of **Jesus.** But they **had** chosen for themselves another father, the evil spirit of hatred and falsehood; and they had renounced the true Father. "He that is of God," says Jesus again (v. 47), "heareth God's words, ye therefore hear them not, because ye are not of God." And again (v. 54), "If I honour myself, my honour is nothing; it is my Father that honoureth me; of whom ye say, that he is your God; yet ye have not known him; but I know him: and if I should say, I know him not, I should be a liar like unto you; but I know him, and keep his saying."

The knowing of the true Father implied loving Him and caring to please Him. And therefore Jesus in other places uses this language also, to describe the condition of the Pharisees towards God. In chap. v., vv. 42—44, we read, "I know you, that ye have not the love of God in you. I am come in my Father's name, and ye receive me not; if another shall come in his own name, him ye will receive. How can ye believe, which receive honour one of another, and seek not the honour that cometh from the only God?"

In dealing then with the religious Jews, our Lord plainly laid the fault of their rejecting Him upon their ignorance of His Father, who was the God of their Covenant and their Law, and whom they were professing to worship. They were not yielding themselves to the Father, or they would have been drawn to the Son.

(2) It is implied in these reproaches, that the Son represented the Father so fully and so closely that to know the one was to know the other. What is

there implied is elsewhere stated explicitly by Jesus. And **in** this light, again, we may consider the truth that those who are to believe in the Son must be **drawn** by the Father.

The fifth chapter of St. John is devoted to the exposition of the relation of Jesus as the Son to the Father. Our Lord vindicates His work of healing on the Sabbath-day **as an** interpretation **of** the Father's work. The Jews sought to kill Him because He not only had broken the Sabbath, but said also that God was His Father, making Himself equal with God. In this charge the Jews showed their ignorance of the very principle of sonship. They thought that Jesus in declaring His Sonship was setting Himself up as *God's equal*. But Jesus reminded them in His answer that it belonged to the very nature of a Son to be subject to His Father, and not to be His rival. The equality of independence He repudiated; the equality of a Son, in all things one with the Father, He claimed. " Verily, verily, I say unto you, the Son can do nothing of himself, but what he seeth the Father do: **for what** things soever he"—the Father—"doeth, these also doeth the Son likewise. For the Father loveth the Son, and showeth him all things that himself doeth: and he will show him greater works than these, that ye may marvel. For as the Father raiseth up the dead, and quickeneth them; even so **the Son** quickeneth whom he will. For the Father **judgeth** no man, but hath committed all judgment **unto** the Son: that all men should honour the Son even as they honour the Father. He that honoureth not the Son, honoureth not the Father which hath sent him." It would be difficult to say which is most strongly expressed here, the absolute subordination of the Son to the Father, or the perfect co-ordination of the will and power and working of the Son with those of the Father. There is nothing in the Son independent of the Father; there is nothing in the Father apart from the Son.

It agrees therefore with the whole testimony of Jesus concerning Himself and His relation to the Father, that He should speak of the Father as bringing those who came to Him, as giving to Him those who were His.

(3) Thirdly, let us look at the case of those who *were* drawn to Jesus.

And let us place first what our Lord Himself says of them. We find that as He declared of those who rejected Him that they did so because they did not know or care for the Father, so He constantly testifies of those who came to Him, that the Father had given them to Him. There is a remarkable passage to this effect in St. John x. 24—30. The Jews came round Jesus, and said, "How long dost thou make us to doubt? If thou be the Christ, tell us plainly. Jesus answered them, I told you, and ye believed not: the works that I do in my Father's name, they bear witness of me. But ye believe not, because ye are not of my sheep, as I said unto you. My sheep hear my voice, and I know them, and they follow me: and I give unto them eternal life; and they shall never perish, neither shall any man pluck them out of my hand. My

Father, which gave them me, is greater than all: and no man is able to pluck them out of my Father's hand. I and my Father are one." In these words we have a totally different figure used to set forth the dependence of His disciples upon the Son of God from that which runs through the sixth chapter. But the spiritual realities remain the same. In the sixth chapter Christ is the Bread upon which His disciples feed; in the tenth He is the Shepherd to whom His disciples are as sheep, and whose guidance they follow. But in both the gift to the disciples is *life*, life eternal; and in both the connecting of the disciples with their Lord is the Father's work.

I need not remind you how frequently the name of the Father is declared to the disciples in the solemn discourses of the night before the Crucifixion. Jesus is evidently striving to lead His friends into a more secure and more enlightened confidence in His Father. He stands forth as expressly the *Mediator*, the connecting bond, between them and the Father in Heaven. Let us mark the commencement of these discourses in the early part of the fourteenth chapter. The first verse stands in our translation, "Let not your heart be troubled: ye believe in God, believe also in me." It is doubtful whether it ought not rather to be (keeping the *imperative* throughout), "Believe in God, believe also in me." But, in either case, the belief in *Jesus* was made the natural sequel or accompaniment to the belief in *God*. The belief in God came first and had the precedence; but, in those who knew God rightly, this was properly followed by a belief in the

Son of God. We are presently reminded that the belief of the disciples in the Father was by no means a clear apprehension. When Jesus had said, "If ye had known me, ye should have known my Father also; and from henceforth ye know him, and have seen him," Philip answers Him as one who had been troubled by the Lord's continual references to the Father: "Lord, shew us the Father, and it sufficeth us;" whereupon Jesus gently rebukes him, "Have I been so long time with you, and yet hast thou not known me, Philip? he that hath seen me hath seen the Father; and how sayest thou then, Shew us the Father? Believest thou not that I am in the Father, and the Father in me? The words that I speak unto you I speak not of myself; but the Father that dwelleth in me, he doeth the works." The time was to come when the disciples should rise out of their perplexities and confusions into a clearer light. The Spirit of the Father and the Son was to make them conscious of their own fellowship with the Father in the Son. But their allegiance to Jesus in the days of His flesh proved at least that their will was to do the Father's will. "My teaching," Jesus had said, vii. 16, "is not mine, but his that sent me. If any man desires to do his will, he shall know of my teaching whether it be from God or whether I speak from myself." The bent of the disciples' will was towards God's will, and therefore they recognised the teaching of Jesus as coming from God: whereas, on the contrary, the will of the unbelieving Jews was to do the lusts of the Evil One. Jesus was, to His

disciples, the true witness and image of the righteous Father in heaven, and for this reason they came to Him and followed Him; and their reward was that their knowledge of the Father, which had been a trembling and uncertain hope, was advanced into clear vision.

In the prayer which Jesus addressed to His Father, recorded in chap. xvii.—that most wonderful of all the sacred records—this blessedness of the disciples is much dwelt upon. "I have manifested thy name unto the men which thou gavest me out of the world: thine they were, and thou gavest them to me; and they have kept thy word. Now they have known that all things whatsoever thou hast given me are of thee. For I have given unto them the words which thou gavest me; and they have received them, and have known surely that I came out from thee, and they have believed that thou didst send me." And the last words of this prayer are these: "O righteous Father, the world hath not known thee; but I have known thee, and these have known that thou hast sent me. And I have declared unto them thy name, and will declare it; that the love wherewith thou hast loved me may be in them, and I in them."

These numerous passages which I have quoted from St. John's Gospel will impress upon you forcibly, I trust, the consistency with which the grand truth of the drawing of men to Christ by the Father is set forth in various forms of language and in diverse applications. It would be possible to dwell at some length upon the indications presented by the history of the disciples, as it is given us in the Gospels, that they were actually drawn to Christ by the Father. But it may be sufficient to touch on the plainest of these indications, such as the prominent confessions of the Apostles. What character was it which they recognised in their Master, when their view of Him was clearest and loftiest and most satisfactory to Himself? Always the character of one *sent from God*—of *the Son of God*. On that night, between the feeding of the thousands and the teaching at Capernaum, when their faith was drawn out by the coming to them of Jesus upon the water, they worshipped Him, we are told, saying, " Of a truth thou art the Son of God." Again, after the teaching at Capernaum, as we read at the end of this sixth chapter, in answer to the mournful inquiry of Jesus, " Will ye also go away?" the answer of the twelve, given by the mouth of Simon Peter, contains the confession, " We believe and are sure that thou art that Christ, the Son of the living God." Once more, the same confession was made by the same leading Apostle on a more famous occasion, when Jesus expressly asked the disciples what they thought of Him : " Thou art the Christ, the Son of the living God." And of this confession Jesus said, " Blessed art thou, Simon Bar-jona ; for flesh and blood hath not revealed it unto thee, but my Father which is in heaven." It is plain that Jesus was to His immediate followers, not some mighty being wielding supernatural powers, but the representative of the living God, the Father in heaven. Their trust in Him grew out of their fear of the living God; their knowledge of Him was made conducive to the knowledge of the heavenly Father. They came to Him, because the Father who sent Him drew them.

Having endeavoured to expound from the scriptures, and especially out of the same Gospel, the truth declared in our text, let me go on to add a few remarks which this exposition suggests.

And first it must occur to us, I think, that this truth does not hold, in the doctrines or religion most familiar to ourselves, the place which it holds in St. John's Gospel. I have had some fear, in bringing together the testimonies which I have recited to you, that the subject might seem to many an unreal or unpractical one, because it does not embrace the religious ideas which we have been taught to consider as most essential.

If you have any such feeling, you must acknowledge that, in any case, the greatest prominence and practical importance are given to this truth in the teaching of our Lord, as St. John has preserved it. The contemplation of our Lord Jesus Christ, not so much as an independently Divine Person, but as the dependent Son of God, in whom the Father manifested Himself because there is nothing in the Father from eternity in which the Son does not share, is made by our Lord and His Apostle the great duty and privilege of the true disciple. The truth that no one can come to Him unless the

Father draw him, that our acceptance of Jesus Christ, and all the benefits which we gain from trusting in Him, depend upon the attitude of our will towards the righteous Father's will, is in the Gospel illustrated by all the faith of the disciples, by all the unbelief of the disobedient. From all, therefore, who reverence the Scriptures as containing the highest and safest teaching of God, these subjects may claim the most devout consideration.

And, if we admitted them thoroughly into our minds, we should see, I have no doubt, that they touch on all that is deepest and most vital and most practical in our common human nature, and in the experience of our lives. What, for example, can be a more universal obligation than the confession of the righteous Father? Think for a moment how the first unconscious rudiments of religion in any human heart must be the acknowledgment of such a Being; how the most advanced attainments in Christian knowledge and in godly living must result in the clearer vision of the same being. Any views or conceptions or doctrines which would lead us away in the least from the simplest filial acknowledgment of the one righteous Father in heaven, must have error and evil in them. The sin that works in us, as our conscience will remind us, is turning away from the righteous Father; all the good in us is the response of our spirits to the righteousness and love of the only God. I would repeat, any doctrines concerning Christ or His work or our own souls, which would tend to make the acknowledgment of the righteous

Father less clear and less living in our hearts, ought to be, on that account, regarded with suspicion.

But may we not also perceive, what most assuredly **is** the doctrine of the scriptures which we have been considering, that the acknowledgment of Jesus Christ whom the heavenly Father sent, who is one with the Father in the spirit of sonship, is in the closest harmony with the confession of the righteous Father, sustaining it, and being sustained by it? We need not embarrass ourselves with the question of *precedence* between these two confessions. Jesus Christ taught, on the one hand, that men came to Him through being drawn of the Father; on the other hand, that He was Himself the way to the Father, and that no one came to the Father but by Him. In these deep matters of the human will and conscience the order of time is of no importance to us, and may be neglected. The great truths work together. In the case of the first disciples, when they beheld Jesus, the name of the Father in heaven revealed itself to them. The Son suggested the Father; the Father commended the Son. And so it is in all ages. It is the office of the Son, as shown to us in the Gospel, to awaken the knowledge of the heavenly Father. The Son becomes dear to those who accept Him, because He represents and reveals the Father. This is our standing, in the face of the whole Divine revelation. Christ, whose history is brought before us from our infancy upwards, *is* our way to the Father. Observing His acts, studying His words, wondering at His sufferings, we learn the infinite nature of the living God, our Maker, who sent His Son into the world. So also, as we honour the Father, as our souls are sensitive to righteousness and love, as we accept with joy the Father's protection, and desire to please Him and live near to Him, we are drawn nearer and nearer to Christ as our Head and Elder Brother, our Saviour and our Lord. We look with awe upon the love with which the Father loved the Son, upon the devotion with which the Son surrendered Himself to the Father's will; and the love of the Father to the Son begins to be *in us*, claiming and conquering us, binding us in the Son of Man to God. We feel that we also are embraced in that wonderful love; that it is our privilege, also, to live, not to ourselves, as independent creatures, but to God in heaven, as depending every hour upon His fatherly goodness and love.

XIV.

FROM THE FATHER AND TO THE FATHER.

St. John vi. 61—63.

'*When Jesus knew in himself that his disciples murmured at it, he said unto them, Doth this offend you? What and if ye shall see the Son of Man ascend up where he was before? It is the Spirit that quickeneth; the flesh profiteth nothing: the words that I speak unto you, they are spirit, and they are life.*"

The saying at which the disciples murmured is our Lord's great declaration concerning Himself: "I am the living bread which came down from heaven; he that eateth of this bread shall live for ever." It was not only the figurative form of the saying which repelled them. Jesus had interpreted the figure. He had explained that to eat the heavenly bread was to come to Him, to believe in Him. He had said that it was the will and the work of the Father to draw men to the Son.

But the saying remained a difficult one to receive. It was not only the ignorant and unsteady multitude that stumbled at it. Nor is that other class here spoken of, which, though better informed and more religious than the multitude, was yet far more disaffected towards Jesus; I mean the Scribes and Pharisees, whose self-sufficiency was wounded by all that Jesus both taught and did. They were "disciples" of Jesus who said, "This is a hard saying: who can hear it?" Many of those who had accepted Jesus as a teacher, and had followed and walked with Him, were startled by the profession which He now plainly put forth. They did not like it when He said that He was to be the life of the world and of every man. They could accept Him as a teacher or master: they were not prepared to recognise Him as the source of a spiritual life which they and other men were to receive through a secret and inward dependence upon Him.

That this want of faith in many of the disciples should have been recorded in the Gospel, is not only a proof of the naturalness and authenticity of St. John's narrative: it also serves as a very welcome support to ourselves of the truth at which they stumbled. For, however familiar the words may be to our minds, however thoroughly we may have been educated to believe them, however unreservedly we may be willing to accept them, it is certain that to many, perhaps at times to all, the truth that our Lord Jesus Christ is our life and the life of the world, will present itself as a hard saying. Those who have never found it so can hardly have realized the force and extent of it. Even when we most thoroughly believe it, the unworldliness of it, the disbelief in it of so many, our own want of conformity to it, must make us willing enough to confess its difficulty. It is a comfort therefore to be told that when our Lord announced this truth it was not received as a matter of course. He Himself knew that it would be a stumbling-block to many, and so it proved. But our Lord proclaimed it nevertheless, and continued to insist upon it, in the face of all the disbelief and murmuring of those who were His disciples, and whom He would have rejoiced to retain.

Let us consider this morning in what manner and with what testimonies our Lord met the murmuring of His disciples. It may be of advantage to us to observe in what light He desired the truth which He had been proclaiming to be regarded by those who found it difficult to receive.

Jesus, we are told, knew in Himself that the disciples were murmuring about what He had been saying. He addresses them therefore in the words, "Doth this offend you?"—that is to say, Do you stumble at this? Is this a difficulty to you?—"What and if ye shall see the Son of Man ascend up where he was before? It is the Spirit that quickeneth; the flesh profiteth nothing: the words that I speak unto you, they are spirit and they are life." It is clear that in these words the reference to *the return of the Son of Man to heaven* is the point of chief importance; **and yet it is** not quite obvious how this reference **is to** be connected either with what goes before or with what follows it.

The reader's first impression of the passage may be that Jesus spoke to the following effect: "If you are **startled** at this doctrine, how much more startled you will be when you see me ascending up into heaven! And after all, what I have been saying is not so very strange, if you take it in a spiritual sense. I only meant it spiritually." But such an interpretation does not do justice to our Lord's explanation of His teaching. If we compare this passage with other places in this Gospel which resemble it, we shall be led, I believe, to a more instructive interpretation of it. To state at once the conclusion to which we shall arrive—Jesus, in speaking of His going up where He was before, is bringing into view His heavenly nature and the great end which was sought by His coming into the world. He is setting the difficult truth of His being the bread of life to mankind, in the light of His return to the Father and of the power of the Spirit to give life to the spirits of men. "Do you stumble at the saying, that I came down from heaven to be the life of those who believe in me? What, then, if you behold the Son of Man returning up to the heaven from which he came down? Will you not then rise to the conception of *a spiritual and heavenly relation to me*, such as will make my language seem natural to you? The whole sphere of what I have been saying is spiritual. It is the Spirit, not the flesh, that gives life: my words, the truths I teach, have a power of the Spirit in them: they are not dead words, they are spirit, and they are life; and if they are really received by your spirits, they will prove themselves a power of life in you."

We have had occasion to see that Jesus, according to St. John's reports, spoke very frequently and emphatically of His having *come down from heaven*. It is one of the great assertions of this chapter. Jesus **is the living** bread, because the Father has sent **Him**, because He has come down from heaven. This **was** the language which He chose in order to convey to the minds of His hearers what He really was. He desired them especially to receive Him as one sent from God, the Son whom the Father had sealed. There was no doubt a danger that His hearers might take such expressions in the most material sense, and suppose that He was speaking of **a** descent of His body from the region of the clouds. Various corrections of such a misapprehension were provided: the people knew Him as having been brought up from infancy at Nazareth; the whole teaching of Jesus was calculated to lead His hearers into worthier conceptions. But our Lord did not abandon the use of that language on account of any danger attending it. He was continually repeating that He had come from the Father, or from heaven, into the world.

Now, if we look forward in this Gospel of St. John, we shall see that from the time of which this chapter treats, our Lord began to speak not only of having come from the Father, but also of His being about to return to the Father, and that He dwells on **this** step with growing fulness and clearness, until at last this return to the Father, and the meaning and effects of it, become the great topic of His discourses. Apparently **in His** earlier teaching Jesus did not speak plainly of His ascending again to the Father; He was content with declaring that He had come from the Father. But on the occasion which we are considering a first intimation of that return is given. "I have been speaking hitherto of my having come down from heaven; what if you should see me go up thither again?" It is evident from subsequent passages that our Lord did not wish to speak too plainly at first of this return. He desired to lead His disciples and the people to think of it. He left them in great uncertainty as to what kind of movement He was contemplating. Thus in the next chapter, at the 33d verse, we read: "Then said Jesus unto them, yet a little while am I with you, and then I go unto him that sent me. Ye shall seek me and shall not find me: and where I am, thither ye cannot come." St. John records the effect of this dark saying on the minds of the Jews: "Whither will he go," they said, "that we shall not find him? will he go unto the dispersed amongst the Gentiles, and teach the Gentiles? What manner of saying is this that he said, Ye shall seek me and shall not find me; and where I am, thither ye cannot come?" I need hardly observe that the Evangelist intends, by relating this perplexity, to call our attention to the saying itself as one which has a peculiar and important significance. It is very interesting to notice the next place in which the saying occurs, and to see how Jesus connects with it the idea of His own heavenly nature, whilst at the same time He turns it into a rebuke of the fleshly mind of the Jews. In the succeeding chapter (viii. 14) Jesus says, "Though I bear record of myself, my record is true: for I know whence I came, and whither I go; but ye cannot tell whence I come, and whither I go. Ye judge after the flesh." Presently Jesus speaks, as usual, of His Father. They ask Him (verse 19), "Where is thy Father?" Jesus answered, "Ye neither know me, nor my Father: if ye had known me, ye would have known my Father also." Again we are told (verse 21) Jesus said, "I go my way, and ye shall seek me, and ye shall die in your sins: whither I go, ye cannot come. Then said the Jews, Will he kill himself? because he saith, Whither I go, ye cannot come. And he said unto them, Ye are from beneath; I am from above: ye are of this world; I am not of this world." We cannot help seeing here, that when our Lord speaks of returning to the Father, He does not mean merely a bodily change of place. He is speaking of spiritual things; of that world to which He essentially belongs.

When we come to the conversations after the Supper on the night preceding the crucifixion, from the thirteenth to the end of the seventeenth chapter, we find the return to the Father mentioned so often, that it is difficult to select the most expressive examples out of so many references to it. Let us take the beginning of our Lord's communications to His disciples, after Judas had gone out to do his deed of darkness. I quote from xiii. 31. "Therefore, when he was gone out, Jesus said, Now is the Son of Man glorified: and God is glorified in him. If God be glorified in him, God shall also glorify him in himself, and shall straightway glorify him. Little children, yet a little while I am with you. Ye shall seek me: and as I said unto the Jews, Whither I go, ye cannot come; so now I say to you. A new commandment I give unto you, that ye love one another; as I have loved you, that ye also love one another. By this shall all men know that ye are my disciples, if ye have love one to another." We learn afterwards how close a connexion this exhortation to love had with the departure of Jesus. At present the connexion is assumed; and after these words, Simon Peter utters the eager question, "Lord, whither goest thou?"—to be answered, "Whither I go, thou canst not follow me now: but thou shalt follow me afterwards." Peter replied, with impatient affection, "Lord, why cannot I follow thee now? I will lay down my life for thy sake." There was some explanation of the reason in the mournful answer: "Wilt thou lay down thy life for my sake? Verily, verily, I say unto thee, the cock shall not crow, till thou hast denied me thrice." This prophecy may well have caused agitation in the little band. In order to reassure them, Jesus proceeds, "Let not your heart be troubled: ye believe in God, believe also in me." And then He recurs to the subject of His return to the Father. "In my Father's house are many mansions: if it were not so, I would have told you. I go to prepare a place for you. And if I go and prepare a place for you, I will come again and receive you unto myself; that where I am, there ye may be also. And whither I go ye know, and the way ye know." This surprises us at first, after what we have read before, as in the query of St. Peter, of the ignorance of the disciples, and their want of power to follow Jesus. And we find it surprised the disciples themselves: for Thomas protests, "Lord, we know not whither thou goest; and how can we know the way?" Then Jesus explains what he meant: "*I* am the way, the truth, and the life; no one cometh unto the Father, but by me. If ye had known me, ye would have known my Father also; and from henceforth ye know him, and have seen him." And then Jesus goes on to speak of some results of His going to the Father, as especially of his sending that Spirit of truth, of whom He says, "the world cannot receive him, because it seeth him not, neither knoweth him; but ye know him, for he dwelleth with you, and shall be [or, and *is*] in you." "If ye loved me," says Jesus, "ye would rejoice, because I said, I go unto the Father."

In the sixteenth chapter, we have the disciples represented as again perplexed and stirred up to discussion and inquiry by a repetition of the same words, "A little while, and ye shall not see me: and again, a little while and ye shall see me, because I go to the Father." The whole matter yet remained dark to the disciples. Some light was thrown upon it at the time by Jesus, when He perceived their difficulty and their wish to learn: but He could not anticipate the hour when they were to be thoroughly taught by the Spirit. He could not make them understand Him until He should have gone to the Father. He could only encourage them to wait in hope for the enlightenment which should then come to them. Let us notice in this chapter, the compendious expression, verse 28, "I came forth from the Father, and am come into the world: again, I leave the world, and go to the Father." This statement combines the two which, as I said, are so prominent in this Gospel.

I might quote the whole of the seventeenth chapter, to show how deep a spiritual significance there was, according to the mind of Jesus, in His reascending to the Father: for this is indeed the topic of these wonderful meditations addressed by the Son in prayer to the Father, in prospect of the completion of the work which the Father had sent Him to do. Those who will read carefully this, and also the preceding chapters, with express recollection of the subject—Christ's return to the Father, and what is implied in it—cannot fail to be struck by the various aspects in which they will be led to view it. At present I must not attempt to do more than to call your attention to some of the sayings which most nearly concern the interpretation of our text. Let me ask you to bear in mind in this chapter, and with reference to the subject now occupying us, the opposition assumed between *the world*, on the one hand, and *heaven*, or *the Father*, on the other. In verses 7, 8, our Lord describes the faith of the disciples as consisting especially in a belief that their Master came from God and spoke God's words. "Now they have known that all things, whatsoever thou hast given me, are of thee. For I have given unto them the words which thou gavest me; and they have received them, and have known surely that I came out from thee, and they have believed that thou didst send me." That account relates to the past and the present: **a** little further on, Jesus contemplates the future, verse **11**. "**And now** I am no more in the world, but these are **in** the world, and I come to thee. Holy Father, keep through thine own name those whom thou hast given me, that they may be one, as we are." . . . "Now come I to thee: but these things I speak in the world, that they may have my joy fulfilled in themselves." There is here some unveiling of the mystery: the desire of the Son of God is that men, by knowing and believing in Him, may be gathered and won *out of the world*, and embraced under the name of the righteous Father. For this *He* came *into* the world from the Father, and returned to the Father out of the world, that He might draw men with Him to form a holy body and family in the Father's house. The disciples were to be *in* and *with* their Master, united so **to** the Father. And in order that this aim of Jesus might not be supposed to be limited to the few who heard Him, He expressly includes all who should believe in Him, and in doing so states His design most fully—this being the conclusion of His prayer: "Neither pray I for these alone, but for them also which shall believe on me through their word; that they all may be one; as thou, Father, art in me, and I in thee, that they also may be one in us: that the world may believe that thou hast sent me. And the glory which thou gavest me I have given them; that they may be **one,** even as we are one: I in them, and thou in me, that they may be made perfect in one; and that the world may know that thou hast sent me, and hast loved them, as thou hast loved me. Father, I will that they also whom thou hast given me, be with me where I am; that they may behold my glory, which thou hast given me: for thou lovedst me before the foundation of the world. O righteous Father, the world hath not known thee: but I have known thee, and these have known that thou hast sent me. And I have declared unto them thy name, and will declare it: that the love wherewith thou hast loved me may be in them, and I in them."

That the love with which the Father loved the Son might be in them, and that the Son might be in them. This was the sum of our Lord's desire for His disciples. The principle of His unity with the Father was love; the glory which He had with the Father before the world, was the glory of love. He came into the world that the love of the Father might descend upon men, His brethren. He returned to the Father, that men, His brethren, might be drawn up in that love to God.

From what we have now seen of our Lord's testimonies we may safely draw, I think, the following conclusions, bearing upon the interpretation of our text. Let me remind you that the question was, as to the truth of the Lord's saying, I am the living bread which came down from heaven. Our Lord says, "Do you stumble at this? what then, if you shall see the Son of Man ascend up where he was before? It is the Spirit that gives life, the flesh profiteth nothing."

(1) **Now we** observe first, that Jesus sets His **return to** the Father against His descent from the Father, as the necessary balance or completion of it. The history of His Incarnation is summed up **in** the statement, "I came forth from the Father, and am come into the world; again I leave the world, and go to the Father."

(2) Secondly, in these two facts it would seem that, according to our Lord's own teaching, His Divine or heavenly nature was most livingly set forth to men. Whilst He was upon the earth, He held fast the consciousness that He was from the Father, and was returning to the Father. His essential and eternal unity with the Father was expressed in His consciousness. At the Last Supper, St. John prefaces the account of the doings and sayings of those final hours, by the marked declaration that Jesus knew that the Father had given all things into His hands, and that He was come from God, and went to God. We might say with truth that St. John's Gospel, as **an** unfolding of the Divine glory of the Son, is an exposition of the twofold statement, He came from the Father, and went back to the Father.

(3) Again, the relation **of** men to Christ set forth **in** the words, "I am the bread from heaven; he that eateth this bread shall never die," is to be understood **in the** light of the truth that He came from the **Father, and** went up again to the Father. That **relation** was partially intelligible to those who, looking on Christ, believed that He was from the Father, and that all His acts and words were not from Him-

self, but were the Father's. But partially only. It was thoroughly understood by the disciples, when they thought of their Master in later days as now with the Father, at God's right hand, and reflected on the marvellous history in which they had borne part. The Son, who was one with the Father, had come down to earth, had been with them as one of themselves, entirely renouncing all honour and glory in Himself, entirely doing the Father's will; and after making Himself known to them as a friend and master, He had laid down His life that He might take it again, and had returned to the Father. As they meditated on Him, thinking now of His unity with the Father, now of His association with themselves, a sense that *they* were in Him united to the Father and embraced in the Father's love, grew strong in them. And this, whilst it was a very solemn, was also a very joyful feeling. It filled them with thankful love to God and to Christ, with a consciousness of the worth of their own nature and of that of their fellow-men, with a longing desire that men in general, for whom this knowledge was provided and intended, should become with them actual inheritors of it. The Son of God and Son of Man, one with the Father in Heaven, one with men upon the earth, proved Himself to them the true Mediator, the living bond between heaven and earth, the actual way to the Father.

(4) And lastly, the disciples in the light of this twofold nature of their Master, learnt the power of the Spirit, and of the Spirit only, to give life. Not till

the Lord Jesus was withdrawn from the world of the senses could they thoroughly know Him, and what He was to the Father and **to** them. When He was gone out of their sight the promised *Spirit* came down to guide them into all truth. It was the work of the Spirit to make them abidingly conscious of the spiritual world, **to** enable them to feel that God was with them and Christ was with them at all times, to make them independent of their senses, and so **to** train them into the highest freedom. In this liberty they had life and strength and vigour. No isolation could drive them to despair, no disappointments or sufferings could overwhelm them, when they knew in the Spirit that they were dwelling in the love of the Father and of the Son. It was the Spirit, they felt, that gave them life. Visible, fleshly, sensible things might have an unspeakable value as instruments and interpretations of the Spirit; but the Spirit gave them their value; in themselves they were nothing. The **flesh and** blood which were worn by their beloved Master must have been inexpressibly dear to the disciples; they knew what it was to feed on that flesh and that blood; **but the** visible body had its glory from the Spirit of which it was both an instru- **ment and** a veil. And so of all the things of sense; **the** believers in Christ were never taught to make light of **them.** They learnt to discern the Spirit in them. **The** things of sense were good and deserved **reverence on** the Spirit's account. If the Spirit were forgotten or denied, the flesh became worse than un- profitable, it was an occasion of idolatry and atheism.

The things true for the Apostles are true also for all those who, through their word, have believed in the same Saviour. We have been learning this morning how we Christians ought to regard the truth that Christ is our life. If we have rightly received the teaching of the Gospel, we are to realize this truth, through a meditation on the twofold nature and history of the Son of God, through contemplating Him as eternally one with the Father, and as having manifested Himself in time and in the world as the Son of Man. Bearing in mind these facts, and remembering always that we are spirits, dwelling in the heavenly world of the Father and of the Son, and drinking in all our real life through spiritual influences and visitations, we too may feed upon Christ as our Redeemer, and may be nourished by Him into freedom and eternal life.

To conclude with one word of warning, we are not to fancy that the putting our relation to Christ in the light of His unity with the Father and of the life-giving power of the Spirit, makes it easy to realize that dependence. It does not make it easy; nothing can make it easy to mortal men, encompassed with the world of sense, tempted continually to be the servants of the flesh. It only shows us where the difficulty lies, and how we are to grapple with it. After our Lord's explanation, many of the disciples departed from Him; one of the few who remained continued to nourish the serpent spirit of a traitor in his heart. But those who went away left Jesus because they were not drawn of the Father, nor cared

for spiritual life. The faithful remained, because they honoured the Father, **and** sought eternal life. The question, therefore, to ask ourselves, the primary conscience-searching question is, Do I honour the righteous Father in heaven? Do I believe in **a** spiritual life which belongs to my sonship **to** the Heavenly Father? Or am I living in the **world** as **one** subject to the world, and caring only for the things of the world? If I am dead to God, I shall also be dead to Christ. If I honour the Father, and seek not the praise of men or the gratifying of the flesh, then I must honour the Son.

If we are brought to put these questions honestly and closely to ourselves, we shall not have studied our Lord's teaching in vain.

XV.

REVELATION THE GROUND OF PRAYER.

St. Luke xi. 1.

"It came to pass, as he was praying in a certain place, when he ceased, one of his disciples said unto him, Lord, teach us to pray, as John also taught his disciples."

IN the last clause of this verse we have an allusion which helps to prove, in conjunction with other indications scattered over the New Testament, that the work of John the Baptist as a religious teacher had a distinctness and a largeness which we are not commonly in the habit of attributing to it. The disciples of Jesus recognise John and his followers as forming a body which might be compared with that of which Jesus was the head. Master, they said, do thou teach us to pray, as John taught *his* disciples. For a certain time, after Jesus had begun to preach and before John was put in prison, a superficial observer might have supposed the two teachers to be heads of rival schools, similar in some main points, but distinguished in others. You may remember the occasion on which the disciples of John came to Jesus, and said, "Why do we and the Pharisees fast oft, but thy disciples fast not?" The disciples of John were evidently not transferred in a body to Jesus, when Jesus began to gather followers about Him. They still remained distinct, and there was an obvious opening for jealousy. Before John had left off baptizing, larger numbers were flocking to Jesus, as John's disciples, apparently with something of complaint in their tone, informed their master. The Pharisees, we are told, observed the same thing, and we conclude that they were turning it to some evil account, or drawing unfavourable inferences from it, because, when Jesus knew that they were aware of it, He left Judea and withdrew Himself to Galilee.

John the Baptist, then, had a distinct school of disciples, whom he taught and trained, and whose customs were not altogether identical with those of the followers of Jesus. He did not attempt to hand them over to Jesus; he did not summarily abdicate his own office as a teacher and master. But he bore witness to Jesus as his superior and Lord. He prepared his followers to see in Jesus the manifestation in the flesh of that heavenly light, of that heavenly kingdom, which he had been constantly declaring to them. He, said the Baptist, is the bridegroom; I am only the bridegroom's friend. He must increase, I must decrease. It is probable that by testimony of this kind he succeeded in preventing any actual rivalry between his disciples and those of Jesus. On His part, Jesus bore witness to John, and took pains to avoid any appearance of collision with him. And before long the Baptist was taken away by imprisonment and death, and his disciples ceased to form a connected body.

But it is useful to bear in mind the very considerable effect which the preaching of John had had upon his countrymen, and to remember, also, the exact character of his preaching, so far as we can ascertain it. And it is interesting to notice the very natural account of the relations between John and our Lord—natural, except that the jealousy which would have been so natural is absent, and that St. John, the wild prophet, the eccentric preacher in the wilderness, who was said by some of his countrymen to be possessed or mad, exhibits a truly supernatural gentleness and humility and insight.

One of the acts of John, whilst he had his disciples about him, as we learn from our text, had been to teach them to pray. It would seem that he had taught them, as Jesus proceeded to teach His disciples, by giving them some forms of prayer which they might use or imitate. Very possibly he had been led to do so by the same circumstance as that to which the recital of the Lord's Prayer by Jesus was owing. The followers of the Baptist may well have seen *him* praying, and have felt some desire to associate themselves with him in this wonderful act, and at the same time have been conscious of a natural ignorance and inability and fear, preventing them from carrying out the impulse. It would be interesting and instructive if we could know what the teaching was which John gave to his disciples, what principles he laid down to guide them, and what desires he encouraged them **to** express to the God of their fathers. But **if** there ever was a John the Baptist's prayer, answering **to** the Lord's Prayer, it has **not** been preserved to us.

We may find it profitable however to reflect upon the parallel here brought before us—John teaching his disciples to pray, and Jesus, also, in imitation of John, giving similar instruction to *His*. The thought to which I am about to call your attention specially, is the connexion between revelation and prayer.

John the Baptist was properly a messenger from heaven. He was not an ordinary pastor whose duty it might be to stimulate devotional habits amongst the people who heard him. He was sent from God, with an announcement or testimony to deliver. He was to proclaim that the Kingdom of Heaven was at hand, and to call his countrymen to the repentance which such an announcement would naturally inspire. "In those days came John the Baptist, preaching in the wilderness of Judea, and saying, Repent ye: for the Kingdom of Heaven is at hand." Or, in the words of another Evangelist, "There was a man sent from God whose name was John. The same came for a witness, to bear witness of the Light, that all men through him might believe. He was not that Light, but was sent to bear witness of that Light." A revelation of God therefore came through John the Baptist. It was given to him to disclose the purposes of God, and to unveil the character which **those** purposes declared. God spoke through John to make Himself known to His people.

We may be sure that the man thus honoured was accustomed himself to hold communion with God in prayer. It is not easy for us to realize the mental condition of a man through whom God spoke one of His most important messages to men, who knew that he was commissioned by the Almighty to speak in His name. But no one will imagine that a man for whom such a commission was a reality could fail to converse much in awe and faith with his God. He must have desired often to confess the shortcomings of his service, the hindrances which his human frailty had put in the way of his mission; and to ask for help and guidance and support amidst the difficulties which encompassed him. We may well believe, further, that he could enter heartily into the feelings of those who have found the contemplation of the Divine perfections the noblest act of the human spirit, and to whom worship has been the highest happiness and reward.

But the same revelation would in an inferior degree call out and demand the spirit of prayer in all by whom it was received. When once men believed that God was seeking them, that He was treating them as His children who had lost knowledge of Him, but who could hear and understand His voice, that God, in short, was revealing Himself to them in relations of kindness and judgment, it was inevitable that their filial hearts should be moved to cry, Abba, Father. Prayer may be thought of as needless, unreasonable, or superstitious, just so long and so far as God is supposed to be divided by an insuperable chasm from men. But let the sound of God's voice be once caught, let it **be** felt that God in heaven is actually making Himself known to men, and there must be a response from men's hearts to God, suitable to their condition before Him. They, **on** their part, **must** speak **to God** as dependent creatures, receivers of light and other blessings, to their Maker, Benefactor, and Inspirer. The great instinct of confession must be awakened, and man must cry, Father, I have sinned against heaven and in Thy sight. The sense of dependence must find some utterance in thanksgivings and petitions. In other words, it is in the nature of a true revelation of God to call forth prayer in men.

And we may say, conversely, that the spirit of prayer needs a revelation to rest upon. How can we pray, without knowing *to Whom* we are praying? It is true that the habit of praying does not wait to be called into life by some unveiling of the nature of the living God. In their deepest darkness what we may call the praying instincts of men have groped about blindly, often making mistakes, addressing themselves to those who by nature were no gods, and fixing on unworthy objects of desire; and in the most superstitious worship which men have ever paid to idols there is a witness of the reasonable worship of the living God. But it is clear that revelation should properly precede prayer; and that men, **when** they speak to God, should have a knowledge of **the** nature of Him whom they address, and should utter their devotions in agreement with His ascertained will.

It is not suitable to the dignity of man, sinner though he be, that he should wildly beat against the bars of his cage in impotent appeals to some supernatural powers which he supposes may have influence over his destiny. He may well ask to have some confidence that he will be heard before he pours out the secrets of his soul in prayer. We know that it has been the design of God to manifest Himself to men as One who hears prayers, before whom the very depths of the human heart may be reasonably laid bare.

These considerations may help to make the simple announcement, that John taught his disciples to pray, more full of life and interest to us. Let us recal, once more, the character of his revelation. He was a Jewish prophet, appealing to the old traditions of his race and to the promises given to the fathers. The phrases he used were not new. He spoke to a generation which was in a singular and inconsistent religious condition. Most of the Jews of that day were in great darkness towards God. Although they had the Scriptures and the Temple, they did not know the God who had given the Scriptures and who dwelt in the Temple. A veil of unbelief had been drawn over their hearts, and they had fashioned for themselves another god, not the God of Abraham, Isaac, and Jacob, to whom they offered an external and mercenary worship. Yet there were high expectations stirring at that epoch in the minds of the Jews. They were looking—many of them idly and ignorantly, a few very earnestly—for the setting up of the Kingdom of Heaven amongst them. Rumours of a coming Messiah were going about amongst the people. The words of John by no means sounded strangely, therefore, to Jewish ears, when he lifted up his voice to proclaim that the Kingdom of Heaven was at hand. But the manner in which he spoke of this kingdom, and the acts by which he bade the people prepare themselves for it, did not fall in with generally-entertained notions. He bore witness of light shining into the inward parts. He spoke of truth claiming the heart as its own. He named a God who was pure and holy, and who sought that His people should be at peace with Him, and who offered to cleanse them from their defilements.

His word found here and there really good ground in which the seed could grow. There were those who received with joy this testimony concerning God; who opened their eyes and saw the Lord God to be faithful and true, One who cared for His chosen people and was coming down to deliver them. Such persons would need something more special in the way of communion with God than the opportunities given by the offerings in the Temple and the meetings in the synagogues. They needed to speak to God just as He had been revealed to them; as to One who was about to manifest Himself to Israel in their own day, and who was there and then calling upon the people to adopt an attitude of awful expectation, to repent and to do works worthy of repentance.

I will not attempt to conjecture with what words the Baptist may have endeavoured to guide the thanksgivings and the petitions of his disciples. We cannot be far wrong if we assume that their prayers corresponded closely to the messages which the Baptist delivered; that they were the fit response of Jewish hearts to the words which God spoke first to them. The prayers would embody the confessions, the trust, the hopes of the Jewish people, answering to the proclamation, "Repent ye, for the Kingdom of Heaven is at hand." They might deplore the faithlessness of the people; they might lay hold of the great mercy of the Lord God: they might plead the promises made of old to the fathers; they might be penetrated with awe in the thought of the nearness of Him who was the God of light and of truth. In some such spirit as this, John taught his disciples to pray.

It would be probable that when our Lord taught His disciples also to pray, the prayers would similarly have reference to the revelation which He was bringing to men. The character of that revelation is summed up in the opening words of the Epistle to the Hebrews: "God, who at sundry times and in divers manners spake in times past unto the fathers by the prophets, hath in these last days spoken unto us by his Son." The Lord Jesus Christ was in Himself the revelation of the Father, by *being* the perfect Son. The Son was the voice or word by which the Father spoke to mankind.

In thinking of the revelation of God that came through Jesus Christ, we must be careful not to assume that the disciples saw as much before His death as was revealed to them after His exaltation by the coming down of the Holy Ghost. It is from the Day of Pentecost that the genuine Christian knowledge of the Son, and of the Father through Him, may be said to date. During the lifetime of Jesus, the disciples were learning to know Him as their Master, and were laying up in their hearts words and works of His which afterwards took new significance in the light of the later revelation. Amongst such words were the names of the Father and of the Son. Jesus revealed the Father, as I said, by *being* the Son. But **He** also named the Father continually. The chief circumstance which distinguished His announcements **from** those of the Baptist was, that the Father was thus incessantly declared. He Himself, He said, was the Son whom the Father had sent. Something of what was implied in these names was understood, no doubt, by the disciples at the time of which we are now speaking. If we are to follow the information given us in the Gospels, we shall conclude that the revelation made to the disciples who followed Jesus consisted in the manifestation of the Son and of the Father's will declared **in** Him, which manifestation was apprehended dimly and fitfully so long as Jesus was in the flesh amongst them.

This revelation, then, would be the basis of the prayers in which the disciples of Jesus could be expected **to** join **with** heart and mind. They must pray to such a Being as they had in some measure learnt **to** know. And you will remember how entirely the Lord's Prayer is governed by the name of the heavenly

Father. That prayer is in truth adapted to the revelation which had been given at the time when Jesus taught His disciples to use it. They who saw Jesus praying, and who said, "Master, teach us to pray," were followers of a prophet who told them that He was sent by His Father in heaven to establish the Kingdom of Heaven amongst them, and to bring them to a true knowledge of the Father. When Jesus Himself was reviewing what He had done for the disciples, He said, "O righteous Father, I have declared unto them thy name." He never tired of repeating that He was come to do and to show the Father's will. If, therefore, the revelation of which Jesus of Nazareth was the minister reached their hearts, so as to draw them to God, their prayers would necessarily have reference to the Father's name and to the heavenly kingdom. What a harmony, then, is to be observed between the language of the Lord's Prayer and the revelation which drew it forth! The disciples of Jesus were taught to approach God with the words, "Our Father, which art in heaven, hallowed be thy name; thy kingdom come." Their first duty was to call God by that name through which He was then revealing Himself to them. God having first said to them, I am your Father in heaven—they were to fall down before Him with the words, Our Father, who art in heaven. Having thus expressed their faith, they were to utter desires corresponding to that work of revelation which was then being wrought upon them and upon the world. "May thy name—the name of the heavenly

Father—be hallowed. May thy kingdom—the kingdom of **the** heavenly Father—come. May thy will—**the** will **of the** heavenly Father—be done upon earth, as it is done in heaven."

Jesus had **led** His disciples to look upon **His** Father and theirs, the Father in heaven, as giving them all things, providing for their needs, caring for His spiritual children more than He could care for the flowers or the sparrows. "Trust to Him who gives the rain and the sunshine, to feed you and to clothe you." It belongs to the simplest and most childlike idea of a father, that he gives his children their daily bread. "If a son shall ask bread of any of you that is a father, will he give him a stone? If ye, then, being evil, know how to give good gifts to your children, how much more shall your Father which is in heaven give good gifts"—and the best gift, His own Holy Spirit—"to them that ask Him?" Therefore, let disciples of Jesus come to the heavenly Father and say, "Give us this day our daily bread."

We might go through the remaining clauses of the Lord's Prayer, and observe a similar harmony between their purport and the truths concerning God which Jesus was imparting to His disciples. We may remember how essentially the revelation that came **through the** Son of God was one **of** Divine forgiveness, **and how** Jesus acted out in His own dealings **with** men the Spirit of His Father; we may remember how often it was implied and proved that the earth was to be won for the Kingdom of Heaven by a real struggle against the evil powers which claimed and ruled it. We shall then feel what an exquisite correspondence there was between what was revealed in Jesus and the prayers, Forgive us our trespasses as we forgive those who trespass against us ; Lead us not into dangerous trials, for which we might be too weak ; but deliver us from the Evil One.

But I must not now dwell upon the significance of the particular clauses of the Lord's Prayer. My purpose has been to lead you to perceive the necessary connexion between revelation and prayer. Of this, as it directly concerns ourselves, let me now speak briefly.

I have said already that the revelation given to the Apostles in our Lord's lifetime was not equal to what was given them through the pouring out of the Holy Ghost. I may say further, that every age must add something to the revelation of God. If the living God is guiding the world and the Church, it is inconceivable that the experiences of generation after generation should go for nothing in making known the mind of God. It would be a strange notion of doing honour to God as a Revealer and Inspirer, to insist that He can have taught men nothing since the age of the Apostles. We, then, are the inheritors of that revelation of God which is recorded in the Holy Scriptures, and of whatever light besides it has pleased God in the after ages to bestow upon His children. Now, according to the view I have been expounding, all the knowledge of God which has been given to us, if it really reaches us, ought to move us to suitable

prayer, as our response to that revelation. The soul **of man** is not to be careless and dead when God **speaks** to it. It **is** not to set to work to speculate with serene self-complacence upon God's words. Its true attitude before a speaking God is to listen with awe, and to reply with reverence. There is something infinitely mysterious in the manner in which God makes himself known to us; there may be an infinite mystery also in the manner of our responding to God. But, as the face of God discloses itself to us, as He makes known to us His glorious designs, it is fit that we should move towards Him, and be interested in His purposes, and desire their fulfilment.

And as God ought not to speak to us without meeting with a response from us, so our prayers should always preserve the character of a response to God, if they are to be such as please God. Our prayers ought **not to** be wilful, self-originating, impelled simply by our own notions of what we should wish for. It was not a sign of dulness and formality when the disciples of Jesus said, Master, *teach us* to pray. Brethren, our prayers ought to be *learnt* from what God has first told us. They ought to be addressed to God as to a Father, because He has made Himself known as a Father. They ought to embody such desires as we know to be in harmony with God's will. There is no spiritual wisdom in the notions of those who think that all prayer should **be** impulsive and spontaneous, and that rules and forms can only kill the life of it.

The Church of Christ, in the training of its children, has always followed the principle which we have been observing. Take our own Church Catechism as an example. We have there, as you know, three principal elements, the Creed, the Lord's Prayer, and the Ten Commandments. The Creed represents the revelation of God which has been given to us. It is a summary of the leading truths concerning God which are revealed to us in Christ. This is that which is first taught. The Lord's Prayer represents that worship of the human spirit which goes up, or should go up, to the God who has made himself known to us. We could not learn to pray by learning the Lord's Prayer only. The most important lessons of prayer are the disclosures of Him to whom we are to pray. But this form is a guide to the ignorance and weakness of our hearts, and shows us how, if we trusted to our own wisdom only, we might go astray even in praying.

If, in our use of the Lord's Prayer, we were limited to the thoughts with which the disciples first used it, it would be very inadequate as an expression of the worship of the Christian Church. But those sacred words, most expressly and admirably as they were suited to the knowledge and hopes of the first disciples, have received without any perversion a rich accession of meaning from all that has been since revealed. We can associate naturally with the expressions of the Lord's Prayer, all the truth which the inspiration of Apostles has bequeathed to the Church, and upon which the experience of the saints may afterwards have thrown light. The name of the Father in heaven ought to be something different to us from what it was to the Galileans who surrounded their Master. But there is nothing higher to us, nothing more suggestive, than the same name. The true Divine revelation has been orderly and gradual. It has expanded and developed, instead of changing and substituting. We know no other God than the Father, the Son, and the Holy Ghost. Only the Fatherhood ought to be wider, profounder, more perfect, in our conceptions; the Sonship deeper, more comprehensive, and closer; the influence of the Holy Ghost more manifold and subtle, and *less* distinguishable in **operation** from the movements of our own wills.

Therefore, let us not cease to ask our glorified Lord, Master, teach **us** to pray. Teach us, by showing whom we have in Heaven above to whom we may address ourselves. Teach us, by making us feel His infinite condescension, His astonishing interest in the difficulties and trials of every one of His children. Teach us, by leading us to see how widely the care of God is spread over His universe, and with what wisdom He can make all things work together for good. Teach us, by proving to our hearts that we have a Spirit with us to inspire even our prayers, and to make us pray acceptably to God, because He knows **the very** mind of God. Teach us, by guarding us from the folly of supposing that we can *change* that glorious and perfect will, which we ought to desire **may be** accomplished in us and in the world. Teach us, by purging our hearts of selfishness and jealousy, and by giving us the family mind before God our Father. Teach us, by all the gracious external discipline which helps and props our infirmities, by the instructions of childhood, by the services of the Church, by those ordinances which thou hast thyself consecrated for the universal use of thy followers. Teach us to pray in spirit and in truth, with trust and hope, mingling thanksgivings with every supplication. Teach us that we have not to enlighten the ignorance or to overcome the reluctance of a God who is indifferent to us, but that our Father knows what things we have need of before we ask Him. Give us Thyself, as the way, the truth, and the life; and enable us all to have access through Thee in one Spirit to the Father.

XVI.

THE SHADOW OF THE PASSION ON THE LIFE OF JESUS.

St. Matthew xvi. 21—24.

"*From that time forth began Jesus to shew unto his disciples, how that he must go unto Jerusalem, and suffer many things of the elders and chief priests and scribes, and be killed, and be raised again the third day. Then Peter took him, and began to rebuke him, saying, Be it far from thee, Lord: this shall not be unto thee. But he turned, and said unto Peter, Get thee behind me, Satan: thou art an offence unto me: for thou savourest not the things that be of God, but those that be of men. Then said Jesus unto his disciples, If any man will come after me, let him deny himself, and take up his cross, and follow me.*"

The fact that **our** Blessed Lord had a foreknowledge of His sufferings, and that He took pains to prepare His disciples for **them** by distinct announcements, is recorded by the Evangelists with some emphasis and repetition. It is desirable for the purposes of study to distinguish between our Lord's own foreknowledge of these events and the information which He thought fit to impart to His disciples. The first belongs to **the sacred and** mysterious history of the experience **of the** Son of God; the second to the discipline which **He used in** training **His** followers.

But the only insight given us by the Evangelists into our Lord's own consciousness is through the communications which He made to others. It is a part of their reverence and simplicity that they know nothing of the mind of their Master except from His own words. Those words were not always addressed to the people about Him; some of the most precious were spoken to His Father in heaven. But when they were uttered audibly it was for the sake of those who stood by, because Jesus wished them thus to learn something of the communion of Himself and the Father. A portion of the words of Jesus are recorded in the Gospels; and these are the only means we have of knowing what passed in His mind. They often stimulate a desire to know more than they tell us; we are obliged to confess that the consciousness of the Son of God in our flesh is a mystery which we are quite unable to fathom. But so far as we have distinct words to guide us, we are intended to study that consciousness, and to feel that we are made acquainted with it.

Thus, in the case before us, from the fact that Jesus mentioned certain future events to the disciples, we learn that they were present to His own mind. St. Matthew, St. Mark, and St. Luke concur in recording two particular occasions, one earlier, the other immediately preceding the Passion, on which Jesus testified concerning the sufferings which awaited Him. The passage I have read from St. Matthew describes the former of these. It followed closely the confession of Simon Peter, "Thou art the Christ, the

Son of the living God." Through that confession, the **truth of our** Lord's mission and nature stood out **more** clearly to the minds of the disciples. After this, when Jesus had stamped the acknowledgment of His Messiahship and His Divine Sonship with particular value and importance, Jesus began to show how He must suffer and be killed. St. Mark's relation, chap. viii. is to the same effect: he adds, that **Jesus** "spake that saying openly," desiring that His disciples should apprehend it clearly and with certainty. St. Luke records the same announcement in his ninth chapter. We do not know how long this was before the Passion. We should reasonably believe that after that plain intimation Jesus touched from time to time upon the evils which He saw before Him. But when the fulfilment was now drawing near, and the Master with His disciples was already on His way to Jerusalem to celebrate the final Passover, He sought again to bring home the scenes they were about to witness to the thoughts of His companions. **St.** Matthew xx. 17, speaks thus: "And Jesus going up to Jerusalem took the twelve disciples apart in the way, and said unto them, Behold, we go up to Jerusalem; and the Son of man shall be betrayed unto the chief priests and unto the scribes, and they shall condemn him to death, and shall deliver him to the Gentiles to mock, and to scourge, and to crucify him: and the third day he shall rise again." The **same words** are given in St. Mark x. 32, but the introductory passage is there very striking: "And they were in the way going up to Jerusalem; and

Jesus went before them: and they were amazed; and as they followed, they were afraid. And he took again the twelve, and began to tell them what things should happen unto him." St. Luke, on the other hand, xviii. 34, adds to our Lord's statement the important reflection, "And they understood none of these things: and this saying was hid from them, neither knew they the things which were spoken."

Jesus, then, for some time at least before His Passion, had distinctly before His mind the sufferings He was to undergo. He knew them so clearly and certainly that He could make them a matter of open and earnest prediction to His followers.

(1) Upon this foreknowledge I observe, in the first place, that it must have constituted a very large portion of the total burden of those sufferings.

It is a fact so common as to be within every one's experience, that the anticipation of any trial or pain is often worse than the actual endurance of it. It is a quality of our human nature, which "looks before and after," that our sufferings come from the past and the future even more than from the present. Pain, like pleasure, has a great deal that is subtle and mysterious in it. It is very dependent upon the imagination. The acutest bodily pain, which seems most outward and measurable, has often been so borne down by some enthusiasm of the spirit as to be scarcely felt. And certainly reflection upon the past and expectation of the future are capable of inflicting the severest suffering. The *fear* of evil seems to be without those compensations which generally accompany the actual endurance of it.

Now the horizon of our Saviour's mind was filled, so to speak, long before with the vision of those cruel and humiliating scenes which constitute His Passion. These scenes were the approaching culmination of the griefs by which Jesus was daily vexed. You observe how, in all the summaries of the Passion, one of the principal points is that the Son of Man is to receive the scorn and the cruelties at the hands of the chief priests and the elders and the scribes. The Messiah of Israel, come to save and to glorify His people, is to be rejected by the representatives of His nation in His own holy city. And with that hostility which could only be satiated by His death, Jesus had to struggle daily. The true Shepherd of His people yearned over the sacred capital. "O Jerusalem," He exclaimed, "Jerusalem, which killest the prophets, and stonest them that are sent unto thee; how often would I have gathered thy children together, as a hen doth gather her brood under her wings, and ye would not!" And again, "When he was come near, he beheld the city and wept over it, saying, If thou hadst known, even thou, at least in this thy day, the things which belong unto thy peace! but now they are hid from thine eyes." When Jesus was in Judea, if not so much when He was in Galilee, day after day saw the schism widening beneath Himself and those who represented the religion and calling of Israel. Day by day He was impelled to denounce some dark superstition or some hypocrisy or cruelty of the Pharisees; and every such attack made them naturally more eager to destroy Him. And all the while Jesus saw in the future the crimes in which the conflict was to end; He Himself necessarily brought nearer and nearer the perpetration of those crimes. The whole evil to come was daily pressing upon His soul.

(2) In the next place it may be observed, that this foreknowledge of His death makes the sacrifice of Christ more plainly *voluntary*.

It was not, indeed, a *self*-willed sacrifice. The Son of God came to do *His Father's* will, not His own. But He yielded Himself with a perfect willingness to His Father's will. His spirit was expressed in the words of the Psalm, "Lo, I come to do thy will, O God: I am content to do it; yea, thy law is within my heart." It was an essential characteristic, then, of the sacrifice of Christ, that it was conscious and deliberate. "I am the good shepherd," he said: "the good shepherd giveth his life for the sheep." "Therefore doth my Father love me, because I lay down my life, that I might take it again. No man taketh it from me, but I lay it down of myself. I have power to lay it down, and I have power to take it again. This commandment have I received of my Father." And when He was nearer to His darkest hour, He uttered audibly the pleading, "Now is my soul troubled, and what shall I say? Father, save me from this hour: but for this cause came I unto this hour." And again, "Father, if thou be willing, remove this cup from me: nevertheless, not my will, but thine, be done."

I say, then, that when we remember how habitually the last and most painful scenes were present to the forethought of Jesus, we gain a stronger sense of this *willingness* of His self-surrender. He saw the hour before Him, and He walked steadily onwards to enter **into it.** However His flesh might shrink from the scourge and the thorns and the nails, however His spirit might tremble to think of the wounding of every affection and of the hiding of the Father's face and of **the** pressure of man's sinfulness, as it was to weigh upon the heart of the Son of God and the Son of Man, yet Jesus humbled Himself and became obedient. He was resolute to do the Father's will, and to work out the redemption of His brethren through suffering and sacrifice. It was for this that He came to the trying hour; for this His filial mind would bear all that was appointed. Contemplate with reverence this utter devotion of the Son of God; meditate upon this mind of self-surrender and sacrifice which was in Christ Jesus. See how the long offering of Himself to the Father's blessed purposes was accomplished by Jesus in the power of the Eternal Spirit. See how the sorrow was increased in order that the voluntary sacrifice might be more perfect. See how the Son of God subjected Himself to the fears and forebodings which form so large a part of the burden of His mortal brethren, and laid down **His** life, not once but a hundred times, on our behalf, without refusing the bitterness of which He tasted so deeply. When the Apostles looked back from the standing ground of their joyful faith in

Jesus risen and ascended, and recalled the steps of the sacrifice through which He entered into His glory; must they not have thought, with awe and wonder and softened hearts, of those days during which He bore not only the present contradictions of sinners, but also the gloom of His impending Passion?

But it was not merely to inform them of what was present to His own mind that Jesus told His disciples how He was to suffer many things, and be rejected and put to death. He desired to bring them into fellowship with His spirit. Let us consider the purpose and method of Jesus as revealed to us in this case.

The discipline of instruction and preparation which was used by our Lord for the benefit of His immediate friends and followers, manifests itself to the reader very strikingly upon a careful study of the Gospels. The twelve Apostles, and perhaps a few others, were admitted into special intimacy by Jesus. Their Master bore in mind the task that was to be committed to them after His Ascension. They were to be *witnesses of Him*; and He sought to make them intelligent and faithful witnesses. He revealed His glory to them as they were able to bear it. He endeavoured to teach them the nature of the truest, divinest, glory. He purged their minds of the natural human errors by which Divine glory was confused with its counterfeits. He nourished in them a knowledge of the Father through Himself as the Son. He presented Himself to them as the way by which they might come to the Father, as the image in whom the Father might be seen.

The Lord Jesus carried out perfectly the character which He found wanting in His enemies but claimed as His own—that of a true Shepherd. The Shepherd, He said, does not separate Himself from His sheep. He goes **in** and out with them: He goes before them and they follow Him. He cares for their interests, **He** encounters their dangers. Such a Shepherd was Christ to the "little flock" which He had always **with** Him. He made His followers *friends* to the utmost possible degree. He kept from them no secrets which they were able to receive. He sought to make *His* mind their mind. He wished them to know Him and hear His voice, and to follow Him through sympathy and love.

And therefore when His appointed Passion was drawing near, He spoke earnestly to the twelve about it, seeking to make them understand Him, and to draw them into the same spirit with Himself. But the attempt was an extremely difficult one. We cannot wonder that it was so.

From the first day of their call, the Apostles were being slowly trained into a reverence for the person of Jesus. They beheld His mighty works; they heard all His discourses; the parables which were cast forth as stimulating images to the multitudes, were to them privately explained; they lived under the perpetual influence of grace and truth; they could prove their Master by secret and familiar observation, **and so** gain the strongest convictions of His perfect nobleness. All this made them ready to believe great things of Jesus. They could willingly confess that

He came from God, and that the Father had sent Him. They gladly acknowledged Him as the Christ of whom the prophets had borne witness. If He had told them of mighty conquests which He would achieve, of astonishing works which He would perform, they would not have been slow of heart to believe Him.

But just when their idea of their Master's nature and power was raised to its highest pitch, instead of promising them triumphs and high places, He begins to tell them that He must suffer and be killed. Is it strange that their feelings underwent something of a revulsion? Is there any human being to whom it would be easy to pass from the thought of a Divine King to that of a sufferer? "I am the Christ," Jesus had said, "the Son of the living God. Upon this rock I will build up a Church, against which the gates of hell shall not prevail." And then He went on to say, "My bitter enemies are about to prevail against me, and scourge and buffet and spit upon me, and put me to death." The Apostles could not receive this saying. When it was plainly repeated the second time, it remained a mystery to them, as St. Luke tells us: "they understood none of these things, and this saying was hid from them, neither knew they the things which were spoken." On the first announcement, Peter, the spokesman of the twelve, exclaimed, "Be it far from thee, Lord: this shall not happen unto thee." Which of us, brethren, can afford to condemn him? Should not we have said the same thing? Nay more, should we condemn ourselves for having so spoken?—Hardly, I think. To have refrained from some such protest would have implied either a deep and a trained insight into our Lord's appointed work, or a cold, unloyal disposition. Our Lord seems to speak with unexampled severity in reply to His follower's exclamation. "He turned, and said unto Peter, Get thee behind me, Satan; thou art an offence unto me; for thou savourest not the things that be of God, but the things that be of men." But perhaps we ought not to think of our Lord as *identifying* Peter with the Adversary. He recognises indeed in Peter's words the enemy's voice; but the very danger of the words consisted not in their patent wickedness, but in their plausibility. From the fervent, loyal lips of the disciple came a protest to which Jesus was *tempted*, we may say, to listen. But had He listened to it, He would have betrayed His appointed work as much as if He had yielded to the Tempter in the wilderness. With a sense of this danger, therefore, Jesus exclaimed so sharply, Get thee behind me, Satan; thou art a stumbling-block in my way. The remonstrance of Peter expressed human and not Divine views. The Messiah from heaven was to manifest His Divine nature by suffering, not by enjoyment. If the disciples were to know and understand Him, the fitness of this manifestation must commend itself to them. They must thoroughly enter into the truth that God could only be known to men in His highest glory, through a fellowship with their miseries.

"It behoved the Christ to suffer;" this was the

Divine truth, which Jesus must exemplify, and which believers in Him must learn, but which was so difficult for human notions to receive. The Apostles would not have been true men if it had cost their Master no pains to teach them this; if it had cost them no time or effort to learn it. We speak too much by rote of the error of the Jews, who expected in their Messiah a temporal Prince surrounded with outward pomp. If we can easily condemn that error, we blind ourselves to the human instincts of our own hearts. It is always a wonder to the ordinary human heart, that the Eternal Son of God should suffer and die. This is still the great difficulty of belief; a stumbling-block, compared with which difficulties as to the infallibility of the Scriptures are but as molehills. It came nearer and was more real to the Apostles than we often allow it to be to us. They were amazed and frightened by it, as St. Mark records; they could not get over it by a phrase. Were they to believe their Friend and Master to be indeed the only-begotten Son of God, into whose hands all things were committed by the Father, the Lord and Judge of all men; and were they to see Him, without a shock of astonishment and doubt, reviled, outraged, beaten, crucified, by triumphant enemies? This at least Jesus declared to them: that whatever pain they might feel at the blindness and brutality of men, however they might grieve with the sorrows of their Master, yet, if they entered truly into the Divine mind, they would see Divine glory in this submission, and Divine ends of mercy to be accomplished by these sufferings.

There was a further truth to be taught them. The glory of patience and self-oblation, which Jesus claimed as Divine, was not to be appropriated by Him exclusively. He would go first; but His sheep, who knew Him and heard His voice, were to follow Him. It was therefore a matter of earnest and affectionate concern to the heart of Jesus that His disciples should see Him without dismay walking upon this road, and should prepare joyfully to follow Him. The passage I have read for our text reminds us that, immediately after the declaration of the sufferings which He was about to meet in fulfilment of His Divine mission, Jesus delivered the solemn warning, " If any man will come after me, let him deny himself, and take up his cross, and follow me." There was a special truth in these words for the disciples to whom they were spoken, and to them they were primarily addressed. No one could become a faithful follower of Jesus without being prepared to renounce everything, without carrying his life itself in his hand. And the first desire of Jesus in speaking those words was undoubtedly to make Peter and the rest of his companions understand clearly the absolute degree of the self-sacrifice which they must make in spirit, if they would be thoroughly associated with the Leader in whom they believed. He was going before them, bearing His cross, submitting beforehand to the ignominy and pain which were to be openly realized; He was thus submitting, not in spite of His Divine nature, but *because* He was the perfect Son of the righteous and loving Father. If His disciples would cherish the high ambition of being His friends and followers; if they would look forward to the joy and the crown by which true sacrifice was to be rewarded—they also must tread in the steps of the Master, they must be content to serve and submit, they must gird themselves to the unreserved offering of *themselves* to God.

The offering of the whole self, if it is real and complete, includes all acts and habits of self-denial. But it is no rare experience that those who are ready to give up life, and who no longer regard themselves as their own, should fall easily into some snare of vanity or ambition. When Jesus and His followers were going up to Jerusalem to the last Passover, no doubt the feeling of the twelve, amidst all their amazement, was that expressed by Thomas, " Let us also go, that we may die with him." But on that very journey, a sad example of selfish ambition and of its dividing effects occurred amongst the twelve. The two sons of Zebedee came with their mother to Jesus, asking that they might have the special privilege of sitting on His right and His left hand in His kingdom. Jesus repels the request with a wonderful mixture of tenderness and correction. But the other ten, when they heard of this unbrotherly conduct of James and John, were naturally indignant. Then Jesus gave them all a lesson in humility, bidding them follow His example, and cherish His spirit. "Whosoever will be great among you, let him be your minister: and whosoever will be chief among you, let him be your servant: *even as the Son of Man came* not to be ministered unto, but *to minister*, and *to give his life* a ransom for many."

Thus our blessed Lord shewed them, and has shewn to us, the true spiritual meaning and worth of His sacrifice. He poured out His blood—He gave up the ghost—He died: but this bodily death was only the last act of a prolonged *self-oblation*. And the offering of Himself was the complete surrender of His mind and will, under the hardest trials, to the gracious will of the Father. It was the triumph of meekness, of humility, of patience, of obedience, of love. In that sacrifice the Lord earnestly invites every disciple to imitate Him. He offers to all the same filial Spirit, in whose power alone the sacrifice of self becomes possible.

XVII.

THE ORIGIN AND AUTHORITY OF THE GOSPELS.

St. Matthew ix. 9.

"*As Jesus passed forth from thence, he saw a man named Matthew sitting at the receipt of custom: and he saith unto him, Follow me. And he arose, and followed him.*"

THERE are no writings in the world so important as the four Gospels. Upon this point there cannot be amongst Christians any difference of opinion. I do not mean only that, as a portion of our sacred volume, they share in that dignity by which the Bible is raised above all other literature. They are the most important part of that volume itself. If other scriptural books were absent, the Bible, we can conceive, might still serve its chief purposes. But without the Gospels the New Testament would be so mutilated as to be almost useless. So long as the Christian Church is founded upon Jesus Christ and exists for His worship, so long the records of His life and death and resurrection must be the most precious and the most indispensable literature of the Christian world.

Each of the names, therefore, by which the Gospels

are headed has a peculiar **and** pre-eminent glory. **The four** Evangelists live in our memory and in our respect because they are the authors of the four Gospels. **One of** them, indeed, St. John, has many **other** titles **to** our reverence. But we should think very little **of** St. Matthew, St. Mark, and St. Luke, if they had not written Gospels. To have written one of the Gospels, however, is so remarkable a distinction, **that we** wonder at its having been conferred upon men not otherwise distinguished.

St. Mark and St. Luke were not of the twelve Apostles, nor companions of the Lord Jesus. They were therefore not themselves eye-witnesses of the things which they relate. St. Matthew was an Apostle, and his call to the Apostleship is all that is recorded of him. He was a collector of customs, and was found by Jesus sitting at the place where dues were paid. The different accounts of his call shew us that **he** bore the name of Levi, " Levi, the son of Alpheus," as well as that of Matthew. Jesus said to him, Follow me ; and Matthew's answer was to rise and follow Him. We read his name afterwards in the lists of the twelve Apostles, and this is all we know **of** him. This Evangelist, like St. Mark and St. Luke, may thus be just identified by one or two facts in the sacred history ; but these are of slight interest compared with the task of composing a Gospel, and they do not suffice to explain the reasons or qualifications **which led** him to that task. There is really no bridge to connect together the name of Matthew the publican and the name of Matthew the Evangelist.

The whole subject of *the origin and composition* of the Gospels is one of much difficulty as well as interest; and I take occasion from the recurrence of St. Matthew's day to make some remarks upon it. It is convenient to separate in our minds the first three Gospels from that of St. John. The three are very like one another, and St. John's is very different from them all. Many things may therefore be said concerning the first three Gospels which would not apply equally to St. John's.

In considering what we know about these Gospels, the most surprising fact is that we know so little. Their origin is lost in obscurity. The Gospels of St. Matthew and St. Mark have no preface to explain who the author is, why he writes, or from what sources he drew his materials. The writer of the Gospel of St. Luke does not tell us his name, but he gives an important preface which identifies him with the writer of the Acts, and from which we learn that "many" had taken in hand the narration of the events orally related by the preachers of the Gospel, by whose example St. Luke was led to use the advantages which he possessed for a similar narrative, addressed especially to one Theophilus. We must recur to this preface. Meanwhile, we observe that the history of the establishment of the kingdom of Christ, contained in the Acts, makes no mention, beyond the allusion at the beginning, of the composition of the Gospels. We read there how Peter spoke and wrought, how St. Paul travelled and suffered and preached the Gospel, but we are not told of any historical Gospel being written or used. Either **no** Gospel was written during the time comprised in the history of the Acts, **or** it **did** not fall within the historian's purpose to make mention of it.

Nor in the Epistles **is** there any allusion to a written Gospel. The facts of our Lord's life are often appealed to, but it is nowhere implied that they were at that time collected in any authoritative record.

We come, therefore, to the following conclusions :—

In the first preaching of the Gospel the Apostles and their helpers did not produce or appeal to *any written document*. They carried their facts in their memories. They gave information to those who received them concerning Jesus of Nazareth, like that which was summed up in St. Peter's address to Cornelius and those about him, but this information was given by word of mouth, and it set forth either what the preacher had seen and heard himself or **what** some other trustworthy person had told him. And this, in truth, was the natural way in which the tidings concerning Jesus would be spread. In an age without newspapers or printed books, it was not the first thought of one who had any facts to announce to put them down upon paper and so to circulate them. The Gospel, we should remember, was spread **in** that, its first age, not by tracts or copies of the Scripture, but exclusively by the personal testimony of those who had a claim to be believed. The earliest believers had no sacred books of their own faith. It may be difficult for us to realize a religion without a Bible : but if we wish to represent to ourselves the life of those first believers, we must not think of them as studying any Scriptures of the New Covenant. In the place of our reading of the Bible was to them the hearing of those who could recite the deeds or discourses of Jesus, the treasuring up of these in their memories, and the relating them to others.

There would be a danger, however, that what was thus carried from mouth to mouth, and depended on the faithfulness and memory of those who repeated it, would before long be wasted through forgetfulness or be mixed with the imaginations of the reporters. Oral tradition was, perhaps, more to be depended upon in the days when it was the chief source or channel of knowledge than it is now: but, under the most favourable circumstances, it was impossible that a series of events and discourses could be long handed down in this way with perfect accuracy. This danger must have been felt and appreciated by many during the lifetime of the Apostles. The necessity of fixing the details of the sacred narrative in writing must have early presented itself to many minds. We are nowhere told that it was so: but it could hardly be otherwise, and the results prove it. We conclude that gradually, and without exciting attention as a great work in the church, the words of the Apostles and other companions of our Lord began to be taken down in writing. Once begun, this work would grow. It was obviously a valuable help to the memory. If done at all, it was highly important that it should be done faithfully and well. Processes of comparison and collection would go on. By degrees, first drafts of a written Gospel would come into existence, owing their origin to **the** reports of eye-witnesses, taking their shape from the general testimony **of the** apostles, and corrected more or less by their express voice.

Assuming what **we** know to be the case, that the Apostles did not begin with presenting any authoritative documents to their hearers, but that they **were** in the habit of giving from their own knowledge long reports of things relating to their Master, which reports were the basis of their appeals to mankind, and obviously of the very highest importance, such a process as I have described is what would naturally take place. Written reports would begin to be handed about, which would tend to coalesce into one, and which would be *edited*, so to speak, with various degrees of authority and accuracy. And this answers **to** what St. Luke mentions. "Forasmuch," he begins, "as many have taken in hand to set forth in order a declaration of those things which are most surely believed among us, even as they delivered them unto us which from the beginning were eye-witnesses, and ministers of the word; it seemed good to me also, having had perfect understanding of all things from the very first, to write unto thee in order, most excellent Theophilus, that thou mightest know the certainty of those things, wherein thou hast been instructed." According to this statement there were many *attempts* at Gospels at the time when St. Luke's was composed. Most of them proved failures, some of them survived.

Of the way in which St. Luke's and its two companion Gospels were selected from amongst all similar narratives, and obtained their present position, we know nothing. When they come before us in ecclesiastical history, in the course of the next century, the work of selection has been almost completed. Between the state of things mentioned by St. Luke, and the appearance of the Gospels according to St. Matthew, St. Mark, St. Luke, and St. John, in the New Testament canon or volume, hardly any intermediate step is made known to us. The early ecclesiastical traditions tell us a little concerning each Gospel, but not much. The books bring their own authority with them. There they are; their contents may be read and compared; these are the records concerning Christ which have emerged out of the obscurity, and have gained the general reverence of the Church; others apparently like them have perished.

I say this is how the Gospels come upon our view as we look back into their history. There is no such evidence of their origin or composition as would have much weight if the contents of the books themselves, and their general acceptance by the Church, did not sufficiently commend them. Whilst the creation and selection of these Gospels was going on, probably those who were engaged in the work were not conscious of the greatness of that work, nor of the power that was using them for it. It was done quietly and without observation, but it was done; and, to the reflective mind, the result itself is a surer and more remarkable sign of the Spirit to whom the work was due, than any more conspicuous *method* of obtaining the result could have been.

Let me mention what we learn from ecclesiastical writers as to *St. Matthew's* Gospel. The Gospel is called by his name, but no explanation is given why he, rather than **St.** Peter **or** St. James, should have written it. **But** an interesting fact is further stated, that the Gospel was written originally, not in Greek as we have it, but in the common language of Palestine, called Aramaic, for the use of the Jewish Christians in that country. We are not told anything as to the translation of the Gospel into Greek, whether St. Matthew had anything to do with it or not. And the original Hebrew or Aramaic Gospel must have early disappeared; no trace of it is now to be found. Possibly that vernacular Gospel was not exactly *translated* into the Greek, but only supplied the principal materials for it. This tradition, that St. Matthew's Gospel was first written in the language of Palestine, is the more likely to be true because it seems a fragmentary and unsupported fact; and it certainly agrees well with the internal character of this Gospel, which is distinguished from the others by its specially Jewish character. It is easily seen by a comparison of the Gospels that St. Matthew, more than the other Evangelists, presents our Lord as the fulfilment of the promises made **to the** Jewish fathers and as the Messiah of the Covenant. This appears especially from appeals to the prophets and allusions to the law which occur in the course of the Gospel. According to

St. Matthew, Jesus was "born King of the Jews;" and in this character, as the true King of the Jews, He is especially set forth in this Gospel. The remembrance of this character will serve as a key to many of the differences by which St. Matthew's Gospel is distinguished from those of St. Mark and St. Luke. The three Gospels have very much in common; so much as to lead us to the conclusion that the authors used the same materials in compiling their narratives; but each of them has also an individual character which it is very instructive to look for and to study. The Gospel of St. Matthew, then, we should remember was written originally in the Jewish vernacular language for the Christians in Palestine, and therefore it addresses itself to the special knowledge and convictions of Jews.

These particulars are interesting, though they are so scanty; and some traditions of a like character exist as to the sources of St. Mark's and St. Luke's Gospel. It is said that St. Mark received instruction from St. Peter, and that St. Luke was influenced by his companionship with St. Paul. These are hints which may help us to a right understanding of the special purpose and character of each of the Gospels.

But they are of little weight with regard to the *authority* of these sacred books. And the question of their authority is sure to arise in our minds when we consider their *origin*. "What claim have these Gospels, the three or the four, to the reverence and confidence with which we regard them?" The first answer to such a question would be, "They are portions of the Bible, and the Bible as a whole is a sacred book." This answer might be sufficient at a certain stage of knowledge and inquiry. But when we are looking back into the history of the Church and the putting together of the New Testament,—as all Christians and readers of the Scriptures ought to do according to their opportunities,—that answer falls to the ground. For we then see the Bible, so to speak, *in pieces*. We observe that the volume called that of the New Testament, or more properly of the New Covenant, is made up of writings which all of them existed separately to begin with, and which by some process or authority were brought together. Each of the Gospels was a distinct treatise. Each of the Epistles was written and sent as a letter. By degrees, and, in the case of some of the books, after a good deal of controversy, the volume of the New Testament was settled in its present shape; its present contents being finally sanctioned as parts of it, and other books of a similar or apparently similar kind being finally excluded from it.

Now in considering *the authority* of the several books we find that the three first Gospels stand on a rather different footing from St. Paul's Epistles, for example. We know St. Paul's life and character, and the great part intrusted to Him in the foundation of the Church of Christ. Any serious and weighty communication proceeding from him would have a claim on our reverence because of its being *his*. But a history of our Lord's acts and sufferings simply called St. Mark's, and without much evidence of being even from him,—St. Mark, moreover, being no eye-witness of the things he relates,—why should this be sacred to us, any more than the histories of "the many" mentioned by St. Luke as having taken in hand similar works?

It is not, in fact, *the authorship* of the three Gospels which makes them sacred and Scriptural. It is not because they were written by St. Matthew, St. Mark, and St. Luke, that we owe them reverence. Their authority rests on two grounds :

First, Their acceptance by the Church.

Secondly, The self-commendation of their contents.

(1) The volume, or canon, of the New Testament grew, as I have already said, in a natural and imperceptible manner. No attention is called to it till the work is almost finished. But, in some way or other, certain books were brought into prominence; others fell into neglect. Probably, some books were cherished in some countries; others, in others. The importance of authentic records of the Saviour's life was increasingly felt. Care and discrimination were exercised. At last, the result comes out plainly before us. We perceive the general acceptance of a volume, as sacred and authoritative, throughout the Church. The hesitation which continued for some time as to the full recognition of certain books, as the Epistle to the Hebrews and the Book of Revelation, proves the carefulness and the sense of responsibility which had prevailed in the gathering together of the other books.

And this work of the Ancient Church we and all

Christendom have inherited from those early days. Since the closing of the canon, or the final settling of the volume, no Church has presumed to alter its contents.

All Churches have confessed the immediate hand **of** God in the formation of our Sacred Book. Since the first preaching of the Gospel by the Apostles, witnesses of the Lord's Resurrection, no work so important has been done in the Church as the making **of** the book, which was to be universally accepted, read, and appealed to, as the book of authentic records **of** the Apostolic age. If in anything the Spirit of God has been with the Church, it must have been in the process of writing and collecting the Scriptures. And the less conspicuous that this process was, the more confidently do we recognise the action of the Divine Spirit in it. That Gospels should have emerged, bearing the comparatively obscure names of Matthew, Mark, and Luke, shews less of human scheming, more of Divine purpose, than if there had been a Gospel of St. Peter, openly professing to have been composed by the chief of the Apostles. We trace, in the acceptance by the Church of these books, a great humility and deference to truth. We infer that the Church submitted to be guided, and felt that the work was not the Church's, but God's.

Even the most Protestant churches of modern times, **therefore,** have accepted the canon of Holy Scripture **from** the **hands of the** Primitive Church, and have maintained with peculiar zeal **the** authority of the **books which** that Church declared to be sacred. And to us at this day the authority of St. Matthew's Gospel depends primarily upon the fact that, through a natural process of selection, it was adopted in the post-Apostolic age into the sacred volume.

(2) But this, though the first in order and the more formal **one, is** not really the weightiest of the credentials which commend the Gospels to us. The sacred books, and the Gospels at their head, *keep their ground,* **and have always** kept it, through their own **intrinsic worth.** This was what commended them to **the Divinely** enlightened conscience and judgment **of the early Church.** And it has continued to commend them to the conscience of every Church and age. Those who **read** these books with simplicity and insight **bow down before** the inspiration that is manifest in them. Other religious and Christian compositions of the primitive ages have come down **to** us: let any man of even common understanding read these by the side of the sacred Gospels, **and** he feels the difference at once. **The** Gospels speak with a Divine voice, and those whose ears are open can hear it. And it is this inward power and authority which is **the** real **strength** of the sacred books. However strictly they **might be** guarded by Church rules, they would have fallen into neglect if they had not life in themselves. And it is this inward life which will practically **preserve** their authority amongst us **in** this age, far more than any theories of inspiration, or any penalties upon criticism.

It is well to add, that there is nothing in the authority of the Gospels, such as we perceive that authority to be, to prohibit reverent criticism of their contents. It does not follow, because the primitive Church thankfully accepted these writings as parts of a sacred volume, and the church in later ages has ratified that acceptance, or because we feel the singular truthfulness and dignity of the narratives, that each of the narratives is in all its details infallible, and that any inconsistency between them is impossible. We should certainly not expect any serious opposition or discrepancy between them; and the piety of devout readers is unwilling to admit that in books so precious and Divine, there is any imperfection at all. But if there is none, it must be shewn practically *by the finding of none*. It cannot be ruled beforehand that in such books none can possibly exist. These books may be all that the voice of the Church has confessed them to be, may be inspired, authoritative, and sacred, and yet may contain human imperfections. It is always, indeed, far more likely that a supposed error or inconsistency may be due to the reader's mistake, than that it really exists in the narrative. But we are not warranted in laying down dogmatically that it is always so. To bind the conscience of a Christian reader of the Bible by a prejudgment that there is no error or inconsistency in the sacred volume, is an arbitrary tyranny; imposing upon men burdens which God has not imposed, for which there is no warrant in Holy Scripture itself, or in the history of the Church of Christ.

It is necessary at the present time to bear this in mind, because the Scriptural books are now subjected to searching critical investigation, and many learned persons are trying to make out the worst against them. When doubts and controversies are abroad, the taking up of a wrong position may expose our faith to needless and most dangerous shocks. Thus, if any one starts with the assumption that the Holy Scriptures are in such a sense a Word of God, that there can be no error or inconsistency of any kind in them, and then is persuaded, rightly or wrongly, that in the eyes of common honesty and intelligence a certain discrepancy with facts or with some other Scriptural statement must be admitted, he is in danger of throwing the Scriptures overboard altogether, and of regarding them as a mere human invention. It is therefore most important that our reverence for Scripture should rest on the true foundation, and that it should not commit itself to any arbitrary dogma. I have been endeavouring to show you what the authority is, with which the Scriptures come down to us —viz. the acceptance of the Church, Divinely guided in so momentous a matter, and the internal self-commending truth of the books themselves. And this authority, whilst it certainly presents the Scriptures to us as most precious and holy, by no means excludes the possibility of human imperfections in their composition. Suppose the writer or translator of St. Matthew's Gospel to have made certain mistakes: it does not follow that the Church was misled at first in receiving the book into the Canon, or that we are foolish in reading the book with a peculiar trust and reverence. It would be a different matter if the book **as a** whole could be shown to be fallacious and worthless. But no critic is likely to prove this.

It is the habit of Christians, and especially of Pro**testant** Christians, in the present age, to lean very exclusively upon the authority and the teaching of the Scriptures. This dependence upon the written documents of our faith is very natural, and, within legitimate bounds, very right. But that there may be a blind and superstitious worship of these books may be shewn, out of Scripture itself, by the example of the Pharisees, who worshipped the books of the Old Testament most jealously, but who were none the better for that worship. It will help much to keep us right in our feelings towards the Scriptures, if we remember the fact I have been dwelling on this morning, that the first believers in Judea, in Corinth, **at** Rome, had no New Testament. And they were yet able to cherish the true Christian faith, and to lead earnest Christian lives. They could not have believed, indeed, or lived as Christians, without a knowledge of Christ. But this knowledge did not come to them in a sacred authoritative volume; it came to them through oral testimony, which they respected and trusted. They learnt what they could about Christ, and believed and cherished it. This they could do without having the fallacious support **of** writings presumed to be infallible. Well: the sacred writings are intended to supply to us the place of the testimony and teaching of eye-witnesses and Apostles. The Bible ought to do for us what oral reports and expositions did for the first believers. It ought to convey to our minds trustworthy information concerning the Lord Jesus Christ, and so to bring us into a real familiar knowledge of Him.

That is to say, the Bible is itself an instrument, and not an end. It is a means of bringing us to Christ. It might do this, so far as we can judge, in spite of many imperfections. And however infallible it were, it would fail to do its work, if we did not use it for its right end, the knowledge of the one true God, and of Jesus Christ whom He has sent. If we place the Scriptures above Christ, they will be to us a mere idol, destined to be broken.

And when we speak of their "inspiration," let the thought of inspiration lead us up to the Holy Spirit, the present and eternal source of light and love. If the Scriptures are inspired, as we believe them to be, they ought to be brought nearer to us, and not put farther from us, by having been written and put together under the moving of that same Holy Spirit, whom we confess as our own Guide, and look to as the only source of all that is good in us.

XVIII.

DIFFICULTIES OF BELIEF.

St. Mark ix. 24.

"And straightway the father of the child cried out, and said with tears, Lord, I believe; help thou mine unbelief."

PERHAPS there are few expressions in the Bible which have been more used or have ministered more comfort in the secret troubles and trials of sincere believers, than this broken confession and appeal. It puts into words for us that which is the true attitude of the universal human heart towards its Lord; it is the voice of a man who proves himself to be a brother to every one of us. Whilst, indeed, we are careless and satisfied with things as they are, we may feel no impulse to believe; we may not be con**scious** of our unbelief. But when we are awakened and aroused, and are girding ourselves to do or to **suffer as** it may be appointed to us, there are no more **natural** words for us to use than these, "Lord, I **believe,** help thou mine unbelief."

The collect for this Sunday* speaks of hindrances which thwart and embarrass us in running the race that is set before us. These hindrances are summed up under the general title of "our sins and wickedness," from which we pray that the Lord, with His mighty help, will deliver us. We greatly need God's help against all our sins, for we are much hindered in our running by all of them. The over-mastering impulses of passion, the greediness of low desires, the meanness of self-seeking and jealousy, the readiness to misunderstand and to be offended, sins like these are continually stopping us or turning us aside in our Christian course. We may well pray also to be delivered from the effect of the sins of others upon ourselves, especially from that discouragement which is caused by the absence of sympathy with our better aspirations. For it is impossible to over-rate the help we gain from knowing and feeling that others are striving together with us, and the hindrance occasioned by seeing others careless and worldly and godless around us. But, even without the hint which St. Thomas's Day suggests to us, we might have called to mind that no hindrances are sorer or more common than those presented by the difficulty of believing. It is in the nature of doubts and perplexities to embarrass and unnerve and distress us. We are consciously more languid and feeble through the want of that faith which doubts seem to keep away from us. And those hindrances

---

* This Sermon was preached on the Fourth Sunday in Advent, which happened also to be St. Thomas's Day.

which are to be traced directly to the lusts of the flesh and of the spirit, have their force and sway through our want of faith; and it is chiefly by a living faith that they are to be overcome.

Practically, then, we are called upon to grapple with difficulties of belief, each with those that come in his own way, and nothing can absolve us from this responsibility. But I feel strongly that it is no easy matter to speak as one ought, or to think as one ought, concerning this class of hindrances. One danger is that of assuming too readily that difficulties have been, or can be, met and removed. Another is that of judging those who differ from ourselves in belief. A third danger is that of acquiescing too easily in a general uncertainty. But the state of mind, of which St. Thomas's hesitation was an example, is brought distinctly before us by the recollection of his history, and so invites our consideration. And, perhaps, without attempting to solve any problems, I may be enabled to set before you some thoughts which may make the remembrance of our own doubts, and of the doubts or disbelief of others, less oppressive and hindering to our minds.

And let me say in the first place, that sincere doubts are neither to be crushed in ourselves, nor to be treated with disrespect in others. No one who **has** any idea of what true knowledge is, can treat **doubt as** essentially an evil thing. Doubts imply **ignorance** and want of assured faith, it is true; but **it** is ignorance seeking to be enlightened, **a** kind **of** faith seeking **to** be made clearer and stronger.

Doubt and disbelief are not by any means the same thing. For example, the assailants of the Christian Faith are generally anything but doubters; they are often exceedingly confident, perfectly sure of their own opinions. But real doubt is the inevitable process to be gone through in the correction of an error. If I have been believing something wrong, doubt must be infused into my mind before my wrong belief can become right. When therefore the question arises in our minds, however it may come there, Is this that I have been accustomed to hold about God, or about Christ, or about the Bible, or about the future state, *true* or not? such a question must be treated with all reverence. I do not say that we ought to become restless and unsettled until we can find a satisfactory answer; but that we are not to stifle the question as a sin. To do so, would make deliverance from error hopeless; and it would suck out all life and reality from our belief. It is not a comfortable state to most minds to have a question presented to them which they cannot answer, and to remain uncertain; but we are not to study comfort first, but the truth. And our loyalty to truth is a very sacred matter, which we must not suffer to be stained or weakened.

But we may maintain this, and so give a kind of honour, as it may be said, to doubt, without glorifying the principle of negation or rejoicing in a chaos of opinion. Mere liberalism, or the freedom of every man to think as he pleases, is but a hollow idol to worship. It may be necessary, in the interest of truth, that such freedom should be recognised, and yet it may be every man's duty to guard against pleasing himself in opinion, and to strive that he and his fellow-men may together believe, not what each man likes, but what is true whether any man likes it or not. It is suspicious, therefore, when a man talks about "his conscience" as directing his belief. His conscience is very likely to mean his self-conceit or self-will. The question for me is not what my conscience has to say, but what is true; that is, what the Eternal God is willing to make known to all men. Whilst I am seeking this in all simplicity, my conscience will retire into the background and not obtrude itself upon notice. Freedom of conscience, then, is an indispensable condition of the worship of truth, and in the interest of truth we should rightly be jealous of anything which tends to crush liberty of opinion; but that liberty in itself is not glorious, and if it assumes to be so, it will probably make itself contemptible and mischievous. Still less is the mere denying of some common opinion to be considered glorious. Such a denial is to be undertaken without fear when truth requires it; but it ought to be undertaken with regret, and with a deep sense of responsibility.

If there is such a thing as truth at all, and it is only for the sake of truth that opinions have any importance, it must be essentially common to all men, the inheritance of the race which is created after one image, the light which is to the spirit as the sun in heaven is to the bodily eye. And therefore it is dishonouring to truth to speak as if a loose variety of private opinions had in it any ideal beauty.

When we come to consider that truth which is most vital, that which has to do with the nature of God and our relations to Him, there is a feature of it which it is most important to bear in mind. The apprehension of such truth belongs to the *life* or to the whole man, and not to the intellect only. In some departments we may perhaps embody truth in fixed conclusions, expressible in words, and drawn from acknowledged premisses. But in the highest departments this cannot be thoroughly done. If we fail to accomplish it to our own satisfaction, or to that of others, the reason of our failure may lie in the nature of things; we may be transferring processes which do very well for one subject to another for which they are utterly inappropriate. This will be better understood if we take an example of it. There are great difficulties as to any theory of *prayer*, difficulties found hitherto insuperable. Unbelievers confidently claim that such a theory should be made out as logical as a rule of arithmetic; and many believers who know better than to refrain from praying are yet disturbed by the feeling that such a demand ought to be satisfied. But the truth is that prayer transcends the capacities of the logical intellect, which knows or ought to know that it cannot comprehend and analyse the whole of what man is and may be, and still less what God is. Similarly, the subject of Inspiration involves what may be called insoluble problems. If we cannot answer questions that are asked about it, the reason may be not that we are believing foolishly and ought to abandon our belief, but that the subject **does** not admit of being embraced within question **and** answer. I mean by Inspiration not only that of the **men** who wrote the various books of the Bible, but that which **we** are all of us taught to confess and to ask for. In either case the difficulty of definition is found to be **very** great.

Now the belief of a Christian, in its simplest and highest **sense,** is the belief of a man in God. What mysteries are involved in this relation! We confess God, with all that has been revealed and that we can know about Him, to be an infinite, incomprehensible Being. We are taught to worship God as Father, Son, and Holy Spirit. This account of the Divine nature is derived from the appearing **of** Him **who** came **as** at this time in our mortal flesh, declaring Himself to be the Son of God from Heaven. This threefold name gives us much knowledge concerning God, but **it** does not make His nature at all more comprehensible than it is without it. It does not enable us to answer the questions of all comers. It only opens to us paths for the fellowship of our spirits with God. And if the great object of human belief is incomprehensible, are we to say that **he who** believes is comprehensible? Only narrow-minded ignorance could think so. The human being, in his height **or in his** debasement, individually or in the race—the **loftiest** saint or the lowest sinner, a man or mankind—transcends the bounds of our understand**ings.** A man does not completely understand **his** neighbour: he does not completely understand himself. And yet we may know one another more or less; we may know something of ourselves; we may know something of human history. We know, in truth, more than we can define or analyse. And this is because our whole being is concerned in knowing. We take in such knowledge through every pore: not only by the calculating intellect, but by the senses, by the affections, by instincts which prove themselves to be alive, but which we cannot lay hold of. The knowledge is real, though it cannot be set out in propositions.

Reflections, then, concerning difficulties of belief must not forget what Christian belief purports to be. It is the affiance of the whole man in God, the personal trust of a living being in a Father, in a Head, in an Inspirer. The creation of this belief in a man may be something different from a demonstration, or from a series of demonstrations. Such a belief, however simple, cannot be a mere superficial assent to certain statements. It must reach to the will, and the affections, and the general tenor of the thoughts. And its reality will not bear any exact proportion to intellectual admissions. A man knowing God and believing in Him, is something quite different from a man having answers ready to questions which may be put to him. What we call doctrines are not the ultimate objects of true faith; they are means of guiding us to Him in whom we are to believe. To know God Himself, and knowing Him to believe in Him, with heart and soul and strength—this is the good we are to gain from creeds and confessions and doctrines, and from the Scriptures, from which these derive their authority.

If we look at the history of the Apostles, we shall learn much as to the nature and growth of true belief. Searching the records of their intercourse with their Master, we do not find Him at any stage demanding of them an assent to doctrinal propositions. What we observe is, that He is gradually training them to the knowledge of Himself, and of the Father through Him. The Gospels are **full** of a personal life, revealing itself in act and word. "We beheld His glory, the glory as of the only-begotten of the Father," is the account which the disciple whom Jesus loved gives of the nature and growth **of** their belief. The disciples were prepared to expect the fulfilment of the promises of the old covenant, partly by the devout study of those promises, but much more through the proclamations of John the Baptist. But their minds were at first in a dim and confused state as to the way in which those promises were to be fulfilled. Jesus did not begin by explaining to them what they afterwards came to know, as to the meaning of the old covenant and its fulfilment in Him. He seems to have kept back verbal expositions, and to have taken care that their intellectual assent was not in advance of their real personal knowledge. His method was to manifest His glory, and so to draw out their belief in Him. We may recognise a wonderful wisdom in this method. In no other way than **that** used by our blessed Lord would it have been possible to lead on the Apostles to such a knowledge of Him, Son of God and Son of Man, as made them efficient witnesses of Him to the world. But by seeing His grace and goodness and power, and by hearing the words of truth and authority which came from His lips, the companions of Jesus, almost without being aware of it, became impressed by the Divine Presence brought near to them in Him, and learnt to love Him with an affection humbled by awe, and to put themselves, body and soul, entirely at His disposal. Even whilst He was amongst them in the flesh, going in and out with them, they could not regard Him as merely one of themselves. They knew that He was sent from the Father, and that the words He spoke and the works He did were the Father's. But Jesus did not anticipate, in the instruction He gave to the disciples, His ascension and the outpouring of the Holy Ghost. Not till after those events did the Apostles arrive at the true spiritual apprehension of Him who had dwelt in flesh amongst them, full of grace and truth. Then they began to know His eternal relation to themselves and to all men. Then they began to worship Him as the universal Saviour, the Word by whom all things were made, the One High Priest of mankind, the Sacrifice which established a perfect reconciliation.

During all the time in which the Lord Jesus was thus training His disciples in personal knowledge of Himself and of the Father, He made use of external signs to draw out and stimulate their faith, but with a special wisdom and caution. He had the power of doing mighty works, and He used that power, and He intended that the observers of it should see the Father's hand in those works: but He did *not* desire that any should accept Him as a powerful Lord on account of mighty works. He therefore expressly restrained and subordinated His action as a miracle-worker. He sought to neutralize that mere effect of astonishment, which it is the nature of marvellous works to produce on the mind. The works were put forward as outward signs of an authority much higher than the wonder-working power, of an authority always present, then in the act of revealing itself to the souls of men. Jesus Christ proclaimed a Kingdom of Heaven, of which miracles were but the humble witnesses. He desired that the Father should be known by men *as* the Father; that He Himself should be known as the Saviour, the giver of life and light. Miracles could not impart such knowledge; they might even do something to hinder it. But they were natural tokens of such a Presence as that of the Word made flesh; and they were capable of doing much service, in opening men's eyes, in breaking the fetters of sense, and disclosing the nature and reality of the spiritual kingdom. These and some other outward evidences of a similar nature, our Lord used graciously, and therefore wisely and sparingly, in the discipline of His followers.

He was tender and considerate to human infirmity, as in other matters, so in this. The Apostle Thomas is a remarkable example of a sincere faith subject to the infirmity of looking for outward evidence. We have no reason to suppose that his state of mind generally towards the Master was different from that of the other ten Apostles. They were all struck down in their hopes by the Crucifixion; they were all surprised by the Resurrection. The ten had seen the Lord after his rising; Thomas had been absent on that occasion. When they told him, We have seen the Lord, he expressed an unwillingness to believe it, and a demand of positive evidence, which indicates something too much of dependence on the outward senses, but which Jesus Himself treated with as much indulgence as censure. And Thomas, when he too actually *saw* the Lord and heard His appeals, was not more sceptical or hard-hearted than the rest. He responded at once with the ardent confession, "My Lord and my God."

Now, I think, dear brethren, that as to our own faith—our belief in God and in Christ—we may learn much by observing the discipline under which the faith of the Apostles was nurtured. I would say at once, that *we* are under a similar discipline. If we know ourselves rightly, we must confess ourselves to be creatures and subjects and children of Him who is revealing Himself personally to our real knowledge, and who seeks to draw out the faith of our total nature towards Himself. In carrying on this work, He uses external evidences, but with a certain sparingness. His wisdom is as remarkable in refusing these signs, as in giving them. For us, the external evidences of our faith are in our sacred books, in the history of the Church, in the triumphs of the Gospel, in an existing Christendom. These are all very remarkable, not to be disposed of except on the hypothesis of a real revelation of the Eternal God in His Son Jesus Christ. But every one who studies the subject, with either favour or enmity, is led to ask, How is it that these evidences just stop short where they do? Why do they just fail of being demonstrative and irresistible to every mind? The answer perhaps is, that it would not have suited the Divine purpose to make them so. They would not in such a case have accomplished that which God seeks to bring about. It is the design of God to train His children to a spiritual apprehension of their Eternal Father, of their sustaining Lord, of the Spirit who moves them. External evidences may do something in this discipline; but God Himself alone knows in what measure they should be used. When we realize, however, what God's design is, how essential it is to His purpose that there should not merely be an assent of our understandings to certain statements, but an affiance of our whole nature in Him as a present God—we shall see a good reason, I think, for the external evidence of the Gospel of Christ being not more overwhelming than it is.

Let me not be supposed to condemn such statements of doctrine as are included in Articles and Confessions. If we say that they are not themselves ultimate objects of our faith, but means of leading us to the one true object, we may be refusing them an honour which they have no right to claim, but we give them a place and a use of high dignity and importance. Such a place and use they will always have, as long as we remain in our present condition. It is chimerical to imagine that Articles and Creeds can be dispensed with. They are necessary witnesses to the truth; but the truth itself is greater and wider and more living.

This, then, is the chief point that I desire to bring before you this morning, in contemplation of difficulties of belief, that our belief is not, according to the whole teaching of Scripture and of the Church, a matter of intellectual assent merely, but a matter of *life,* a relation of knowledge between mysterious human beings and their still more mysterious Maker. We must look to Him for the revelation of Himself to our spiritual nature. Whereas, generally, when we speak of the difficulties in the way of belief, we are forgetting the real state of the case, and assuming something imaginary.

At the same time the question will be a very pressing one, and one not to be put by. Supposing that the Christian's belief is the knowledge of the Invisible and Eternal Being communicated to the human spirit, how are we to know whether we are believing rightly of God—whether our conceptions of His nature and of our relations to Him are *true* or imaginary? What are the criteria of our knowledge in Divine things? With reference to this question, I must content myself with giving briefly two hints.

(1) It is not unreasonable to ask, What will be the *alternative* of our belief? What is involved in our ceasing to believe as we have been taught to do? If

an opponent says, I show you **a** logical anomaly in **your** belief, and therefore call upon you to abandon that belief, we may answer, A still more formidable inconsistency, a much more insuperable difficulty, awaits us on responding to your summons. We will not be frightened by a logical difficulty from clinging to a belief, the abandonment of which would plunge us directly into more serious embarrassments. We hold this *alternative* to be a sign that substantially we are **not in** error, although some of our conceptions may be unworthy, and all of them may be inadequate.

(2) Secondly, the great criterion of such belief as that of the Church of Christ purports to be—of that vital relation between the spirits of men and the Divine nature—is, whether the belief actually proves itself in experience and history, whether it can be *lived* by. This affords us no compendious method of proving or disproving a doctrine; but it is the real and positive test of all great beliefs. Our lives, and the life of humanity, are sacred things; they are under Divine guidance. If we could only read it aright, there is no more Divine voice than that which they utter. But because it is very difficult to read their witness, we must be very humble and cautious in interpreting it. But we may be sure that this is the most genuine and real criterion of all doctrine. The question put to every professed revelation of **the** Invisible is this, Does it explain and help and guide the life of men and the course of things? Does the Being who leads on the life of the world,

and the lives of human beings, bear *His* testimony to the doctrine?

Such is the test which the Gospel of Christ, the revelation of the Eternal Father in the Son of His Love, who was made flesh and dwelt amongst us, will have to stand. It claims to be tried by that test with the utmost stringency. It offers to set right and restore and develop all human and created existence. We are invited by it to ask ourselves, whether we should be truer and better, by confessing a righteous and loving Father of our souls, who seeks to make us anew in the image of His Son Jesus Christ, by confessing a Lord and Elder Brother, in whom as our Head we are members both of Him and of one another, by confessing a universal Spirit of Truth and Peace, who strives to make us all one; or whether this confession will lead us astray into confusions and darkness and hopeless contradiction to facts. Let us ask ourselves in all seriousness and honesty this great question. And the Gospel also bids us ask, whether communities of men, churches and nations, and the whole human race, are following a true light of heaven, in confessing the one Father, the one Lord, and the one Spirit, God blessed for ever—whether history says, This is the fundamental truth upon which society stands, by which it is held together and prospers; or whether the course of things tends really to discredit the revelation of God in Christ, and compels men to believe in themselves only, or in chance. By the practical answers to such questions the Gospel will stand or fall.

XIX.

ONE GOD AND FATHER OF ALL.

EPHESIANS IV. 6.

"*One God and Father of all.*"

IT is important that we should ask ourselves what is meant by "all," in this Apostolic article of faith. Is the word to be taken simply in its widest sense, or is it to be limited by some conditions which the nature of the case supplies? Did St. Paul preach a God who was the God and Father of all *men*, in every country and of every generation; or a God who was the Father of *Christians* only; or, to narrow the reference still further, a God who was the Father of *true* Christians only? It is desirable to press the question, because there is a very considerable reluctance amongst Christians to give his words the sense which they naturally bear. There is a feeling that, whilst on the one hand philanthropy and toleration would persuade us to recognise the loving and fatherly relations of God with man as prevailing between the Supreme Ruler and *all* men, on the other hand, from a religious point of view, it is dangerous to give way to such a laxity of belief, and logically necessary to make God the Father only of those who know Him as a Father through Christ.

This fear of the word "all"—this suspicion of those articles of faith which speak of all mankind—this disposition to charge with infidelity such views of God's Fatherhood as would overleap the barriers within which the speculations of men have circumscribed it—has always existed in the Church. It has always assumed to be pre-eminently religious; it has always taken the liberty to force and compress the language of Scripture so as to suit its own conceptions. It is generally supposed that we have a symptom of this tendency in a slight alteration which took place very early in the latter part of this verse. St. Paul wrote, there is no doubt, "One God and Father of all, who is above all, and through all, and in all." In the last clause "you" was slipped in, and the reading "*in you all*" became generally adopted in the copies of the New Testament. The few alterations of this kind which have corrupted the text of Scripture, have been produced by the desire to make Scripture *safer*, more orthodox. Thus, to speak of God as "in all men," not to say, "in all *things*," seemed dangerous. Some reader, feeling sure that St. Paul must have meant Christians only, thought it would make the meaning clearer, and preserve it from being misunderstood, if "you" were inserted. The insertion answered to a general feeling, and was accepted. So that, as we have the passage in our translation, there is a delusive appearance of a distinction between the comprehensiveness of those Divine relations which are expressed by "above" and "through," and the limitation of that which **is** expressed by "in." St. Paul really speaks **with** his characteristic manner of repetition, and with **his** characteristic fondness for terms which imply universality, abundance, and fulness. He winds up his brief confession of faith, with the unhesitating and unreserved proclamation of One who is the God and **Father of** all, who is over all, and through all, and in all. With a similar feeling, and with much resemblance **of** meaning, he concludes in another Epistle an outburst of admiration for the mystery of God's boundless mercy, and of God's unsearchable wisdom, with the confession, " For of Him, and through Him, and unto Him, are all things : to Him be glory for ever and ever, Amen."

It is true, however, that when we come to consider the passage in which the words of our text occur, **we** find no necessity in *the bearing of St. Paul's argument*, for making his words refer to any except Christians. He has been enlarging, in the first part of the Epistle, upon the nature and the glories of that calling which had been made known to men in Christ, and to which the Ephesian believers had responded. He has been opening out to them what it means to be *a Christian*. He is himself filled with awe and rejoicing as he contemplates the Divine mysteries revealed in Christ, the mysteries of God's motive, of God's end, of God's grace and love, the mystery that human beings, who **are born and** die, are made the children of the Infinite **God in His** Eternal Son. To St. Paul, the whole duty **of man is** wrapped up in this revelation. What man is to *do*, what he is to *feel*, is involved in what he *is*. His Maker and Father has already prepared the works in which he is to walk. The believer who "considers" Christ, as the Son who makes the Father known, and who believes himself to be a member of Christ, will have the true principles of his daily conduct gradually disclosed to him. He will see plainly what kind of a spirit he must cherish, why he must act in this way, and must not act in that way. St. Paul's primary exhortation, therefore, when he seeks to enforce the practice of Christian morality, is the following appeal to the Christian standing, "I beseech you that ye walk worthily of the vocation wherewith ye are called, with all lowliness and meekness, with longsuffering, forbearing one another in love; endeavouring to keep the unity of the Spirit in the bond of peace. There is one body and one Spirit, even as ye are called in one hope of your calling; one Lord, one faith, one baptism, one God and Father of all, who is above all, and through all, and in all." St. Paul then is evidently enforcing a spirit of unity upon Christians as a fulfilment of filial piety towards their common God and Father. He is not setting forth the condition of men in general, but urging that special Christian unity which was involved in a common fellowship with one God. We shall not do justice to the passage, unless we bear in mind this distinct *argument* into which St. Paul is throwing his thoughts.

At the same time it is impossible for any one who reflects upon these words themselves, especially when he compares them with other expressions in which the same Apostle delighted, not to see that they *must* bear the widest sense which we can put upon them. **His** words would naturally be understood in his day, as they would in ours, to bear such a sense. The heathen were in the habit of speaking **of** the chief god as the **father of** all men, as St. Paul reminded the Athenians when he said, "The Lord of heaven and earth hath made **of** one blood all nations of men for to dwell on all the face of the earth, and hath determined the times before appointed, and the bounds of their habitation, that they should seek the Lord, if haply they might feel after him and find him, though he be not far from every one of us: for in him we live, and move, and have our being; as certain also **of** your own poets have said, For we are also his offspring." St. Paul, being familiar with these thoughts concerning God's relation to men universally, could not have gone on repeating One God and Father of *all*, who is above *all*, and through *all*, and in *all*, with this free delight in the word "all," without the slightest restriction or condition attached to it, if he had not been perfectly willing that that word should be taken in its natural and accepted sense, and that he should be regarded as a preacher of that large theology which refuses to shut out the actings of God's nature from any part of His created universe.

I conclude, then, that in this passage St. Paul, whilst he is thinking of the obligations imposed upon **Christians in** particular by the calling which has **been** made known to them in Christ and which they have confessed, is declaring truths which apply not to Christians only, but to men as men. The One Lord whom he proclaims is Lord of things in heaven and things in earth and things under the earth. The One God and Father whom he proclaims is the God and Father of all men, is over all, through all, and in all.

The Apostle who uses habitually this and similar **language, and** who says nothing that can even plausibly **be set** against it to contradict it, cannot have been **inspired by that fear of** universality which has constantly haunted the most orthodox portion of the Church, **and which gives** rise to much uneasiness and to many warnings and threatenings at the present day. I will endeavour to explain more fully what I mean; **but let me ask you** first to observe how wonderful this *breadth* in the Apostle's doctrine appears, when we put it by the side of the character of that body to which St. Paul belonged.

It is not uncommon to assume that *breadth* of this **kind is the result of** modern knowledge and modern civilization, of the discovery of countries of which the old world was ignorant, **of the** acquaintance which has been gained with **lines of** history which did not meet in that old world, of the enlightened appreciation of the various modes of thought and modes of worship which have prevailed in different lands and times. We can pardon, it is thought, the narrowness **of** our forefathers' views, their readiness to excommunicate those who did not believe with them, their disposition to keep **the** living God of this universe to themselves. They knew nothing of America, nothing **of** China, nothing of Indian philosophy and mythology.

nothing, properly speaking, of the philosophy of history. A little community in the old world, ignorant in the midst of an ignorant society, might well, so men reason, have its exclusions and its definitions, could not help having its hundred limitations of thought and doctrine. It is our business to correct this early narrowness, to retain only that part of primitive Christianity which is compatible with the inevitable liberality of the present age.

So men argue with some truth, and with more appearance of truth. The world at the time when St. Paul wrote and lived was unquestionably ignorant of much that it has been given to us to know. Men's notions of the universe were full of a now exploded absurdity. The Jews had even less of science than the Greeks and the Romans. It was entirely to be expected that a small Jewish sect should be exclusive and intolerant in its way of regarding those who did not belong to it. The sect of Christians was full of a singular confidence and determination, and was yet despised and persecuted—a twofold condition which has always shewn a tendency to make the doctrine of such a sect stern, thorough, and inconsiderate. Moreover, this sect of Christians was eminently aggressive and proselytizing, a character sufficiently represented in the life of St. Paul and his missionary efforts. How earnest were the labours of the first believers in Christ, how affectionate the sympathy shewn, how great the sacrifices made, in endeavouring to win men to the knowledge of Christ, and to draw them into the fellowship of the Christian body! But religious communities which are anxious to gain converts are naturally induced to make out the worst possible case for all who do not belong to them. "What success," it has been asked, "can Christian missions amongst the heathen expect, if you do not maintain that every one who is not a Christian must be eternally lost?" The Pope of Rome in a recent pastoral has thought it necessary to re-affirm solemnly, that all those who deliberately remain outside of the Church of Rome have no chance in the world to come.

To lay down such principles is very natural to religious communities, and would have been not less natural to a society placed in the circumstances in which the first Christian believers found themselves than to any other. Yet we observe that St. Paul, the most zealous and eager of Christian missionaries, the believer who was most thoroughly possessed and penetrated by his Christian faith, had the most special delight in the broadest and most expansive declarations of God's fulness, of His infinite and all-embracing mercy, of His fatherly government of the whole world, and of His fatherly interest in all mankind. When he came amongst heathens we perceive that it was not his custom to speak to them of the doom impending over all who should not become Christians, but of the witness which the Universal Father had given of Himself to all nations, in that he did good and gave them rain from heaven and fruitful seasons, filling their hearts with food and gladness,—or of that providence and inspiration with which He who had made all men guided and attracted towards Himself the indwelling God, each nation placed on the earth according to His design. Let me just remind you of the intense enthusiasm with which the Apostle contemplated the opening of the older covenant to all mankind, and that unrestricted scope and range of God's redeeming and adopting and reconciling grace, which was manifested in the Person of the Son of God made man, crucified, and raised again for men. I say that it is very remarkable to find this breadth and freedom in apprehending God's nature and relation to mankind universally, in the utterances of one who represented a small, struggling, earnest sect, composed of ignorant men who longed to persuade Jews and Greeks and Romans to forsake their old ways, and to cast in their lot with them.

I have already intimated that there are many circumstances affecting ourselves in this day which urge us towards what we might call religious liberalism. The principle of political toleration, the habit of living in social intercourse with those whose faith differs widely from our own, the observation of foreign countries, close alliances with Roman Catholics or Mahometans or members of the Greek Church, the uncertainty of mind upon questions **of** faith which has come **over** Christian nations so widely in these days, these and similar causes make it very difficult for us **to** limit **God's** interest in men to our own communion, to the Church of England, to Protestants, or even to Christendom. These causes would lead us to speak of the **One** God and Father of all, who is over all, though we might not naturally go on **to** speak of Him as *through* all and *in* all. It seems reasonable and inevitable to contemplate God's providence as universal, His teachings as going forth to different nations of various faiths, His loving purposes as not being exclusive but all-embracing.

At the same time this tendency also occasions uneasiness to those who cherish a strict and firm religious belief. There appears to be some opposition between so wide an estimate of God's rule and mercy and that dogmatic reception of Christian truth which we have been taught to be necessary both for ourselves and for all other men. Texts are recalled, with more or less misapprehension of their purport; such as, "he that believeth shall be saved . . . he that believeth not shall be damned;" "he that believeth on the Son hath everlasting life: and he that believeth not the Son shall not see life; but the wrath of God abideth on him." This, it is urged, is the plain testimony of Scripture, whatever human reason may have to say to the contrary. And then a feeling of opposition grows up against liberal conceptions of God's relations to men, as being carnal and worldly, and devices of the Evil One to lull men into a godless security. The Gospel, instead of being a rich and tender message of grace, contracts hard features of condemnation. Jesus Christ is come into the world to condemn the world, first; and, afterwards, to save some few out of its ruins. In daily and social life, the more generous impulses are in danger of being looked upon with suspicion. Religious people think it their duty not to foster such impulses in the young, but to be perpetually cautioning them against the danger of indulging them, and to impress on them the necessity of holding, as matters of faith, opinions concerning the outer world from which conscience and humanity revolt.

And while this spirit of narrowness and fear infects the religious world, the more sceptical and liberal acquire the habit of looking on theological doctrines as primitive fetters from which the world has now broken loose. They regard with a mixture of anger and contempt the efforts of the religious part of society to maintain the influence of dogmatic creeds by appeals to the fears and superstitions of mankind. They are confident that as culture goes on and becomes more general the thoughts of men will be widened by civilization and philosophy, and the old creeds, with their definitions and exclusions, will gradually die out.

And a great number of persons who desire to be sincere and consistent in their convictions are disturbed and distracted by this antagonism, being unable and unwilling on the one hand to resist the influences which lead them towards a liberal way of thinking, and on the other hand feeling inwardly and devoutly what a terrible loss it would be to give up their faith in the Lord Jesus Christ as the one Saviour of men, and in a pure Apostolical Christianity as the one religion for the world.

Now, I have endeavoured to show you this morning that St. Paul, the servant and Apostle of Jesus Christ, and the preacher of Him crucified, was wont to exult, without any of the neutralizing restrictions and uneasy balancings with which we are familiar, in the most free and boundless apprehensions of God's relations to men. At the very moment when he is urging the little flock of believers to be true and consistent believers he points them to the one God and Father of all, who is over all. And observe that he does not say, "In a certain distant sense God is over all men; but His nearer and closer relations are limited to you who believe in Him." He goes on to say that the one God who is over all is also *through* all and *in* all. I cannot now attempt to bring out the meaning of these remarkable and difficult expressions. They describe mysteries, not mysterious doctrines, but mysteries of fact and being. They point to the deep, inexplicable, unfathomable relations that exist between the spirits of men and the Father of spirits, between us who are endowed with reason, conscience, affections, will, and Him in whom, according to the testimony of heathen poets and Christian Apostles, we live and move and have our being. It is impossible to use stronger language than this. Whether you understand it or not you cannot exceed the force of it. If you wish to describe close and intimate relations between God and men you could not say more than that God is through all and in all, that in Him we live and move and have our being.

Shall we say, then, that St. Paul was taught by his knowledge of Greek literature and his own philosophical instincts to correct the narrowness of his Jewish creed? Might we put his views in a form like this? "Although I preach a crucified Man **as the** Son of God and the Lord of Glory, and call upon Greeks and Romans to forsake their worship and to **be** baptized into the service of Jesus, yet, **as** an educated man and a man of the world, I know very well that we cannot think **of** the Divine Being according to the narrow Jewish conceptions of Jehovah, I cannot withhold some sympathy from those Pantheistic ideas which are to be found in the writings of enlightened Greeks." Such an account of St. Paul's views would be utterly mistaken and false. His Greek training, if it had succeeded, as we know it did not succeed, in quenching his narrow Jewish faith, might have made him loosely tolerant, passively and contemptuously sceptical, like the Gallios to whom all religions were equally inevitable and equally fictitious. But this sort of spirit could never have given birth to that joy and adoration with which St. Paul contemplated the largeness and universality of God's fatherly and spiritual dealings with men. The truth is, and St. Paul knew it well in his own heart, that it was the knowledge of Christ which had itself awakened in him these glorious apprehensions. Christ was revealed to him inwardly. He saw the Eternal **Maker** manifesting and proving His fellowship with human beings in the flesh of Jesus Christ the Son of God. What a mystery, what a glory for humanity! **He saw in the** person of Jesus Christ, the genuine and peculiar character of the Divine Nature. He saw condescension **and** sympathy—all the wonder that this word *sympathy* or fellow-feeling strives to express:

he saw a desire not simply to make a man happy by shutting off from him the avenues of pain, but to raise man, through his spiritual consciousness and freedom, to the dignity of a child of God. This elevation he saw could only be brought about by delicate and spiritual methods. Such methods he perceived to be those of God in Christ. He beheld God appealing to man through love and knowledge, drawing him with human cords, changing him into a better nature through the contemplation of that higher Divine nature to which he as man was attached. As he looked up into heaven and the heaven of heavens, where the loving Saviour whom he had persecuted was sitting at the Father's right hand, he could gaze upon the mysteries of God shining out in the face of Jesus Christ. And to one so gazing all separations and distinctions of men disappeared. All, as he felt with shame and sorrow, were sinners alike. All were the objects of a natural affection on the part of the heavenly Father; all were united by a heavenly relationship to that Son of God in whom they were all reconciled to the Father, in whom they all had wisdom and righteousness and sanctification and redemption.

What, then, was St. Paul's inference from these discoveries? Did he say, "Inasmuch as the heavenly Father of all cares for all, and there is a Son of God who has shown by His death what the measure is of His love for His brethren, I, for one, may take my ease and be happy. It is all right. One creed is evidently as good as another, and no doubt in the end each will be shown to have had its truth and its use"? You know how different from this was the Apostle's practical conclusion. He thought within himself in this way: "The Father, **who has** begotten men as children **in** a spiritual relationship to Himself, and who desires to bring them all to know Him and to love Him, has manifested Himself in His Son Jesus Christ. The Son of God has appeared to me and claimed me as His servant. He bade me go forth to carry His name amongst men, labouring and suffering for His sake. This is now the business of my life. To proclaim the Gospel of a Son of God who died and rose from the dead for men, is henceforth the work to which I am devoted. In the strength of my Lord I will do His bidding."

St. Paul was wont to remind himself and others that his Apostolic ministry was a commission which he dared not and could not put off. **But we** know that he found abundant joy and reward in his work. It was a sufficient stimulus and recompense to him to see that, when the Word of God was spoken by his voice, although many mocked and many doubted, yet some everywhere came out of darkness into light, out of strife and jealousies into unity, out of despondency and despair into a blessed hope. The Apostle saw more clearly every day that it was the purpose of the wise Father to awaken and to raise His children *through the Word*. He bade that the Word should be spoken; He confirmed **it** with signs following; and He caused the Word to bear fruit in faith **and joy and** peace, in pure and holy lives. And therefore St. Paul earnestly, undoubtingly, rejoicingly, gave himself to the ministry of the Word.

Is there anything unreasonable or inconsistent or unreal in such a history? Does it not seem to us most reasonable that St. Paul should thus be led through Christ to the knowledge of the one Father of all, and that because he knew the goodness of that Father, he should devote himself to drawing other men to the same knowledge?

Brethren, let us put ourselves at St. Paul's point of view. Let us consider Jesus Christ. Let Him be to us a real way to the Father. It is not the work of Christ to contract and dim the glories of a Father in whom the natural man has hoped. It is the work of Christ to reveal a Father of whom the natural man has hardly dreamt, a living Father, a Spirit, who speaks to the hearts of men, and hears what they say to Him. Let us open our minds without misgivings to the unveiling of such a Father. As we come to know Him for ourselves, we shall be sure that He is also a Father to other men. We cannot rest in a partiality, of which we are to find the evidences in ourselves. We must repose on the absolute righteous love of Him who has made and who sustains us. And as we allow this love to shine upon us, it will more and more constrain us into an answering love, and bind us to all our duty. We shall be ashamed of our wanderings and rebellion, of our hardness of heart, of our thwartings of God's good purposes. We shall feel drawn towards our brethren whom the same Father has made. We shall know it to be a sin against **God to** indulge in pride and jealousy, in an exacting and unforgiving temper towards **our** fellow-men. We shall desire to be frank, generous, unselfish **with our** neighbours; to think not each man of his own things, but every one also of the things of others.

It is true that whilst we thus resolve to believe in the one **God** and Father **of** all men, we may find much to perplex and confound us in the sins and miseries which prevail upon this earth, in the wide prevalence of darkness, and in the slow progress of light. But let us remember that St. Paul and his fellow-labourers had at least as much to perplex and distress them. Let us take refuge, where they took refuge—in the unsearchable wisdom and absolute righteousness and love of God. When baffled by the scenes of earth, let us look upwards again to heaven, where the Son, the mediator between God and men, sits at the Father's right hand. Let us repeat the Gospel **of** redemption to our own hearts, and endeavour to make it credible by our lives and deeds to others. Let us confess it to be an honour and a delight to give ourselves up, body, soul, and spirit, to the service of such a Gospel.

XX.

THOU SHALT LOVE THE LORD THY GOD.

ST. MATTHEW XXII. 37, 38.

"*Jesus said unto him, Thou shalt love the Lord thy God with all thy heart, and with all thy soul, and with all thy mind. This is the first and great commandment.*"

Our Lord is not here professing to enact a new law. He is summing up the teaching of that old Law which had been given by Moses to the Jewish fathers. The same interpretation of the Law had pervaded the appeals of every Jewish prophet. Coupling a second commandment with this first and greatest, our Lord truly says, "On these two commandments hang all the law and the prophets."

It is obvious, indeed, to any one who studies the records of Jewish history, that this devotion to Jehovah as the God of the chosen people was the main principle of Jewish life. Not that such devotion was an irresistible instinct in the Jewish nature—a kind of physiological phenomenon distinguishing the Hebrew race from other races of mankind. According to all the testimony of their history, the natural tendency of the Jews was to forget and desert Jehovah their God. They needed to be continually reminded of Him. They had not chosen Him, but He had chosen them. He had revealed Himself through acts of bounty and deliverance. He had been the guide and helper of the seed of Abraham. He had shown His power to give them over to dreadful punishments when they forsook Him and would not obey His laws. But for all this they rebelled more and more. The false gods of the nations round about them seemed to them more agreeable objects of worship than the righteous Jehovah who claimed them for His own. Cruel, lustful, unequal, selfish gods seemed to them less awful, easier to influence by prayers and gifts, more likely to give them pleasure, than the just and gracious God who inhabited eternity. They continually forsook Jehovah to follow after such Gods. In reading the Jewish history, we are astonished at the perverse infatuation by which the people in every age were led astray into idolatry. To the rulers who were faithful to Jehovah, and to the prophets who were raised up to speak in His name, it seemed a weary and almost a hopeless task to keep the people to their allegiance. Severe and far-reaching punishments were often inflicted upon the idolatrous; the books of the prophets are full of the passionate appeals, the reproachful upbraidings, the promises and the threats, by which those godly men endeavoured to sway the hearts of their countrymen, and to guard them against the temptations which so strongly beset them. Yet, in spite of all these arguments, the Egyptian calf, and Baal, and Ashtaroth, and even Moloch, would draw away one generation after another and pollute them with their sensual rites.

But notwithstanding this proneness of the Jewish people to idolatry, it remains true that the vital principle of their history is devotion to Jehovah their God. It was through the call of Jehovah that they became a peculiar people; it was through the redemption wrought by Him that they were delivered out of slavery; it was by His gift that they received a land to dwell in; it was under His laws that they were organized. The will of Jehovah created the people, and sustained them after they were brought into being. All that was vital and strong in the national existence was connected with the relation established between Israel and Jehovah. The tendency to idolatry lay in the natural animal impulses: the bond which united the people to Jehovah consisted in the gradual revelations made to them, in the voices which spoke to the conscience, in the power which protected and guided, which rewarded and punished, the people. When the Jews were faithful to Jehovah, they were strong and prosperous; when they forsook Him, they fell into internal corruptions, and became object to oppressors. Every man who was a true loyal Israelite, every man whose eyes were opened, whose hands were clean, whose heart was pure, was a devout worshipper of Jehovah; the seeds of all decay, the stains of all pollution, were the signs and fruits of idolatry. And therefore the one great historical lesson for the Israelite to learn, was to flee from idolatry, and to cleave to Jehovah the

God of his fathers, with all his heart **and** soul and strength.

Jesus, then, was announcing no novelty when He gave out the **two** great commandments, Thou shalt love the Lord thy God with all thy heart, and thou shalt love thy neighbour as thyself. He was simply interpreting, in the briefest possible form, the purport of the old Law. He shewed on this occasion, as he did on many others, that He was not come to destroy the Law and the prophets, but to fulfil them.

There is a difference, no doubt, between the faith of the Christian and the faith of the Jew under the old covenant. This difference has given rise to a very exaggerated notion as to the manner and the degree in which Christianity superseded Judaism. People think and speak as if Christ and his Apostles had forsaken the Jewish religion and sought in their ministrations to convert men from that to a religion called Christianity. This is a very erroneous view. Neither Christ nor His Apostles ever abandoned the faith which they inherited, or tried to persuade their countrymen to change their religion. And when we look into the books which tell us how Christ lived and taught, we may well be puzzled to detect any signs of a change of religion. If it was the vital principle of Jewish faith, to be true to the God of Abraham, Isaac, and Jacob, the God of Moses and David and Isaiah and the other prophets, there was **no** one in whom that principle was so perfectly embodied as it was in Jesus of Nazareth. He declared Himself to be the Son of that God whom his countrymen worshipped. It was His Father who had called out Abraham, who had spoken by Moses, who had chosen Jerusalem as a holy city, and who heard in the temple the prayers of devout worshippers. It was the honour of this God which Jesus vindicated against the mock-religion of the Pharisees, who pretended to serve Him, but who knew nothing of Him in their hearts. And who ever fulfilled as Jesus did the great commandment of the Law? The one all-inclusive characteristic of our Lord's life was devotion to His Father, that is, to Jehovah the God of Israel. His meat and drink was to do the will of that Father. His desire was to glorify his Father in all things. The most sifting temptations could not draw Him from filial devotion to his Father; the severest sufferings could not induce him to prefer His own will to his Father's. In Jesus, then, the first and great commandment of the law found the perfect fulfilment, for which, till Jesus came, it had waited. Righteous and good men, genuine Israelites, had found strength and joy in loving the Lord God. They had felt how foolish it was to withhold from Him such love as he himself desired, how blessed it would be to love Him with all their heart and soul and mind. But this they had never been able to attain to. Only the Son of God, knowing the Father in the fellowship of an eternal unity, could surrender himself utterly a perfect sacrifice to God.

It was impossible that one in whom the law was thus fulfilled should seek to diminish the faith of His countrymen in Him who had given the law. His one complaint against them was, that they did no[t] believe in Him enough nor love Him sincerely. "[I] know you," he said, in one of his most commanding rebukes to the Pharisees, "I know you, that ye have not the love of God in you." "How can you believe," he asked, "you who receive honour one from another and seek not the honour that cometh from the only God?" It was unquestionably the purpose of Jesu[s] to re-affirm to the utmost the principle of the law. That which had been the cherished commandment o[f] the Israelites, Thou shalt love Jehovah, thy God, with all thy heart and soul and strength, so far from being repealed, was to become the universal law for mankind.

The Christian who receives this commandmen[t] differs from the Jew of old, not in having anothe[r] God to worship, nor in having different demand[s] made upon him, but in having the same God mor[e] fully revealed to him. The God whom we worshi[p] is the God of Abraham and Isaac and Jacob,—th[e] Jehovah of the national Jewish covenant. But, unde[r] the new covenant, we do not call Him Jehovah. [A] Christian ought to have wider and deeper conception[s] concerning God than were possible to a Jew. W[e] ought to think of Him more habitually as the Go[d] of the universe and of the whole human race, lovin[g] His children impartially, and dealing with the[m] equally. Such thoughts are in harmony with ou[r] **wider** range of knowledge, with the acquirement and habits of modern civilization. But, as I endea[-] voured to show last Sunday, Christian views of th[e] nature and character of God, such as recognise most largely the all-pervading operations of the Divine love and justice, have not grown out of the science and the culture of modern times. They are due to that revelation of the Father which was made in Christ. As the first believers studied the nature of God, not in books, however holy, nor in commandments, however imperative, but in the person of the Son of Man, the horizon of their thoughts was inevitably widened. They saw all mankind embraced in the Son of Man. They discerned the lofty and spiritual character of the relation between God and men. They saw what a perfect fatherliness there is in the love of God towards men; they saw that men's love towards God must be free, enlightened, and spiritual. To the Israelite of old God was known primarily as the Being who had given a promise to Abraham and to his seed, then as the Jehovah, or I AM, from whom the law proceeded. He gained his acquaintance with the name and nature of the invisible God through national forms and symbols, and through acts of providence and government which especially concerned his nation. Various limitations necessarily attended such a knowledge of God, and these limitations are associated with the Jewish name of God. But to the Christian, God is primarily the Father of our Lord Jesus Christ, the Father of the Son of Man. If we could associate Jesus Christ with any race or sect or class of men, to the exclusion of the rest, then we might also limit in our thoughts the fatherhood of God. If we can see anything superficial in the relation between the Father and Christ, then we may also think of the bond between the Father and men as a loose and slight one. But Christ is the Brother and Head of all men; and His Father is the Father of all men. The Father was united to the Son in an eternal spirit of love, the Father knowing the Son and the Son knowing the Father; and Jesus prayed that His disciples might be united to Him and to God, as He was one with the Father.

This ampler and deeper knowledge of **the** same true and only God is what distinguishes the faith of the Christian from the faith of the Jew. It would seem, therefore, that the law, Thou shalt love the Lord thy God with all thy heart and with all thy soul and with all thy mind, so far from having been weakened, must have become only more stringent and absolute. The Jew was commanded to love God because God had called out his race and had delivered it from bondage, and placed it in a good land, and continually manifested Himself in new favours to his people. *We* are called upon to love God because He has so loved us as to send His only-begotten Son that we might be reconciled to Him and might have the life of sonship, and because by His Spirit He is ever speaking words of grace and comfort and hope to our souls. In the name of such mercies and privileges **we** are commanded and besought to give thanks **in** everything **to** God, to love Him as He has loved us, to devote ourselves, body, soul, and spirit, to God's service.

It may seem sometimes that it was easier to a Jew, who thought of Jehovah almost exclusively in reference to his own race and land, to cherish towards God a personal love and devotion, than it is for us, in whom it would be wrong so to limit God's operations. It may seem that our own individual relations to God are lost in His infinitude, in the boundless multitude of souls which may call Him Father, in the universality of His presence, and the impartial distribution of His care and love. When a deity is localized there is a certain familiarity in the local worship with which he is honoured. The god or the patron saint of a city or a district seems to be bound more closely to his clients than a Being who calls all the earth his own. The most famous piety of old heathen times has had this local character. At the present day, in Roman Catholic countries, local saints and Madonnas draw out the more vigorous external manifestations of worship. Any help that may be gained by thus limiting the object of worship to a place or a nation, we are bound, as Christians, to renounce; and at the same time we are called upon to give the deepest homage of our hearts to Him whom we confess as the God and Father of all.

The Scriptures evidently recognise the danger of our losing the one God in the infinite distance of His perfections. The words of Christ Himself declare a certain natural impossibility of coming to the Father. "No man cometh to the Father, *but by me.*" The eternal Father *is* distant, incomprehensible. *But* He has revealed Himself in the Son. It is in Christ that we have the means which God has provided for us, to make our knowledge of Him close and personal and vital. God comes near to us, not through arbitrary associations with mountains or groves or **sacred buildings**, but through the flesh and blood **of the Son of Man. And** in order that Christ, in whom we know and come to the Father, may Himself be real to us, God has given us the records of His life which we have in the Gospels, records of priceless value on this account: that is, not primarily as documents of instruction or a rule of life, but as enabling us to know Jesus Christ in His life and history, as leading us to Him who leads us to the Father.

Here then we have our protection against the vagueness that haunts the worship of the one Universal God and Father, against the desponding consciousness of our inability to climb to so inaccessible a height. We are not commanded to climb up **to** the Heaven of heavens. God has come down to us. He has visited us and dwelt among us. He who is gone up into the heavens that he may fill all things is the same who descended into these lower parts, and tabernacled in flesh and blood, who lived our human life, and died our human death.

Dear brethren, the contemplation of Jesus Christ has been proved in tens of thousands of hearts to have a power beyond that of any local mythology, to make God's love real and near to man, and to stimulate in man a vital undoubting love of God. As the Apostles testified, there are *treasures* in Christ which may be drawn upon without limit in human experience. The *Person* of One, in whom dwelt the fulness of the Godhead bodily, who gathered up in Himself also all the true nature of man, has depths which none of our sounding-lines can fathom.

And therefore, whilst the obligation of loving God with a strong and hearty devotion is laid upon us under the new covenant with only the more force, we are at the same time enabled to meet that obligation as none but Christians could be enabled. A Spirit has been given to us, the Spirit of the Father and the Son, in whose power we may know Christ, and through Him may ascend to the Father. Our duty and our hope consist now, not in looking to earthly and sensuous associations for the support of our religious affections, but in living and walking in the Spirit, as members of Christ who is in Heaven. Let us try whether, thus sought in the Spirit, God is not still to be found not far from any one of us. Let us try whether He does not more tenderly commend His love to us, and constrain us to answer him with a reverent and grateful love. God is not the less One,—not the less the object of a devout personal affection, because He is infinite. In these mysteries which surpass our comprehension, let Christ be an assurance to us,—He whom the Father so loved, and whose love to the Father was the one principle of His existence.

There is another cause, besides that of God's infinity, which may weaken to our minds the force of this commandment, Thou shalt love the Lord thy God. I mean the faint degree in which it is obeyed upon the earth. Even the best persons may not appear to us to be prompted continually by love towards God. We may slide into the notion that love towards God belongs to an exalted **and** exceptional sanctity, instead of being the vital principle of human life, for all men and for all circumstances.

It is true that this commandment is comparatively silent. The principle of love towards God does not assert itself loudly or obstinately in human affairs. It speaks according to its nature, with a certain delicacy of appeal. But the commandment does assert itself in our ears without any modification of its thoroughness.

Thus, it is bound up in our faith and our worship. Everything in virtue of which we call ourselves Christians upholds the testimony that God loves us with a spiritual love, and bids us *love* Him heartily and utterly in return. Just so far as we refuse to admit that we ought to live in the daily constant love of God, so far we are also rejecting the conditions of our calling as Christians. Think how we are baptized in infancy into the name of God, Father, Son, and Holy Ghost, in answer to this claim upon us, and receive his seal, that we may thenceforth grow up in the Spirit, in the fellowship of faith with the Father and the Son. Our earliest Christian instruction informs us of this our consecration to God; it tells us that we are members of Christ, children of **God, and** inheritors of the heavenly kingdom. It **bids** us, therefore, live truly and loyally to God. It recites to us those commandments of which our Lord gave the spirit and the kernel, when He summed them up in the duty of loving God supremely, and our neighbour as ourselves. When we are of an age to take part in the worship of our fathers, we find ourselves members of a Church founded upon Christ, called out of the world into communion with God, cherishing a life not of this earth, but of heaven. Our common prayers testify to us that we are constantly failing in our duty towards God, but that our blessedness lies in seeking forgiveness and returning to God. The most sacred act of our Christian worship, that Sacrament in which every Christian is invited to partake, speaks to us of a union with God in the person of Jesus Christ, which can only be one of love and sympathy. It offers us from heaven the grace of such a union; it commands us to regard ourselves as not our own, but as persons bought with a price, and bound to glorify God with our bodies and with our spirits which are His.

There is something grave and solemn in all this testimony. It is not lightly to be disregarded. It bids us ask ourselves whether it is not practically true. Is it not right for us to love God with all our heart and with all our soul and with all our mind? Let it be true that we have lived thus far with a very imperfect, perhaps with a scarcely appreciable fulfilment of the first and great commandment. Still, thinking of the one only God as the fountain of truth and righteousness and love, may we not trace to a respect for Him, a respect of which we are not always distinctly conscious, whatever has been good in our past life? Does not the mutual affection by which human life is kept together, the honour of parents, the regard for justice, the sense of obligation, contain within itself this principle of the **love of** the perfectly righteous and gracious Being? **And** if we acknowledged ourselves as altogether the children and the servants of God, bound to renounce all other masters and objects of worship, that we might follow Him only at whatever cost, if we made faith alone towards the unseen Father, the ground of our daily conduct, should we not find our life purer, stronger, more useful, and more happy? Such questions are urged upon the honest mind by the consideration of this great commandment, Thou shalt love the Lord thy God. But they are also urged upon us by the special character of our inward moral history. For, as our Christian teaching tells us, we are subjects of a spiritual struggle. Whilst God, the Just and the Good, is claiming us as His, and appealing to us to render ourselves up in our voluntary freedom to Him, other lords are seeking to have dominion over us. There are three powers named to us in our childhood, of whose assaults we are conscious, whose claims we know to be usurpations, to whom we confess it would be ruin to give ourselves up without reserve. The world, the flesh, and the devil, desire to make us their own. We are tempted to grow *worldly*, to grow *sensual*, to grow *false and malicious*. Who is not conscious of these temptations? Who does not know the exceeding subtlety with which they can approach him? Who has not listened to the powerful arguments which would furnish him some excuse for a slavish conformity to the world, for the indulgence of some mere appetite, for the admission of some insincerity or jealousy? And in whom, again, has not a voice been heard replying to these arguments, the voice of the only God, saying, "Thou art mine; thou art a son of righteousness and goodness; thou must not, thou shalt not, confess the dominion of the world, of sense, of the false and dividing spirit?"

Brethren, in these painful conflicts, so often ending in our shame, we may find, if we will, helps towards a simple and a vital love of God. Those enemies of God and of our souls may drive us towards our true Father. We can only renounce them and gain the victory over them through His grace. Looking to Him, and inspired by Him, we may set them at defiance. We may overcome them by faith. This is the victory that overcometh the world, and equally, the flesh and the devil,—even our faith. And our faith is to believe that Jesus is the Son of God, and that we sinful, mortal creatures are made children of God in Him. Let every temptation, therefore, nerve our faith. Let the allurements of the world, the amazing influence of public opinion and of fashion, be resisted in the strength of our allegiance to that Heavenly Kingdom in which the Son of God is Lord. Let the snares of the flesh be trampled under foot in the consciousness that we are spiritual beings, entitled to communion with the Father of our spirits, that our bodies are temples of God, dwelling-places of the Holy Ghost. Let the besetting inducements to dishonesty and ill-will be repelled in the faith that we **are** made members of one another in Christ, that Christ died and rose again to be made the head of **a** Society in which no man should deceive or hurt **his** brother, in which the members should sorrow and rejoice together, **in** which each one should **seek** his neighbour's good to edification.

All these beliefs are gathered up in the expression **of our one duty** towards God, to love Him with all our **heart, and** with all our soul, and with all our mind. Let this simple but awful commandment be continually before us. May it lead us to dwell upon the nature of Him who is altogether worthy of our love. The love of God is the child of the knowledge of God. Let us endeavour, with the use of all means and opportunities which it pleases God to put in our way, to grow in a real knowledge of God. By being sincere with ourselves, sincere in the confession of our uncertainties as well as of our convictions, let us strive that our knowledge may be *real*, and not artificial. Let us make stepping-stones of our very sins by which we may rise out of the dark region to which they belong into light and life. In every effort that we make let us be sure that God Himself is with us and urging us. In ourselves we are weak enough, and the more we are conscious of our weakness the better: **for** the grace of God is all-sufficient, and that is made perfect in our weakness.

APPENDIX.

THE TESTIMONY OF THE CHURCH AND OF SCRIPTURE AS TO THE POSSIBILITY OF PARDON IN THE FUTURE STATE.

It is said by many to be a fundamental doctrine of Christianity, that those who die impenitent are from that moment fixed in impenitence by a Divine necessity, which excludes the possibility of repenting and being forgiven, through the endless ages of futurity. The question to be asked in the following pages of our Anglican formularies and of the Sacred Writings, is whether they impose upon us this belief? I do not present this doctrine in the garb of horrors in which it has usually been dressed. I deal with the moral aspect of it. If a man die without being reconciled to God, are clergymen bound to maintain that by the justice of God he is precluded from reconciliation for ever?

Let us inquire first what the Church of England says in answer to this question; and with this view let us examine her principal formularies in order.

(*a*) The Articles of Religion claim the first place. The Declaration prefixed to them affirms that they "contain the true doctrine of the Church of England." What then do we find here? That the condition of men after death is not set forth in any one of the Thirty-nine Articles. The subject appears to be wholly omitted from this document. The ninth Article states that sin "deserveth God's wrath and damnation;" but the wrath and damnation of

God clearly belong to this life as much as to the next. There is simply no dogmatic statement in the Articles, either primary or incidental, as to the possibilities that may lie hid in the future state.

(*b*) The Three Creeds may be supposed to be formally next to the Articles, for a clergyman of the Church of England; as Catholic authorities they of course stand much higher than the Articles. Two of the Creeds, the Apostles' and the Nicene, have no single expression from which any inference in favour of the ordinary doctrine of future torments could be drawn. The Athanasian Creed, on the other hand, contains the clause, "They that have done good shall go into life everlasting; and they that have done evil into everlasting fire." These latter words have appeared to many to bind upon the clergy the doctrine that a portion of mankind—"they that have done evil"—are to suffer in the next world without cessation and without hope for ever.

We shall return to this clause in the Athanasian Creed, the solitary one that we have to deal with in the Articles and the Creeds, when we have gone through the other formularies.

(*c*) The Catechism is the Church's appointed form of instruction. The only clause in the Catechism bearing upon our subject is that in which the petition, "Deliver us from evil," is explained. "I pray unto God that He will keep us from all sin and wickedness, and from our ghostly enemy, and from everlasting death."

(*d*) The Communion Service involves the profoundest doctrine of the Church relating to sin and redemption. We ought, therefore, to search this service early in our present inquiry. But the most diligent search will find in it nothing that speaks of a hopeless future.

(*e*) The Baptismal Services, again, though it is their express office to set forth a state of salvation (or perhaps, *because* that is their office), are similarly silent.

(*f*) In the Burial Service we pray, " Deliver us not into the bitter pains of eternal death." And the same phrase occurs in the form, " Shall not die eternally." On the other hand, this Service speaks with what has been thought an unwarranted and dangerous hopefulness concerning the promiscuous multitude of those over whose graves it is used.

(*g*) We might perhaps expect some intimation in harmony with the common doctrine in the Collects for Good Friday and Easter Day, or in the Office for the Visitation of the Sick. But there is none. The Litany has the expression, " From Thy wrath and from everlasting damnation, good Lord, deliver us." Throughout the whole of the remaining prayers and services of the Church, if I am not mistaken, we cannot find any statement which even appears to forbid hope to sufferers in the life to come.

As the fruit, then, of our search through the authorized formularies of the Church of England, we have the three or four places which speak of " everlasting or eternal death," of " everlasting damnation," and of " everlasting fire."

The two last of these phrases are taken from Scripture. But the exact expression, " eternal or everlasting *death*," is not to be found in the New Testament. It might however be fairly treated as Scriptural, inasmuch as its equivalents are to be found there; and its logical opposite, " eternal *life*," occurs in passages too numerous to quote. But what is the sense of this term, " eternal death ?" If we had nothing but the words themselves to guide us to their meaning, we should think most naturally of *extinction* or annihilation. The expressions, " to die,—to perish, —to be destroyed,—for ever," are most simply understood as setting forth final disappearance or extinction. It would be a waste of words to quote illustrations of this sense. And I have no hesitation in saying, at this point of the argument, that a far stronger case could be made out from Scripture in support of the extinction of the condemned, than in support of their prolonged and hopeless torment. But I think we are not shut up to that most obvious sense of the word "eternal death." It is a very plain and safe proposition that "death" is the negation of "life." And "eternal life" is named so frequently, and with such varied and definite explanations of its meaning, that we are enabled from it to understand what "eternal death" must be. "This is life eternal," said the Saviour, "that they might know Thee the only true God, and Jesus Christ whom Thou hast sent" (John xvii. 3). "This is the record," says St. John, "that God hath given to us eternal life, and this life is in His Son. He that hath the Son hath life; and he that hath not the Son of God hath not life" (1 John v. 11, 12). "We show unto you that eternal life which was with the Father, and was manifested unto us" (1 John i. 2). In exact harmony with these statements, our Church confesses in one of our daily Collects, that "in the knowledge of God standeth our eternal life." In the face of these and of a multitude of similar passages, no one will contend that "eternal life" means nothing more than endless felicity. It is plain that the life spoken of is *spiritual* life, life for the soul, not dependent upon the changes and chances of this mortal life, but dependent upon fellowship with the Divine Father. It is plain that it belongs to the present stage of existence, as well as to the future. It is plain that it is called "eternal," not to define its duration, but to intimate its kind or quality. It is contrasted with mortal life, animal **or** psychical life. Eternal life is the life of children of the eternal God, the Father and Begetter of their spirits. We are not left at sea therefore, when **we are driven from** the vulgar sense of death, in the phrase "eternal or everlasting death." **We** are enabled to conclude **that this phrase denotes the** condition of souls which are **not enjoying** "eternal life." It is the state of not knowing **God,** of being **out** of fellowship with God, the state **of darkness and** isolation in self. Much misery, much punishment, may attend this state; but suffering is not its essence. What the ultimate extremity of this state may be, whether there is such a thing as an ultimate extremity of "eternal death," any more than of "eternal life," who shall say? What we are now concerned to ob**serve is this,** that the dissolution of the body is nowhere spoken of **as** the beginning or as the fixing of these states. It is implied that they belong to this life, in which escape **and** forgiveness are possible, as well as to the next.

We have interpreted "eternal death" as the negation of eternal life. In the Athanasian Creed, the opposite of eternal or everlasting life is "everlasting fire." We should conclude, therefore, that, if they are not identical, eternal death and eternal fire may be predicated of the same condition. **Now** fire is a great Scriptural symbol. Any one **who calls up to memory** the most striking examples of its use in Scripture, will feel how necessary it is to be cautious **in** the interpretation of it. Let us suppose that in such a place as the Athanasian clause, fire stands for the wrath of God, which is probably the ordinary opinion. God's wrath is against sin. That wrath cannot be inconstant and variable, subject to passion or persuasion. It must be eternal, **as the** nature of God Himself. *It is the eternal* **aspect of the** *Divine nature towards evil.* There is nothing more reasonable therefore, than that if the wrath of God **is** called fire, the fire should be characterized as eternal. **But it** does not in the least follow that the sin, which is the object of the eternal wrath of God, should be fixed without the possibility of repentance in a man's soul, in the next world more than in this.

If we refer for a moment to Scriptural analogy, we find that "everlasting fire" appears to be used interchangeably with "unquenchable fire" (compare St. Matt. xviii. 8, with St. Mark ix. 45), and that Sodom and Gomorrha are represented as suffering the penalty of "eternal fire." (St. Jude, 7). And we are surely led thus to think of eternal as characterizing the fire itself, declaring **it to be** consuming and irresistible, a true type of the Divine wrath, rather than as defining the endless duration of time for which a human being must be subject to it.

But the whole passage in the Athanasian Creed needs **to** be carefully considered. The ordinary interpretation of it is as arbitrary in one part as in the other. The sense commonly put upon it would be, I conceive, as follows :— They that, at the moment of death, are in a state of peace with God through faith and repentance, will at the Day of Judgment enter upon a state of immeasurable and endless felicity ; they that, at the moment of death, are in their natural state and not reconciled to God, will at the Day of Judgment enter upon a state of fearful and endless misery. But the Creed makes no allusion to the state of the soul at the moment of death. Its two classes are, "they that have done good," and "they that have done evil." Is there any one so good as not to have done evil ? St. John and the universal human conscience reply, " If **we** say that we have no sin, we deceive ourselves, and the **truth is** not in us." On the other hand, where can we point to a brother-man of whom we can say that he is so evil as never to have done good? If then human beings in general have done both good and evil, how are we to separate the two classes which are to inherit such different destinies? The question is no easy one. It will be answered very differently. It may be said that God's infinite wisdom is able to strike a balance between the good and the evil that a man has done, and that, according as the good or the evil preponderates, he will be classed with the doers of good or the doers of evil. But who will be satisfied with such an account of God's dealings with men? Another view will be, that true faith, with the forgiveness that follows it, blots out previous evil works; that one who has the true faith is considered as a righteous man and therefore as a doer of good for Christ's sake; and that when a man dies a true believer these benefits accrue to him, however recently he may have come to the state of faith. Let us suppose this to be sound theology; but can it for a moment be said to be the literal grammatical interpretation of the Athanasian article? Any departure from current interpretations is sure to be proscribed as a forcing or straining of the words interpreted; but I ask, can we easily imagine any more violent treatment than the words "they that have done good" must undergo, if they are to yield such a sense as that?

The right principle of interpretation for this clause appears to be one which we must necessarily apply to many passages of Scripture, as well as to a large portion of ordinary human sayings. It is common to lay down general propositions about the good man and the bad man, the strong and the weak, the rich and the poor. When we come to apply them to actual persons, we must speak of the man so *far as* he is good or bad, rich or poor. Very likely the same man may be in different ways or senses, *both* good *and* bad, both rich and poor. **St.** John contains striking examples of this simple and necessary **way** of speaking. "He that committeth **sin** is of the devil; . . . whosoever is born of God doth not commit sin, for his seed remaineth in **him, and he** cannot sin, because he is born of God" **(1** John iii. 8, 9). He says this after having warned his readers that if we say that we have no sin, we deceive ourselves. The only choice in the interpretation of such a passage is, either to assume that St. John was using very exaggerated language, and only meant that one who was born of God does not sin so much as other men or without repenting of it afterwards; or to hold that what he says is strictly true, and that the true son of God does not sin, but at the same time to admit that in any given person there is an "old man" as well as "the new man," and that whilst "the new man," the begotten of God, sins not, there may be much sin to be put down to the account of the "old man," the tendency which confesses the Evil One as its father. Similarly we may believe, that it is the strictest possible law of God's judgment, that they who have done good shall go into eternal life, and they that have done evil into eternal fire (or, as our Lord expresses it, into "condemnation"—St. John v. 29); whilst it may well be true, that the life and the fire, the praise and the wrath, may touch the same person, and that every sinner on the earth, *so far as* he has been a doer of good, shall be rewarded, and *so far as* he has been a doer of evil, shall be punished.

The phrase "everlasting damnation," in the Litany, is identical with the "eternal damnation" of St. Mark, iii. **29,*** and the "eternal judgment" of Hebrews vi. 2.

---

* There is a remarkable "various reading" here, which some critics prefer as more genuine, ἁμαρτήματος **for** κρίσεως. "An

The *act of judging* or condemning is called eternal. This usage is itself enough to suggest that the word "eternal" was not meant to denote simply an endless duration of time. It is not to be transferred from the thing which it qualifies,—the judgment,—to the condition of the human beings who may be brought under it. It expresses a quality in the judgment,—that it is without appeal, *un*temporal, absolute, or *Divine.*

I do not think it can be fairly said that these are attempts to "explain away" the proper meaning of the passages to which they refer. But if they are true, they undoubtedly explain away whatever in those phrases appears at first sight to imply that all human beings who come under condemnation are kept by Divine wrath in endless torments. And these are the only passages I can find in the Prayer Book which seem to require such an explanation; and it follows that the Church of England, in her authorized formularies, says no single word in affirmation of the doctrine for which we are searching. If, however, the reader is not quite satisfied with the interpretations which have been given, let him consider how the case stands. Let him endeavour to realize the momentous nature of that doctrine as it has been commonly taught. Let him observe how other doctrines which are important for us to believe are defined and set forth and involved in our Church formularies. Then let him think of the phrase "eternal death" as occurring some three times with nothing dogmatic said about it, and of the one dogmatic statement, open and subjected to various interpretations, in the Athanasian Creed. And let him ask

eternal sin or offence" has a novel sound; but it may be explained, in harmony with the views here expressed, as a sin against the very nature of God, involving an "eternal" or absolute opposition to Him.

himself whether he can regard such a basis as sufficient for such a doctrine, whether any one has a right to affirm that the English Church has bound her ministers in conscience **and** by penalties to preach it.

It may be contended that the absence **of** clear unquestionable declarations on this subject is due **to** the fact that the ordinary doctrine was taken for granted by the Church **of** England, and therefore indirectly bears witness to the certainty and necessity of that doctrine. But it is impossible to maintain such a position. Imagine that a hearty believer in the doctrine of a hopeless futurity of torment and rebellion awaiting the great mass of mankind, is set to compose a whole body of prayers, services, and dogmatic articles : can you believe that he will omit that doctrine from his work? We know very well the kind of place it would have. We know, too, that other ecclesiastical compositions have contained the doctrine in a very unquestionable form. I will only take two examples. The Larger Catechism, drawn up at Westminster, and received as authoritative by the Presbyterian Church of Scotland, contains the following question and answer :— " What are the punishments of sin in the world to come? The punishments of sin in the world to come are everlasting separation from the comfortable presence of God, and most grievous torments in soul and body, without intermission, in hell fire for ever." And in the Articles of Religion agreed upon in a Convocation of the Irish Church, held in the year 1615, the following clause occurs :— " The souls of the wicked are cast into hell, there to endure endless torments" ("Hardwick on **the** Articles," p. 357). But what proves beyond the possibility **of** doubt that the silence **of** our own Church was deliberate and intentional, is the fact that in **the** Articles adopted **in** the year 1552, there was one relating to this very subject, which afterwards was simply omitted. This Article, the 42nd and last of that earlier code, was headed, "All men shall not be saved at the length," and ran as follows:—"They also are worthy of condemnation who endeavour at this time to restore the dangerous opinion that all men, be they never so ungodly, shall at length be saved, when they have suffered pains for their sins a certain time (*definito tempore*) appointed by God's justice" ("Hardwick," p. 318). It may have been perceived, that an Article referring to "this time" was not suited in form to be permanent; but so important a dogmatic statement would not have been dropped without a substitute on this ground. It must have been felt that it was better for the Church not to pronounce anything dogmatically as to the possibilities of the future life. The moderate and cautious tone of that Article is itself striking: there are few of us who would not admit, as I should for one, that the doctrine it condemns is unauthorized and dangerous. But the Article was wholly withdrawn in the course of ten years. And the Church of England has virtually pronounced that no dogma on the subject of future punishment shall be binding upon her clergy or her members.

The position of the Church in this matter is therefore a neutral one; the question is within certain limits left open. For I fully admit that there is no passage in the Articles or the Prayer Book which holds out a hope to those who die impenitent. The Church formularies are in this respect more cautious and reserved than the New Testament. But then the Church of England proclaims with fearless freedom that Gospel of grace and redemption which, by revealing to us the nature of the righteous and loving God, forbids us to believe in what is contrary to righteousness and love. The Church has taught us to acknowledge a Will which is righteous and gracious towards all men, and has allowed no arbitrary barriers **to be set up,** saying to that Will, " Hitherto shalt thou come, **and** no farther."

We proceed now **to** consider the testimony **of** Holy Scripture, that is, **of** the New Testament, concerning the possibility of forgiveness in the future state. The Old Testament is silent on the matter. Where so little is said of the life beyond the grave, **we** could not expect to find anything declared as to its remoter contingencies.

The New Testament is not like the Prayer Book in supplying very few passages which call for consideration. There are many places which appear to speak strongly on the one side ; there are some which seem to speak more definitely on the other. But by grouping similar sayings together, we may abridge our inquiry within very moderate limits.

Nearly all the passages in the New Testament which speak of future punishment are *figurative*. Certainly this character does not make them unmeaning ; **it** was our Lord's custom to teach the most important truths by means of figures. But in order to understand such passages rightly, we must recognise them as figurative and not treat them as literal definitions; and we must endeavour to ascertain what **the** figures **are** intended to convey. Now certain images frequently recur **in** the Scriptural language relating to future punishment, and it will be convenient to detach these and to consider them separately.

(1.) The most important of them is the " Hell," or " Gehenna," of the New Testament. Of this we find the following account in the " Dictionary of the Bible." Gehenna, or the Valley of Hinnom, was a deep narrow glen to the south of Jerusalem, where the idolatrous Jews had once offered their children by fire to Molech. In consequence of these abominations, the Valley was polluted by Josiah, and became the common laystall of the city, where the dead bodies of criminals, and the carcases of animals, and every other kind of filth, were cast, and, according to some authorities, the combustible portions consumed with fire. From its ceremonial defilement, and from the detested and abominable fire of Molech, if not from the supposed ever-burning funeral piles, the later Jews applied the name of this valley, Ge Hinnom, Gehenna, to denote the place of torment, and some of the Rabbins fixed here the "Door of Hell."

When therefore our Lord used the name of Gehenna, the word suggested, first, a well-known valley devoted to abominations; and secondly, it called up the associations popularly connected with it,—associations due not to the Scriptures of the Old Testament, but to later Rabbinical traditions. We have very imperfect means of knowing what the Jewish notions of future punishment were in our Lord's time, and it is certain that they had no really authoritative expression by which they were defined. But the popular apprehensions of a doom symbolized by the valley of refuse and fires are undoubtedly recognized in some degree by our Lord's use of the popular figure. The terms, "Where their worm dieth not, and their fire is not quenched," appear to have been borrowed as literally applicable to Gehenna from the passage at the end of the Book of Isaiah.

(2.) The image of *Fire* is closely connected with that of the Valley of Hinnom, but it is also used without reference to that valley. In many Scriptural places, its brightness is the key to its interpretation; but its con-

suming and its *purifying* properties **are** those which we have to bear in mind. One of the first thoughts of a Jew concerning **fire** was that it consumed sacrifices; another, that it purged away the dross of metals. Fire does not seem to **have** been thought **of** as *giving pain without destroying*.

(3.) *Outer darkness* is a frequent image in our Lord's predictions of punishment. It implies a lighted house with a feast going on within it. Outer darkness is the dark **of** the night outside the house. Those who are shut out are sometimes described as wailing and gnashing their teeth in the bitterness of disappointment and envy.

(4.) According to a common way of speaking, the due amount of punishment is sometimes represented in the Gospels as a *debt* which must be discharged.

There are few of the well-known passages relating to threatened punishment in which one or other of these figures does not occur. These figures have acquired from **a** long tradition the property of suggesting to our minds the whole system of a place of torment and misery to which the lost are to be consigned, and in which they will curse God for ever without the possibility of repentance or forgiveness. For example, it is assumed that the word "hell" means such a place and condition, and that if this word is seen in Scripture, the testimony of Scripture is a settled matter. It is necessary for the candid reader to **be on** his guard against this assumption. The question **now** raised is, whether that notion of hell be the Scriptural one, and therefore whether the passages which seem to imply it do really mean that and nothing else. Now **we say** that where the word "hell" occurs as the rendering of Gehenna, *the word* means the Valley of Hinnom near

Jerusalem in which refuse was thrown out and the carcases of criminals exposed. It does not therefore of itself include or sustain the common notion attached to it.

Besides the figurative language of the passages we are considering, some of them have another characteristic which introduces an element of uncertainty into their interpretation. They are declarations of punishment and destruction, the fulfilment of which belongs to that coming of the Lord which is to take place within a generation. Let the following passages be compared:—

"What is a man profited, if he shall gain the whole world, and lose his own soul? or what shall a man give in exchange for his soul? For the Son of man shall come in the glory of his Father with his angels, and then he shall reward every man according to his works. Verily I say unto you, There be some standing here which shall not taste of death, till they see the Son of man coming in his kingdom."—(St. Matt. xvi. 26—28. See also xxiv. 33, 34.)

"The Son of man shall send forth his angels, and they shall gather out of his kingdom all things that offend, and them which do iniquity; and shall cast them into a furnace of fire: there shall be wailing and gnashing of teeth."—(St. Matt. xiii. 41, 42.)

"Whosoever shall be ashamed of me and of my words, of him shall the Son of man be ashamed when he shall come in his own glory, and in his Father's, and of the holy angels. But I tell you of a truth, there be some standing here which shall not taste of death, till they see the kingdom of God."—(St. Luke ix. 26, 27.)

Very important and difficult questions are raised by these predictions. Did our Lord and His Apostles really foretell a speedy coming of the Son of man, to be attended by acts of judgment and retribution? Did such a coming take place? If it did not, how are we to regard those prophecies? If no such coming took place, we seem to be shut up to the alternative of supposing the prophecies to be the offspring of a delusion, or of taking them in some non-natural sense. But the more the real history of that generation is studied, the more it may be felt that the phenomena of the time do indicate the "end of an age," the winding-up of a dispensation, a true proclaiming of the Son of man as Lord. Whether all the expressions to be found in Scripture which apparently relate to that proximate Advent can be held to have been fulfilled to the letter, will still seem questionable to most readers. But it is surely better to recognise, if we can, the substantial truth of the New Testament predictions, though we may fail to see the fulfilment of all the language in which they are expressed, than to vindicate the letter of Scripture by the help of arbitrary and non-natural interpretations. In any case, those who candidly consider these predictions will not feel inclined to press their terms in support of a logical theory as to the future state.

The Gospel of St. Matthew contains most of those sayings of our Lord which are thought to threaten hopeless and endless misery after death. Let us consider the most prominent of these.

It is scarcely necessary to dwell on the denunciation addressed by John the Baptist to the Pharisees and Sadducees who came to his baptism.—(St. Matt. iii. 7—12.) The Baptist is evidently speaking of judgments hanging over his hearers and that age, which would have the effect of consuming barren trees and worthless chaff. No serious argument in support of a hopeless existence through the endless ages would be drawn from this passage. But in the fifth chapter we come to some of our Lord's most marked declarations on the subject of punishment.—" Ye have heard that it was said by them of old time, Thou shalt not kill; and whosoever shall kill shall be in danger of the judgment: but I say unto you, That whosoever is angry with his brother without a cause shall be in danger of the judgment; and whosoever shall say to his brother, Raca, shall be in danger of the council: but whosoever shall say, Thou fool, shall be in danger of hell fire" (v. 21, 22). The gradation here presented must be rather startling to those whose only notion of "hell fire" is that of a hopeless futurity of torment. But let us see how an orthodox commentator explains the passage. Dean Alford says, "There were among the Jews three well-known degrees of guilt, coming respectively under the cognizance of the local and the supreme courts; and after these is set the γέεννα τοῦ πυρός, the end of the malefactor, whose corpse, thrown out into the valley of Hinnom, was devoured by the worm or the flame. Similarly, in the spiritual kingdom of Christ, shall the sins even of thought and word be brought into judgment and punished, each according to its degree of guilt; but even the least of them before no less a tribunal than the judgment seat of Christ. The most important thing to keep in mind is, that there is no distinction of *kind* between these punishments, only of *degree*. In the thing compared, the κρίσις inflicted death by the sword, the συνέδριον death by stoning, and the disgrace of the γέεννα τοῦ πυρός followed as an intensification of the horrors of death; but the punishment is one and the same,—death. So also in the subject of the similitude, all the punishments are spiritual; all result in eternal death; but with various degrees, as the degrees of guilt have been." "Gehenna," then, was used by our Lord in this passage as meaning the local valley near Jerusalem. And it appears that this solemn warning says absolutely nothing as to hopeless misery after death. Its intention is to mark guilt, and the degrees of it. The precise nature of the punishment to be inflicted on spiritual guilt is supplied by commentators from elsewhere; it is not stated here.

The justice of the impression derived by the English reader from this and similar passages may be tested in some degree by the mere substitution of its more exact equivalent for the word "hell." Thus, in the 29th verse of the same chapter, we read, "If thy right eye cause thee to stumble, pluck it out and cast it from thee; for it is profitable for thee that one of thy members should perish, and not that thy whole body should be cast into the Valley of Hinnom." This is now obviously a parable throughout. The body, a principal member, the hated doom of the malefactor's body,—are types of the spirit, of a cherished tendency or affection, of the horror and shame of spiritual reprobation. What the consequences of this reprobation may be is not stated. The same image occurs in a warning of our Lord's, given by St. Matthew, xviii. 8, 9, and by St. Mark, ix. 43—48. Jesus is speaking of the sin of causing "little ones" to stumble; and He implies that the man who would corrupt little ones must be himself corrupted first. He therefore urges the most decided acts of self-denial, typified by the excision of a member, in order that the whole man may not go to shame and ruin. In St. Matthew the expression, τὸ πῦρ τὸ αἰώνιον, the eternal fire, occurs once in the place of Gehenna. St. Mark renders this into τὸ πῦρ τὸ ἄσβεστον, the unquenched fire, where their worm dies not, and the fire is not quenched. And the fact that this fire of Gehenna is a symbol of spiritual horror and punishment,—of God's wrath,—is made more obvious by the use of the phrase "to enter into life." Although it might be contended that even in these passages there is no departure from parabolic language, it ought, I think, to be admitted that the spiritual reality nearly breaks through the imagery,—that the life spoken of is hardly to be distinguished from spiritual life, and that "the eternal fire" is almost a direct expression for that wrath of God which burns eternally against sin. But that the eternal wrath of God against sin forbids men to repent in another life, when its declared aim is to drive men to repentance in this life, certainly cannot be inferred from these places.

There are two parallel passages, in which the meaning of "Gehenna" becomes still more distinctly spiritual. "Fear not them which kill the body, but are not able to kill the soul; but rather fear him which is able to destroy both soul and body in Gehenna."—(St. Matthew x. 28.) "I will forewarn you whom ye shall fear. Fear him, which after he hath killed hath power to cast into Gehenna." (St. Luke xii. 5.) It seems to be plainly implied in these warnings, that, beneath and beyond any harm that can happen to the body, there is a state of horror into which souls may enter through sin. Upon this point our Lord's language is very clear; but it is straining sayings like these beyond the meaning they naturally bear, to see in them any affirmation of the endlessness of an impenitent state.

A comparison of the Scriptural places in which the image of *fire* occurs would show strikingly with what freedom and variety, as well as frequency, the greater natural phenomena are used in Scripture for purposes of illustration. But we have to do with those passages only in which it sets forth *punishment* **or** *pain*. When the element of fire is seen at its work, it generally appears to **the** eye to *burn up* what it lays hold of; things burnt disappear from the sight. At other times, as especially in the case of metals, fire works changes which are said to leave the material *purer* than it was before. Dry wood is burnt up, gold is refined, **by the** action of fire. Accordingly in Scripture **fire** represents a power that consumes or that purifies. The fire of God is spoken of as continually burning in the world, consuming the ungodly and their evil works. The Old Testament is full of such uses of this image; and it is applied with the same breadth and simplicity by our Lord and the New Testament writers. In most places, the thought appears to be rather that of sweeping out of the world,—destroying as dry wood or chaff is destroyed,—than of any torment after death. It would be easier to infer total extinction than never-ending torment from these passages. But in truth to infer either is to push the image too far. If we look beyond the "destruction," we must seek other materials for forming our expectations.

I have already referred to some of the best known places in which destruction by fire is threatened. The words of John the Baptist **are** illustrative enough to represent all sayings of this class: "Now also the axe is laid unto the root of the trees: therefore every tree which bringeth not forth good fruit is hewn down and cast into the fire. . . . . He that cometh after me . . . . shall baptize you with the Holy Ghost and with fire. Whose fan is in his hand, and he will throughly purge his floor and gather his wheat into the garner; but he will burn up the chaff with unquenchable **fire**" (St. Matthew iii

10—12; St. Luke iii. 9, 16, 17. Compare also Matt. vii. 19; xiii. 42, 49; Mark ix. 49). There is a remarkable saying of our Lord's which ought to be specially noticed "I am come to send fire on the earth; and what will I if it be already kindled?" (Luke xii. 49.) These passages speak of destroying the evil and saving the good. There is no carefulness to distinguish between the fire by which the good is purified, and the fire by which the evil is consumed. There is no reason for placing the operation of this fire in the life beyond the grave more than in this present life, but the contrary.

In St. Matthew viii. 11, 12, we read as follows:— "Many shall come from the east and west, and shall sit down [to a banquet] with Abraham and Isaac and Jacob, in the kingdom of heaven. But the children of the kingdom shall be cast out into *outer darkness*: there shall be weeping and gnashing of teeth." (Compare xxii. 13, xxv. 30; St. Luke xiii. 28, xiv. 24.) The meaning of these passages turns upon the phrase, "the kingdom of heaven." The punishment is exclusion from the light and privileges of that kingdom. Gentiles would enter into it; Jews, the natural children of it, by their unbelief would shut themselves out. Now, it is needless, I believe, in the present day, to prove that the kingdom of heaven does not mean a place of infinite happiness on the other side of the grave,—that it has to do with this earth as well as with the invisible region or the future state. The admission of Gentiles and the shutting out of Jews, so far from referring *only* to the future life, referred primarily to the present life. How then should any argument as to the special hopelessness of the future state be drawn from these passages?

There are two of our Lord's parabolical sayings which

may be considered under this head, inasmuch as they both imply exclusion from the shelter and enjoyments of a house. One of these is to be found in Matt. xxiv. 45—51, and in Luke xii. 42—48. Our Lord is declaring the punishment with which the master will visit a profligate and riotous steward. "The Lord of that servant shall come in a day when he looketh not for him, and in an hour that he is not aware of, and shall cut him asunder and appoint him his portion with the hypocrites [or, with the unfaithful]; there shall be weeping and gnashing of teeth." The word διχοτομήσει presents some difficulty here. It is translated quite faithfully in the English version; and both in Greek and English it might no doubt mean, "shall cut him bodily in two pieces," like those spoken of as being sawn asunder (Heb. xi. 37); but this meaning seems too violent for the context. It sounds strange to speak of a man thus cut into two parts, as having his portion with hypocrites that wail and gnash their teeth. More probably, therefore, it is to be taken in the sense, "shall cut off or divide asunder utterly from the lord's establishment." Then the punishment is the same as that indicated by being driven into the outer darkness, where also is wailing and gnashing of teeth, the bitterness of disappointment and envy. The other saying is reported in Matt. vii. 13, 14, and in Luke xiii. 23—30. The disciples are exhorted to "strive to enter in at the strait gate." The strait gate and the narrow way lead "into life," in St. Matthew; into a house where an entertainment is going on, in St. Luke; into the kingdom of heaven, we may add from similar passages. Our Lord saw "few" really entering in at that narrow gate; many walking along the broad way leading to destruction. He knew that some, under the pressure of punishment, would try to thrust themselves irregularly into the safety of His kingdom. To these He would be compelled to say, "I never knew you." It is, perhaps, worth while to mention that the original expression in the question, "Are there few that be saved?" is οἱ σωζόμενοι. "Are they few who are being saved, who are escaping into safety?" Every scholar knows that in such a case the present tense is not used carelessly for the past or the future.

We return to the fifth chapter of St. Matthew, to consider those threatenings which involve the figure of *debt* and its payment. The first example of these is in verses 25—26. "Agree with thine adversary quickly, whiles thou art in the way with him; lest at any time the adversary deliver thee to the judge, and the judge deliver thee to the officer, and thou be cast into prison. Verily I say unto thee, Thou shalt by no means come out thence till thou hast paid the uttermost farthing." (Compare xviii. 34, 35; St. Luke xii. 59.) These passages all appear to relate to making up a quarrel with a brother. Our Lord's teaching is, that if we are exacting towards our brother, God will be exacting towards us. With what measure we mete, it shall be measured to us withal. Now certainly if God requires of us strictly all that is due from us to Him, we can never pay it, and we must remain for ever in prison. But God is ready at any time to remit the payment, when our mind towards our brother changes; and if the possibility of such remission in this life is not excluded by our Lord's threat, what is there to exclude a similar possibility in the next life? Our Lord draws here no distinction between the two lives. Dean Alford's comment is instructive: "These words, as in the earthly example they imply future liberation, because an earthly debt can be paid in most cases, so in the spiritual counterpart they amount to a negation of it, because the debt **can** never be discharged." That is, the natural meaning of **the** image must here be inverted, in order to make it agree with a doctrine supposed to be derived from other sources.

I have reserved for concluding remarks two grand passages, relating to judgment and the punishment to follow, which are used as the chief supports **of** the doctrine of endless and hopeless torment. Two chapters in St. Matthew, xxiv. **and** xxv., contain a discourse, or a series of discourses, delivered by Jesus in answer to the question, "Tell us, when shall these things **be?** [the casting down of the buildings of the temple:] and what shall be the sign of thy coming and of the end of the world?" These discourses wind up with a scene of unexampled sublimity, in which Jesus describes the judgment which the King, the Son of Man, shall pronounce and execute at His coming. Now, the first observation which a reader would naturally make upon this prophecy is this, that it applies to the time when the temple was to be destroyed. The prophecy is strictly continuous. The marks of time in it are peculiarly emphatic and distinct. The subject of it from the beginning is the coming of Christ and "the end of the world" (or the winding-up of the age, $\dot{\eta}$ συντέλεια **τοῦ** αἰῶνος). Jesus proceeds to announce what the signs of that coming will **be.** They relate **to** Judea and "the holy place," to the persons actually standing before Jesus, to the generation which had already begun. In xxiv. 31, 32, Jesus declares that the Son of Man will come in the clouds of heaven with power and great glory, and will send His angels to gather together His elect. Then without any interval He proceeds: "Now learn a parable of the fig-tree: when his branch is yet tender, and putteth forth leaves, ye know that summer is nigh: so likewise ye, when ye shall see all these things, know that it is near, even at the doors. Verily I say unto you, This generation shall not pass, till all these things be fulfilled. Heaven and earth shall pass away, but my words shall not pass away." Every succeeding paragraph of this wonderful prophecy is closely connected with its subject, both by the time-mark "Then," and by the terms in which the coming of the Son of Man is expressed. To judge by a simple straightforward reading of these chapters the scene of the Son of Man sitting upon the throne of His glory belongs as properly to the time of the destruction of the temple, as the fleeing of those in Judea into the mountains.

Critics who do not care whether our Lord's words as reported in the Gospels have proved themselves true or not, see clearly enough the unity of subject in these chapters. They have no difficulty to overcome. But Christian readers have been perplexed by what they have assumed to be the fact, that the greatest of the events which our Lord predicts did not occur at the time of the destruction of Jerusalem. They have said, Whatever in this prophecy was not then fulfilled, must be awaiting fulfilment at a later coming, and we must take it as having been spoken with reference to that more distant time. In the discourses themselves they can find no shadow of a reason for making such a distinction. They have no criterion enabling them to say, This relates to the destruction of Jerusalem, this to the coming which has yet to take place,—except the popular notion of what was fulfilled in that generation and what was not. They are manipulating the words of Scripture in a most arbitrary manner, in simple obedience to a supposed exigency of faith.

The real question for the pious reader and interpreter cannot be any longer, which verses are to be referred to one coming, and which to another; but, how far can we trace in the events of that age a real fulfilment of this whole prophecy? I **do** not deny that there will be **much** difficulty in giving a literal fulfilment **to** all the expressions applied **in** Scripture to the Coming of the Son of Man. Still less do I deny that we of these later ages are warranted in looking for a yet future judgment. But I **do** contend that our business with passages like these **in** Matt. xxv. 31—46, is to trace their relation to the Divine dealings with men at the close of the Jewish dispensation and of the old world. Approaching this scene from such a point of view, or indeed from any point of view, we might reasonably see in it something of a *dramatic* character. Few interpreters would contend that the scenery is a literal transcript of fact. If it is not, who is to determine the exact degree of licence to be permitted in the explaining of it? But we need not ask for licence, we may desire to do full justice to every word of this written picture, if we accept it as setting forth in its own manner the strict *principles* upon which the Son of Man did then judge the old world, and always will judge nations, churches, and individual men. We see, then, two opposite habits of life described, represented in doing and refusing to do acts of charity towards brethren of the Son of Man. We see judgment pronounced upon these habits of life by the Son of Man. We see rewards and punishments meted out. Inheritance in the kingdom of the Father and of the Son of Man is freely given to those who have been kind and generous to human beings; exclusion from that kingdom, separation from the Son of Man in his glory, partnership with the evil spirits in the eternal unquenchable fire of the Divine wrath, is the lot of those who have *not* ministered to human wants and sufferings.

Let it be admitted that at first sight the words "eternal fire," and still more, "eternal punishment," might naturally be taken to imply that the condemned would be kept for ever hopelessly in torment. But then we may urge on the other hand that the analogy of these phrases elsewhere, (as in St. Jude 7,) suggests a different meaning; that we are always led to think rather of the *nature* of that which is called eternal, than of the length of time during which human beings may be subject to it; that the judgment in this case might be maintained to come upon communities rather than upon single persons; and lastly, that the disciples were plainly taught to look for the judgment at the proximate coming of the Son of Man. These considerations are surely sufficient, if not to establish the right interpretation of the passage, at least to prevent its being used as an irresistible proof of the hopelessness of the future state.

The story of the rich man and Lazarus, in the 16th chapter of St. Luke, belongs to the same class with the scene we have just been considering. It is not exactly a parable, but it is dramatic, and requires to be interpreted upon the same principles as a parable. Like so many of our Lord's parables, it was aimed directly at the Pharisees, and threatened them with downfall and discomfiture. The imagery is that of the common Jewish notions in our Lord's time. The representative poor man is shown to be an object of heavenly care by being carried by the angels into Abraham's bosom; the rich man goes down to Hades and finds himself in torments. An appeal of the rich man to Abraham is met by a stern rebuff, in which, however, we observe that Abraham addresses him as "Son." A great gulf is said to be fixed between Abraham and Lazarus on the one side, and the rich man on the other. Then the rich man is represented as pleading, in an admirable spirit, for his five brothers, desiring that they may repent. Not satisfied with one repulse, he continues: "Nay, father Abraham, but if one went unto them from the dead, they will repent."

The first thing which strikes one in this story is perhaps its peculiarly Jewish complexion. It is an *argumentum ad hominem* addressed to the Pharisees, appealing against their inhuman pride and selfishness to father Abraham, to Moses and the prophets, without any mention of God or of the Son of Man. The next remarkable point in it is the singularly unqualified way in which the fortunes of the rich and of the poor are represented as reversed in another world. And then there is something very striking in the effect produced by his sufferings upon the rich man. The proud man is humbled, the hard and selfish man is filled with concern about his five brethren. Looking at these features of the story, it would seem very forced indeed to deduce from it the ordinary doctrine of future punishment. The theory of a purgatory would find here much more support. But we are reminded of the expression, "Between us and you there is a great gulf fixed:" does not this imply, it is asked, that the doom of the departed, once assigned, cannot be altered? Not necessarily, we must answer, if this saying is about to be applied to the proof of an important doctrine. It implies that the difference in the conditions of the rich man and Lazarus was real and decisive. There was no moving backwards and forwards between the two. But this is all that is affirmed, and all that is needed, for the lesson of the story. No affirmation whatever is made as to the possibility or impossibility of a change during an endless future.

On the whole, a rapid survey of our Lord's teaching, with especial reference to the subject of punishment, leaves upon the mind the impression that He was accustomed to proclaim a real and effective retribution, to a degree not at all recognised in the ordinary notions of that teaching. Those who think of Christ as an utterer of mild precepts, must shut their eyes to the stern threatenings which form so large and so marked a feature of His discourses. It shows an equal ignorance, to speak of the retributions of the New Testament as contrasted with those of the Old, in referring only to the future life, or in dealing with individuals instead of communities. Our Lord's great threatenings were against the Pharisees and Jerusalem, to be carried out in the sweeping away of the Jewish nation and polity. But this aspect of the Christ of the Gospels has become unfamiliar to our eyes; and the ideas of righteous Divine retribution now take root less easily in religious minds than in those of a secular and political bias.

To what cause is this fading out of the ideas of retribution to be ascribed? Perhaps to nothing so much as to the prevalence of the ordinary doctrine of endless misery and endless bliss. The mind feels it absurd to think or speak of just reward and punishment in the presence of this doctrine. If the normal destiny of mankind be a hideous and hopeless doom, from which certain individuals are happy enough to escape into an infinite felicity, how idle it must be to look for evenly just recompense, for the few stripes or the many stripes, for promotion from ruling over few things to ruling over many things! If when you say that God is perfectly just, you mean that one single sin, or an inherited taint, naturally and justly brings upon a human being an endless existence of rebellion and torment, and that a belief in Christ at the time of death justly changes this prospect into one of unspeakable happiness, you may be very eager to win the happiness and escape the misery; but you no longer retain any real idea of justice, of justice to be trusted in or to be imitated. The retributions which come to men in the ordinary course of the world must seem to be quite apart from the justice of God as defined by theology.

The natural antagonism between the belief in retributive justice and the belief in an alternative of hopeless misery or secure happiness is strikingly confessed by a sagacious writer who holds firmly to the latter. In "The Restoration of Belief," Mr. Isaac Taylor asserts strongly the necessity of "*fixedness*" in the two future states to produce a sufficiently powerful effect upon the hopes and fears of the mass of mankind. After contending to this effect he admits that "the sense of fitness, order, and justice, demands *a doctrine of quite another sort*." This moral necessity is satisfied in the teaching of Christ when "He gives expression to the doctrine of an exactly adjusted and an evenly meted-out retribution," "such as shall approve itself to all well-constituted minds." "This doctrine stands before us on the one hand quite as sharply defined as does the other doctrine on the other hand." "But now do we not discern an incongruity in these two beliefs? Does not the one doctrine cut across the path of the other, and seem to contradict or to dislodge it?" Mr. Taylor will not attempt to reconcile them; he thinks that a pious reader of the New Testament, accepting each separately, will derive benefit from both. "On the one hand, the prospect of an absolute and irreversible alternative of happiness or woe takes effect, with unutterable force, upon the religious instincts, giving power and intensity to the religious life. On the other hand, the counter doctrine, which is not less distinctly set out to view, meets the requirements of a healthy reason, and of a conscience sensitive, well-informed, and exercised among and upon the duties and trials of real life." But hitherto logic has succeeded in shutting out one doctrine or the other. "Why has not Christ's teaching concerning an impartial and rigorous future retribution, touching all men, hitherto taken the prominent place which of right belongs to it in our theologies? Why? because we could not allow it to come into any such position without risk to the counter-doctrine of an absolute alternative of good or evil." Mr. Taylor's advice is, that we should believe both equally, without regard to logical consistency, Christ Himself not having said a word "to fill up the chasm in his religious system." But the advice, though tempting, is dangerous; for the antagonism is not, as Mr. Taylor assumes, only logical, but at least as much moral. And there is no such chasm to fill up in the religious system of Christ, if the very passages which have been loosely read as affirming the "irreversible alternative," the "fixedness" of the two states, are those in which the idea of a just retribution shines most clearly. It is the general impression, to judge from ordinary arguments, that the two ideas are, not antagonistic, but identical. Those who are repelled by the doctrine of an irreversible alternative of happiness or woe, are charged with disliking the thought of a rigorous future retribution. But the truth is, as Mr. Taylor says, that the former doctrine has actually dislodged the latter. [See "Restoration of Belief," pp. 276—282.]

In looking for the Scriptural passages upon which the prevalent doctrine bases itself, we have little occasion to go beyond the three first Gospels. St. John's Gospel, the

Acts, and the Epistles, contain altogether but few phrases or statements likely to be adduced; and these, with the more numerous passages from the Apocalypse, might be classed with one or other of those which we have considered in the earlier Gospels. We are led, therefore, at this point to observe, that the threatenings of eternal fire and destruction belong to the most strictly *Jewish* portions of the New Testament; they are expressed in Jewish imagery, and they relate mainly and primarily to judgments on the Jewish people. In the other parts of the New Testament, although the idea of retribution and judgment is never wanting, it is expressed in language to which the prevailing doctrine cannot pretend to appeal.

In St. John's Gospel, "eternal life" might almost be said to be the key of our Lord's discourses, and there is an abundant recurrence of the thought of "condemnation." But then it is placed beyond all doubt that eternal life describes a state upon which men may enter before death, and that condemnation also affects this life as well as the next. "He that believeth not is condemned already" (iii. **18**). "He that believeth on the Son hath everlasting life; and he that believeth not the Son shall not see life; but the wrath of God abideth on him" (iii. 36). From which saying it may, with precisely the same truth, be argued that on this side of the grave there is no escape from that eternal and abiding wrath into the state of faith, as that there is none on the other side of the grave. Nothing whatever is said or implied as to death being the commencement of irreversible conditions. Our Lord says, indeed, in another place (v. 28, 29), that "they that have done good shall come forth unto a resurrection of life, and they that have done evil unto a resurrection of judgment." But we have seen these **words,** *life* and *judgment* (or damnation), used freely of this life as well as of the future; and therefore we do not see in them, as they stand, an assertion of anything irreversible in the condition of those who enter into the life and the judgment. And I have already contended, in considering the similar clause in the Athanasian Creed, that such statements are to be held as distinct and peremptory assertions of principles, rather than as defining sharply the total condition of living persons. There are no human beings who have done good only; perhaps there are none who have done evil only; but in every case the doing of good shall be rewarded with life, and the doing of evil shall come under judgment. The same person may be a subject both of quickening and of judgment.

In the Acts of the Apostles I have not found any passage which calls for consideration.

In the whole series of St. Paul's Epistles, there is one place certainly to which we should be at once and confidently referred; but I think not more than one. At first sight, perhaps, the glorious assertion of God's even-handed justice in Romans ii. 2—16, might be supposed to favour the view of an irretrievable state of impenitence and misery; but on closer observation, it will be seen to belong to the contrary side of Mr. Isaac Taylor's pair of opposites. And will not that other passage to which I have alluded really range itself upon the same side also? Let us read it, in 2 Thess. i. 6—10, "Seeing it is a righteous thing with God to recompense tribulation to them that trouble you, and to you who are troubled rest (ἄνεσιν) with us, when the Lord Jesus shall be revealed from heaven with His mighty angels, in flaming fire taking vengeance on them that know not God, and that obey not the gospel of our Lord Jesus Christ; who shall

be punished with everlasting destruction, from the presence of the Lord and from the glory of His power; when **he** shall come to be glorified **in** His saints, and to be admired in all them that **believe**." Who does **not** see here that we have **a** prediction **of** the same class with those **in** our Lord's prophecy **of** his coming, professedly relating to the age of those who were addressed, declaring in high prophetical language the triumph of the Son of Man, and the establishment of his kingdom? It is needless **to** dwell at any further length upon this passage.

We might class with this as throwing light upon it, the words in the Epistle to the Hebrews (x. 26—31), denouncing, in the spirit and with the solemnity of our Lord's threatenings, real and severe, but at the same time just vengeance upon apostates from the faith of Christ. An argument might be drawn, as is well known, from this passage, and others in the same Epistle, especially the awful words in vi. 4—8, in support of the impossibility of repentance and forgiveness *in this life* for those who have fallen away: but it would be monstrous to argue that, because the writer speaks of repentance as impossible in this life, it *is* possible in this life, but impossible in the next.

In the book of Revelation the image of fire recurs in more terrible and more brilliant forms than it wears in any other book of Scripture. It is associated with many other images of less certain significance. We read of Babylon the great being utterly burned with fire; of the beast and the false prophet being cast alive into a lake of fire burning with brimstone; of death and hell being cast into the lake of **fire**. Any one who reads the whole book **or the** chapters containing these words will feel assuredly **that** there is some awful significance **in** them; but, if he is reverent and cautious, he will shrink from building upon them any general doctrine which is not elsewhere stated in plainer language. Who indeed would venture, in confessed default of other Scriptural proof, to infer one of the most important of doctrines from the most figurative chapters of the Apocalypse, from the judgments denounced on the beast and the false prophet and Babylon? I am quite content to appeal in this case to the very general sense of uncertainty as to Apocalyptical interpretation. But I will at the same time express the belief—a growing one amongst the more reasonable interpreters—that the prophecy of this book relates, in the main, to those same "days of vengeance," of which our Lord spoke as coming on the earth, "that all things which are written may be fulfilled" (St. Luke xxi. 22). It appears to be a prediction of the triumph of the kingdom of the Son of Man over the two powers, having their centres respectively at Jerusalem and at Rome, which sought to destroy it.

It has not been the object of the present inquiry to consider the whole Scripture doctrine of rewards and punishments. We are only sifting the testimony of Scripture upon the question, whether the future condition of one of the two divisions of mankind must be believed to be absolutely hopeless and given up to a persistent impenitence. We have had under review the principal passages which seem to point to the affirmative conclusion; and concerning these we have seen reason to think as follows: that they are mostly *figurative*, using images drawn from Jewish rabbinical traditions; that they are mostly limited to the scope of Jewish prospects, threatening a destruction to come in that age upon systems and communities which set themselves up against the Son of Man; that they set forth a genuine vengeance of God, pursuing what is inhuman and ungodly to the utmost; but that they cannot, without diverting them entirely from their natural meaning and application, be interpreted as defining the nature of human existence during the endless ages of futurity. **We** have seen that the parts **of** Scripture less imbued with what may be called local Jewish colouring, such as the fourth Gospel, the Acts, the Epistles, hardly furnish any passages of a similar character, but that the idea of punishment which they set before us is that of a discriminating retribution, vested in the Son of Man. Looking at this side alone, does not the candid reader feel that we are really free from the oppression which has been put upon us in the name of Scripture? But we are now to ask what Scripture says on the other side.

I of course anticipate the comment, that the passages hitherto discussed have been strained with more or less ingenuity from their straightforward, which is their popularly-accepted, meaning. Any change of interpretation, even from the most forced to the most natural sense, is liable to this charge at the hands of those who do not sympathize with it. But, apart from fairness and truth, it is very much the interest of those who may agree with the present writer to claim that the most straightforward and natural sense of Scriptural assertions should be accepted. The passages now to be quoted would need to be very much strained indeed before they can be brought into harmony with the popular doctrine.

The three first, or so-called Synoptic, Gospels hardly **contain** any direct hint of the possibility of recovery or repentance in the future state. **But** there is one remarkable saying of our Lord's which may be quoted here.

The three Evangelists all contain Christ's fearful sentence upon blasphemy against the Holy Ghost. In St. Matthew (xii. 32) the following words occur: "Whosoever speaketh against the Holy Ghost, it shall not be forgiven him, neither in this world, neither in the world to come." This seems to imply that in the world to come, as in "this" world, *other* offences might be forgiven. The inference would not be a strong enough foundation for a positive belief; but it has been thought such a clear and fair inference, that some commentators (as Olshausen), holding firmly to the doctrine of an irreversible condition after the Judgment Day, have expressed an opinion that *between* Death and the Judgment Day forgiveness may be possible.

There is more of direct assertion in the saying recorded by St. John (xii. 32), "I, if I be lifted up, will draw all men unto me." It is not obvious why our Lord should have said "*all* men" if He only meant *some*. But perhaps it may be legitimately explained; and as the emphasis is rather upon the 'drawing' than upon 'all men,' it would imply a distressed theology to make much use of this text.

St. Paul is the sacred writer who speaks with real explicitness on this side. It is not upon particular intimations and promises that a wide and unrestricted hope as to the future can be grounded. The Saviour might have given these, but he has not done so. Such a hope grows out of a contemplation of the Eternal Mind and Will of God. St. Paul, to whom the Gospel of Christ was glorious and precious, because it was a revelation of God's eternal purpose, could not help believing in the real and satisfactory fulfilment of that purpose. He has no universalist theory about a future of happiness for every one after a certain time or quantity of suffering; but he trusts in the continued energy of that will of God which was manifested in Jesus Christ. He studied the will of God in the person of Christ; in Him he **saw no** limitations **of** righteousness or love, no dividing of the human race into two sections. He saw the whole human race gathered up in Christ, the object of Divine love, reconciled to the Father in the Son. He therefore spoke words of faith and **hope** which a modern preacher of popular orthodoxy would never dream of repeating—which he would not quote if he could help it, and never without neutralizing them by qualifications.

Thus, in Romans v. 12—21, St. Paul expressly makes the work of grace in Christ co-extensive with the work **of** sin. "Death," he says, "passed upon all men, for that all have sinned." But then the grace of God has the more abounded, "For if by one offence death reigned through one man, much more they which receive the abundance of grace and of the gift of righteousness shall reign through one, Jesus Christ. Therefore as by the offence of one [judgment came] upon all men ($\text{εἰς πάντας ἀνθρώπους}$) to condemnation, even so by the righteousness of one [the free gift came] upon all men ($\text{εἰς πάντας ἀνθρώπους}$) unto justification of life. For as by one man's disobedience many (*the* many, οἱ πολλοί) were made sinners, so by the obedience of one shall the many **be** made righteous. Moreover the law entered that the offence might abound; but where sin abounded, grace did much more abound: that as sin hath reigned unto death, even so might grace reign, through righteousness, unto eternal life, by Jesus Christ our Lord." I am aware that theologians are not to be surprised by the quotation of this or similar passages; **they** are quite ready with some explanation of them. They will say that we are of course to take the condemnation as *in esse*, the forgiveness as only *in posse*. They will say that πολλοί in one clause means "all," in the other it means "some." "A common term of quantity is found for both, the one *extending to its largest* numerical interpretation, the other *restricted to its smallest.*" Or they will say that all this in which St. Paul glories is *conditional* upon the due repentance in this life. Well: when there is any mention of modifying the natural sense to meet the exigencies of theological opinion, let these explanations be borne in mind.

The subject of the rejection of Israel, discussed in chapters ix.—xi. of the Epistle to the Romans, leads St. Paul to speak of God's final purposes. He has great heaviness and continual sorrow in his heart because of his brethren according to the flesh. He has seen God's mercy, to all appearance, transferred from the chosen people to the Gentiles. He bows before God's dealings, being sure that they must be right. But he does not acquiesce in the rejection of Israel. He saw, in the acceptance of himself and of other Jews, an earnest that God yet remembered His own people. He hoped for the time when Israel might recover from his blindness. "For I would not, brethren, that ye should be ignorant of this mystery, lest ye should be wise in your own conceits; that blindness in part is happened to Israel, until the fulness of the Gentiles be come in. And so all Israel shall be saved. . . . For as ye in times past have not believed God, yet have now obtained mercy through their unbelief; even so have these also now not believed, that through your mercy they also may obtain mercy. *For God hath concluded them all in unbelief, that he might have mercy upon all.* O the depth of the riches both of the wisdom and knowledge of God! How unsearchable are his judgments, and his ways past finding out! . . . *For of him, and through him, and unto him, are all things*: to whom be glory for ever. Amen." Here was an example of wrath and rejection on account of unbelief, which were to end in greater mercy. Thus would God wonderfully justify His own nature: thus would all things redound to His glory.

If we go on now to 1 Cor. xv. we find a passage strikingly parallel at the beginning to that which we quoted from Romans v. " Since by man came death, by man came also the resurrection of the dead. For *as in Adam all die, even so in Christ shall all be made alive*. But every man in his own order: Christ the firstfruits; afterward they that are Christ's, at his coming. Then cometh the end, when he shall have delivered up the kingdom to God, even the Father; when he shall have put down all rule and all authority and power. For he must reign, till he hath put all enemies under his feet. The last enemy that shall be destroyed is death. For he hath put all things under his feet. And when he saith, All things are put under him, it is manifest that he is excepted which did put all things under him. And when all things shall be subdued unto him, then shall the Son also himself be subject unto him that put all things under him, that God may be all in all" (1 Cor. xv. 22—28). Will any one contend that the Pauline conception in the latter verses would be satisfied by the endless existence of the majority of the human race in misery and sin? Has Christ "subdued" those who gnash their teeth at Him, because he makes them suffer? Is this "the working whereby he is able even to subdue **all** things unto himself?" Will God " be all in all," when vast multitudes of His creatures are in impotent but obstinate rebellion **against** Him?

The three Epistles, to the Ephesians, the Philippians and the Colossians, written towards the close of St. Paul's career, will show us whether his experience as a preacher of the Gospel led him to suppress his wide hopes as to the future, or to declare them more firmly. He is dwelling more than ever, when he writes these Epistles, upon the Will and Purpose of God as manifested in Jesus Christ. It is from this revelation that he draws his conclusions. Let us take a passage from each of these Epistles.

"Having made known unto us the mystery of his will, according to his good pleasure which he hath purposed in himself; that in the dispensation of the fulness of times *he might gather together in one all things in Christ, both which are in heaven, and which are on earth*, even in him" (Eph. i. 9, 10). "Wherefore God also hath highly exalted him, and given him a name which is above every name; *that at the name of Jesus every knee should bow, of things in heaven, and things in earth, and things under the earth; and that every tongue sould confess that Jesus Christ is Lord, to the glory of God the Father*" (Phil. ii. 9, 10, 11). "For it pleased the Father that in him should all fulness dwell; and, having made peace through the blood of his cross, *by him to reconcile all things unto himself; by him, I say, whether they be things in earth, or things in heaven*" (Col. i. 19, 20).

It surely cannot be denied that this language is freer, bolder, more hopeful, than that of modern orthodox theology. It seems to me to prove that St. Paul was not willing, and would not have been willing, to regard the redeeming and reconciling work of Christ as restrained by any fixed limits. I think that to say, This universal reconciliation is what *might have* been, only that the unbelief of men has barred and baffled it for ever, and has made the work of Christ in the main a failure,—not only does considerable violence to the words, but contradicts the *spirit* in which St. Paul wrote, and makes his rejoicing impossible.

It would be easy to quote important passages in which the idea of strict and proportionate justice is set forth, and in which the unchangeable character of God's rule and judgment, manifested now in blended mercy and severity, is declared. The tendency of these is, as we have seen, to expel from the mind the thought of an irreversible destiny. But they do not directly affirm the possibility of repentance and reconciliation in the future world.

It is admitted that such affirmations, putting that possibility in clear and unambiguous terms, are wanting in Scripture. The fact should be fairly recognised, and the proper inferences drawn from it. I should conceive that a reader having no interest or bias on either side, after considering the arguments adduced from Scripture, would be inclined to say, "Scripture has no plain dogmatic statements at all as to the possibility or impossibility of repentance after death. There are terrible threats of a Divine vengeance that shall overtake the ungodly; there are a few distinct utterances of a hope embracing all times and existences and states. But the specific question at issue does not appear to be raised in Scripture." Let us suppose that this is a fair account of the bearing of Scriptural testimony on the controversy, and that the Church has for herself maintained a neutral silence, cautiously repeating, without development or further definition, the expressions to be found in the Bible. To those who may think such a representation not wholly untrue, I would earnestly commend the following reflections:

(1) If there is any belief to be offered to the minds of human beings in the name of a good and righteous Ruler of the universe, which ought to be expressed in perfectly unambiguous terms, and to be supported by clear irresistible evidence, it is surely that which we are now discussing. The presumptions against it are, to say the least, very strong. I will refrain from applying to it the language which rises to the lips from a thoughtful human heart—language, let me only say, of horror and of eternal protest. But I would entreat my readers to contemplate the doctrine steadily, whilst they think of their friends and neighbours, of departed relatives, of the nature of Him whom all men are invited to call Father, of the sacrifice of the Redeemer. Let them ask themselves what the force of Scriptural authority should be, by which such a belief should be imposed upon unwilling consciences; and then let them remember what the Scriptural authority actually is.

(2) For ordinary religious teaching, the wisest course will be to follow the guidance of the Bible and of the Church. We need not, in that case, dogmatise about the future condition of mankind. The great principle set before us by those authorities, and one to which no school or party has borne a sufficiently earnest witness, is, that God will punish and reward with clear and unimpeachable justice. We may teach that eternal life, in this world and in the next, is the sure reward of those who believe and who do the works of faith; that darkness and shame and anguish, in this world and in the next, will be the certain lot of those who disobey God, and who deny the Son of Man in his brethren. We must above all things be true to the Gospel. The Gospel is able to take care of itself; we must not spoil it with our qualifications. We

must preach that the Eternal God has sent **His** Son to be the Saviour of the world; that He came, not to condemn the world, but that the world through Him might have life; that God was in Christ when He gave Himself up on the cross, reconciling the world unto Himself, not imputing their trespasses unto them. With this Gospel we must invite and summon men to repentance. We have no right to tell them that repentance will be made pleasanter in the world to come than it is here; we have every reason to think that it must be more awful and trying. We may continue to ask men how they can expect to repent more easily to-morrow, on their death-bed, in the next world, than **to-day**. We may warn them with Scriptural solemnity of the danger of falling away. Not only will Scriptural promises gain life and new brightness, but the salutary terror of Scriptural threatenings will also be revived, when we can testify without reservation or misgivings, that God is Light, and in Him is no darkness at all.

NOTES.

NOTE 1.—I have not dealt directly with the argument, that we must cling to a belief in the endless misery of those who die impenitent, *because* otherwise we should have no assurance of the endless felicity of those who die penitent. The truth is, that I trusted we should never hear this argument again. It is with shame that I now refer to it. What? If a proposal were made to the few who die penitent, that, at the price of some possibility of loss to themselves, a ray of hope should be permitted to pierce the horrible gloom of the many who die impenitent, would they not gladly, eagerly, accept it? And do all their hopes for themselves depend upon a controverted sense of the adjective "eternal"? Is the Nature of God nothing to rest upon? Is God's Love to be counted as nothing in the estimate of the prospects of the saved, lest it should reach beyond them to the perishing also? If the believers in hopeless punishment feel compelled to say, The Scriptures forbid us to entertain the slightest hope for our brothers who die unreconciled, let them have the decent humanity to add, We would willingly make some sacrifice to have it otherwise.

NOTE 2.—It is startling to find how confidently even highly-educated English ecclesiastics are now affirming that eternity can mean nothing but an indefinite extension of time, and that the Son of God is called everlasting in the sense that His existence will never come to an end. Such language would once have been condemned as heretical. If any one supposes that to distinguish Eternity from **Time is** modern mysticism, let him look at the writings of St. Augustine; as, for example, the volume of the Confessions, edited in English by Dr. Pusey. He will there find it stated, over and over again, that Time is a created element, depending absolutely on succession or change; and that to speak of the Life of God as in Time is to deny His Divine all-creating nature. "If eternity and time are rightly distinguished, in that time exists not without a varying changeableness, whereas in eternity is no change, who seeth not that times could not have been, had no creature come into existence, which should vary something by some change?" (P. 247, note.) "In the Wisdom by whom all things are made, 'to have been' and 'hereafter to be,' are not, seeing she is eternal. For 'to have been' and 'to be hereafter' are not eternal." (P. 174.) "Thy To-day is Eternity; therefore didst thou beget the Co-eternal, to whom thou saidst, This day have I begotten thee." (P. 234.) Eternity, Truth, Love, are the Divine Trinity; and "we were created in the image of our Creator, whose is True Eternity, Eternal Truth, Eternal and True Love, and He is the Eternal and True and Loving Trinity." (P. 121, note.) "Thou, O Lord, art my comfort, my Father everlasting, but I have been severed amid *times* whose order I know not; and my thoughts, even the inmost bowels of my soul, are rent and mangled with tumultuous varieties, until I flow together into Thee, purified and molten by the fire of Thy love." (P. 247.)

BY THE SAME AUTHOR.

BAPTISM, CONFIRMATION, AND THE LORD'S SUPPER;

As interpreted by their outward signs. Three expository addresses for parochial use.

1s. 6d.

"Fresh and thoughtful."—*Guardian.*

THE WORK OF CHRIST;

Or, The World reconciled to God. Sermons preached at Christ Church, St. Marylebone. With a Preface on the Atonement Controversy.

6s.

LIFE IN CHRIST;

Sermons. 5s.

TRACTS ON MIRACLES,

"THE SPIRIT GIVETH LIFE," and THE DEATH OF CHRIST, in TRACTS FOR PRIESTS AND PEOPLE.

1s. each.

ST. PAUL AND MODERN THOUGHT;

A Criticism of Professor Jowett's Commentary on St. Paul.

2s. 6d.

THE WORSHIP OF GOD AND FELLOWSHIP AMONGST MEN;

Sermons by the Rev. F. D. MAURICE, T. J. ROWSELL, D. J. VAUGHAN, and J. LL. DAVIES.

3s. 6d.

THE REPUBLIC OF PLATO,

Translated by the Rev. J. LL. DAVIES and the Rev. D. J. VAUGHAN.

Second Edition, 10s. 6d.

THEOLOGICAL WORKS

PUBLISHED BY MACMILLAN AND CO.

CAMPBELL (J. McLeod) ON THE NATURE OF THE ATONEMENT. 8vo. 10s. 6d.

CAMPBELL'S (J. McLeod) THOUGHTS ON REVELATION. Crown 8vo. 5s.

DAVIES (J. Ll.) THE WORK OF CHRIST; OR, THE WORLD RECONCILED TO GOD. Fcap. 8vo. 6s.

HARE'S (Archdeacon) CHARGES. Three Vols. 8vo. £1 11s. 6d.

HARE'S (Archdeacon) VICTORY OF FAITH. Second Edition. 8vo. 5s.

HARDWICK'S (Archdeacon) CHRIST AND OTHER MASTERS. Second Edition. Two Vols. Crown 8vo. 15s.

HARDWICK'S (Archdeacon) HISTORY OF THE CHRISTIAN CHURCH DURING THE MIDDLE AGES AND THE REFORMATION. Two vols. Crown 8vo. 21s.

McCOSH (Dr.) METHOD OF THE DIVINE GOVERNMENT. 8vo. 10s. 6d.

McCOSH (Dr.) THE SUPERNATURAL IN RELATION TO THE NATURAL. Crown 8vo. 7s. 6d.

MAURICE (Rev. Frederick Denison), THEOLOGICAL ESSAYS. Second Edition. Crown 8vo. 10s. 6d.

MAURICE (F. D.), WHAT IS REVELATION? Crown 8vo. 10s. 6d.

MAURICE (F. D.), THE GOSPEL OF ST. JOHN. Second Edition. Crown 8vo. 10s. 6d.

MAURICE (F. D.) THE EPISTLES OF ST. JOHN. Crown 8vo. 7s. 6d.

MAURICE (F. D.) DOCTRINE OF SACRIFICE. Crown 8vo. 7s. 6d.

MAURICE (F. D.) LECTURES ON THE APOCALYPSE. Crown 8vo. 10s. 6d.

O'BRIEN (Bishop) ON THE NATURE AND EFFECT OF FAITH. Third Edition. 8vo. 12s.

THEOLOGICAL WORKS—*continued.*

PROCTER'S ELEMENTARY HISTORY OF THE BOOK OF COMMON PRAYER. 18mo. 3s. 6d.

PROCTER'S HISTORY OF THE BOOK OF COMMON PRAYER. Fifth Edition. Crown 8vo. 10s. 6d.

TRENCH'S (Archbishop of Dublin) NOTES ON THE PARABLES OF OUR LORD. Ninth Edition. 8vo. 12s.

——— ——— NOTES ON THE MIRACLES OF OUR LORD. Seventh Edition. 8vo. 12s.

——— ——— SYNONYMS OF THE NEW TESTAMENT. Fifth Edition. Fcap. 8vo. 5s.

——— ——— SYNONYMS OF THE NEW TESTAMENT. Second Part. Fcap. 8vo. 5s.

——— ——— ON THE AUTHORIZED VERSION OF THE NEW TESTAMENT. Second Edition. 7s. 0d.

——— ——— COMMENTARY ON THE EPISTLES TO THE SEVEN CHURCHES IN ASIA. Second Edition. 8s. 6d.

VAUGHAN'S (Dr. C. J.) LECTURES ON THE EPISTLE TO THE PHILIPPIANS. Crown 8vo. 7s. 6d.

VAUGHAN'S (Dr. C. J.) LECTURES ON THE REVELATION OF ST. JOHN. Two Vols. Crown 8vo. 15s.

VAUGHAN'S (Dr. C. J.) EPIPHANY, LENT, AND EASTER. Second Edition. Crown 8vo. 10s. 6d.

VAUGHAN'S (Dr. C. J.) REVISION OF THE LITURGY. Second Edition. Crown 8vo. 4s. 6d.

VAUGHAN (Dr. C. J.) THE BOOK AND THE LIFE, and other University Sermons. Second Edition. Fcap. 8vo. 4s. 6d.

WESTCOTT ON THE NEW TESTAMENT CANON. Crown 8vo. 12s. 6d.

WESTCOTT, INTRODUCTION TO THE STUDY OF THE GOSPELS. Crown 8vo. 10s. 6d.

WESTCOTT, THE BIBLE IN THE CHURCH. A Popular Account of the Reception of the Sacred Scriptures in the Christian Church. 18mo. 4s. 6d.

MACMILLAN AND CO., LONDON AND CAMBRIDGE.

WORKS

BY

WILLIAM ARCHER BUTLER, M.A.

Late Professor of Moral Philosophy in the University of Dublin.

I.

SERMONS DOCTRINAL AND PRACTICAL.

First Series. Edited by Thomas Woodward, M.A. Dean of Down, with a Memoir and Portrait. Sixth Edition. 8vo. 12s.

"Present a richer combination of the qualities for Sermons of the first class than any we have met with in any living writer."—*British Quarterly Review.*

II.

SERMONS DOCTRINAL AND PRACTICAL.

Second Series. Edited by J. A. Jeremie, D.D. Regius Professor of Divinity in the University of Cambridge. Third Edition. 8vo. 10s. 6d.

"They are marked by the same originality and vigour of expression, the same richness of imagery and illustration, the same large views and Catholic spirit, and the same depth and fervour of devotional feeling, which so remarkably distinguished the preceding Series, and which rendered it a most valuable accession to our theological literature."—*From Dr. Jeremie's Preface.*

III.

LETTERS ON ROMANISM.

In Reply to Dr. Newman's Essay on Development. Edited by Thomas Woodward, M.A. Dean of Down. Second Edition. Revised by Archdeacon Hardwick. 8vo. 10s. 6d.

"Deserve to be considered the most remarkable proofs of the Author's indomitable energy and power of concentration."—*Edinburgh Review.*

IV.

HISTORY OF ANCIENT PHILOSOPHY.

A Series of Lectures. Edited, with Notes, by William Hepworth Thompson, M.A. Regius Professor of Greek in the University of Cambridge. 2 vols. 8vo. 1l. 5s.

"The Author's intimate familiarity with the metaphysical writings of the last century, and especially with the English and Scotch schools of psychologists, has enabled him to illustrate the subtle speculations of which he treats in a manner calculated to render them more intelligible to the English mind than they can be made by writers trained solely in the technicalities of modern German Schools, or by those who disdain the use of illustration altogether. Of the Dialectic and physics of Plato they are the only exposition at once full, accurate, and popular, with which I am acquainted."—*From Prof. Thompson's Preface.*

MACMILLAN AND CO. LONDON AND CAMBRIDGE.

23, HENRIETTA STREET, COVENT GARDEN

London and Cambridge.

MACMILLAN AND CO.'S

DESCRIPTIVE CATALOGUE

OF

THEOLOGICAL WORKS.

WORKS BY WILLIAM ARCHER BUTLER, M.A.

Late Professor of Moral Philosophy in the University of Dublin.

1.
SERMONS
DOCTRINAL and PRACTICAL.

First Series. Edited by THOMAS WOODWARD, M.A., Dean of Down, with a Memoir and Portrait.

Fifth Edition. 8vo. (1859) **12s.**

"Present a richer combination of the qualities for Sermons of the first class than any we have met with in any living writer."—*British Quarterly Review.*

2.
SERMONS
DOCTRINAL and PRACTICAL.

Second Series. Edited by J. A. JEREMIE, D.D., Regius Professor of Divinity in the University of Cambridge.

Third Edition. 8vo. (1859) 10s. 6d.

"They are marked by the same originality and vigour of expression, the same richness of imagery and illustration, the same large views and catholic spirit, and the same depth and fervour of devotional feeling, which so remarkably distinguished the preceding Series and which rendered it a most valuable accession to our theological literature."—*From Dr. Jeremie's Preface.*

3.
LETTERS on ROMANISM.

In Reply to **Dr.** NEWMAN'S Essay on Development. Edited by THOMAS WOODWARD, M.A., Dean of Down.

Second Edition. Revised by ARCHDEACON HARDWICK.

8vo. (1858) 10s. 6d.

"Deserve to be considered the most remarkable proofs of the Author's indomitable energy and power of concentration."—*Edinburgh Review.*

4.
HISTORY OF ANCIE[NT] PHILOSOPHY.

A Series of Lectures. Edited, Notes, by WILLIAM HEPWO[RTH] THOMPSON, M.A., Regius [Pro]fessor of Greek in the Unive[rsity] of Cambridge. **2 vols.** 8vo. (1[858]) 1l. 5s.

"The Author's intimate familiarity [with] the metaphysical writings of the last [cen]tury, and especially with the English [and] Scotch schools of psychologists, ha[s en]abled him to illustrate the subtle spe[cula]tions of which he treats in a manner [cal]culated to render them more intelligi[ble to] the English mind than they can be [made] by writers trained solely in the techn[icali]ties of modern German Schools, o[r by] those who disdain the use of illustr[ation] altogether. Of the Dialectic and physi[cs of] Plato they are the only exposition at [once] full, accurate, and popular, with which [I am] acquainted."—*From Prof. Thomp[son's] Preface.*

THE LETTER AND T[HE] SPIRIT.

Six Sermons on the Inspiration [of] Holy Scripture. By CHARL[ES] P. CHRÉTIEN, M.A., Re[ctor] of Cholderton, late Fellow [and] Tutor of Oriel College, Oxfor[d.] Crown 8vo. *cloth* (181 pp.) 1861.

The last few years have greatly alt[ered] the general state of feeling and informa[tion] with regard to Holy Scripture. Ther[e is] now no longer the same unthinking ass[ent] even on the part of many thinking mind[s to] sweeping and unproved assertions as to [its] nature and functions. Enquiry on these [sub]jects has now become a necessity. It [has] been attempted in these Sermons to a[id] that the necessary researches may be [con]ducted without the distraction of pai[nful] doubts and the bitterness of excited con[tro]versy. The Author has had the wis[h to] comfort anxious souls who are strugg[ling] for life among deep waters.

WORKS BY JULIUS CHARLES HARE, M.A.
Late Archdeacon of Lewes and Chaplain-in-Ordinary to the Queen.

1. CHARGES

Delivered during the years 1840 to 1854.

With **Notes on the Principal Events affecting the Church during that period, and an Introduction, explanatory of his position in the Church with reference to the parties which divide it.**

3 vols. 8vo. *cloth*, 1*l*. 11*s*. 6*d*.

These Charges **have now been collected because, by their fulness in** dealing with **the several** important questions which have affected the Church of England during **a** most eventful period in her history, they **may be said** to constitute the ECCLESIASTICAL HISTORY OF ENGLAND during fifteen **years.** None of **these** questions are **as** yet **obsolete**: they are still required **to be** understood and grappled with **by** clergymen and laymen who **would not be** unfaithful to their **callings.**

THE CHARGE **FOR 1840** contains Notes on the Duty of the State to provide for the Religious Instruction **of** the People—Pews in Churches—Church Restoration—Place of the Pulpit—Training Schools—Union with National society—Clerical Societies—Rural Chapters—Appropriation of Cathedral **Stalls.**

THE CHARGE FOR 1841 contains Notes on Restoring the Laity to discharge **of** their proper duties in the Church—On the Use of the Bible in Schools—Duty **of** Proprietors to educate the Children **on** their estates—Evening Schools—The Duty of the State in educating all its members—Parochial Missionary Associations—Baptism during Divine Service—Frequent Administration of the Lord's Supper—Mutilation of the Burial Service—The importance of having efficient Churchwardens—Heating of Churches.

THE CHARGE FOR 1842 contains Notes on Impartiality **in** Ecclesiastical History—

CHARGES—*continued.*

The Slanderous character of our Religious Literature—Illegitimate Births—Means of Supporting Training Schools—Missionary Societies—On the Bishoprick of Jerusalem—Revival of Convocation.

THE CHARGE FOR 1843 contains Notes on the Position of the Church since the Reform Bill and the Increase of Bishops.

THE CHARGE FOR 1845 is devoted to the discussion of Romanizing Fallacies.

THE CHARGE FOR 1846 is on **the Romanizing** Tendencies of the Age.

THE CHARGE FOR 1849 contains **Notes** on the admission of Jews to Parliament—The National Society and the Committee of Council—On the Obligation of the Levitical Law—Marriage with a wife's sister—The Baptismal Controversy—Schools for the Middle Class—Religious Newspaper.—The Sterling Club.

THE CHARGE FOR 1843 contains Notes on the Right of the Crown in appointing Bishops—The Management Clause of National Schools' Union—The Clergy Offences Bill—The Proviso for making the 39 Articles the legal Test of Heresy—The beneficial effects of the French Revolution—The Pantheistic parodies of Christianity—Prospects of the German Protestant Church.

THE CHARGE FOR 1851 is on **the** Contest with Rome, and contains Notes especially in reply to Dr. Newman on the Position of Romanists in England, also on a Court of Appeal in the Gorham case—The Supremacy of the Crown—The need of a Synod—The Exeter Diocesan Synod—On Schools for the Middle Class.

THE CHARGE FOR 1854 is more especially directed to the subject of THE REVIVAL OF CONVOCATION.

2. MISCELLANEOUS PAMPHLETS

On some of the Leading Questions agitated in the Church during the Years 1845—51. 8vo. *cloth*, 12*s*.

3. The VICTORY of FAITH.

Second Edition. 8vo. (1847) 5*s*.

ARCHDEACON HARE'S WORKS—continued.

4. THE MISSION OF THE COMFORTER.

Second Edition. With Notes. 8vo. (1850) 12s.

5. VINDICATION OF LUTHER

From his English Assailants. In Reply to Sir Wm. Hamilton, Mr. Ward, Mr. Hallam, and others.

Second Edition. 8vo. (1855) 7s.

6. PARISH SERMONS.

8vo. (1849) 12s.

7. SERMONS

Preacht on Particular Occasions. 8vo. *cloth*, 12s.

The two following Books are included in the Three Volumes of Charges, and may still be had separately.

8. THE CONTEST WITH ROME

With Notes, especially in answer to Dr. Newman's Lectures on Present Position of Catholics.

Second Edition. 8vo. *cloth*, 10s. 6d.

9. CHARGES

Delivered in the Years 1843, 1845, 1846. Never before published. With an Introduction, explanatory of his position in the Church with reference to the parties which divide it. 6s. 6d.

10. PORTIONS OF THE PSALMS

In English Verse. Selected for Public Worship.

18mo. *cloth*, 2s. 6d.

WORKS BY THE REV. JOHN McLEOD CAMPBELL,
Formerly Minister of Row.

1. THE NATURE OF THE ATONEMENT

And its Relation to Remission of Sins and Eternal Life.

8vo. (1856) 10s. 6d.

CONTENTS: The Ends contemplated in the Atonement awaken the expectation that we are to understand its nature. Teaching of Luther. Calvinism as taught by Owen and Edwards. Calvinism as recently modified. Reason for not resting in the conception of the nature of the Atonement on which these systems proceed. The Atonement to be seen by its own light. Retrospective aspect of the Atonement. Prospective aspect of the Atonement. Further illustration of the fixed and necessary character of Salvation as determining the nature of the Atonement and the form of the Grace of God to man. The Intercession which was an element in the Atonement considered as Prayer. The Atonement as illustrated by the details of the Sacred Narrative. How we are to conceive of the sufferings of Christ during that closing period of which Suffering was the distinctive character. The Sufferings of Christ, in which the Atonement was perfected, considered in their relation, (1) To His witnessing for God to Man, and (II) To His dealing with God on behalf of Men. The Death of Christ contemplated as His tasting Death and for every Man. That God is the Father of our Spirits, the ultimate truth on which Faith must here ultimately rest.

2. THOUGHTS ON REVELATION

With Special Reference to the Present Time. Crown 8vo. (1862) 5s.

"One of the most wisely conceived and soundly reasoned works on the Divine Authority of Revelation, that has appeared in the whole course of recent controversy on the subject.. It is a refreshing and strengthening book."—*Nonconformist.*

"This little book is the ablest, the most clear, and by much the most interesting we have read on the confused subject of the principles at issue."—*Spectator.*

"Characterised by soundness and faithfulness."—*Evangelical Christendom.*

WORKS BY CHARLES HARDWICK, M.A.

Late Archdeacon of Ely, and Christian Advocate in the University of Cambridge

1. CHRIST AND OTHER MASTERS.

A Historical Inquiry into some of the Chief Parallelisms and Contrasts between Christianity and the Religious Systems of the Ancient World: with Special Reference to Prevailing Difficulties and Objections. Revised, with the Author's latest Corrections, and Prefatory Memoir, by FRANCIS PROCTER, M.A., Vicar of Witton, Norfolk, Author of "History of the Book of Common Prayer." Second Edition, 2 vols. Crown 8vo.

CONTENTS: Part I. INTRODUCTION. Part II. RELIGIONS OF INDIA. Part III. RELIGIONS OF CHINA, AMERICA, and OCEANICA. Part IV. RELIGIONS OF EGYPT AND MEDO-PERSIA.

"Never was so difficult and complicated a subject as the history of Pagan religion handled so ably, and at the same time rendered so lucid and attractive."—*Colonial Church Chronicle.*

2. HISTORY OF THE CHRISTIAN CHURCH

DURING THE REFORMATION. 459 pp. (1856). Crown 8vo. *cloth*, 10s. 6d.

This Work forms a Sequel to the Author's Book on The Middle Ages. The Author's wish has been to give the reader a trustworthy version of those stirring incidents which mark the Reformation of the Church throughout Europe.

"The utility of this work consists in bringing the greater and minor histories connected with the Reformation into a single volume and a compact shape, as well as presenting their broad features to the student. The merit of the history consists in the penetration with which the opinions of age, the traits of its remarkable men, and the intellectual character of the history are perceived and the force with which they are presented."—*Spectator.*

3. HISTORY OF THE CHRISTIAN CHURCH

DURING THE MIDDLE AGE, A.D. 590—1520.

With 4 Maps, constructed for this work by A. K. JOHNSTON. Second Edit. Cn. 8vo. (1861) 10s. 6d.

Edited by the Rev. FRANCIS PROCTER, M.A.

This history of the Mediæval Church commences with the time of Gregory the Great, because it is admitted on all hands that his pontificate became a turning-point, not only in the fortunes of the Western tribe, and nations, but of Christendom at large. A kindred reason has suggested the propriety of pausing at the year 1520,—the year when Luther, having been extruded from those Churches that adhered to the Communion of the Pope, established a provisional form of government and opened a fresh era in the history of Europe.

"As a manual for the students of Ecclesiastical History we know of no English work which can be compared to this."—*Guardian.*

THE DECALOGUE

Viewed as the Christian Law with Special Reference to the Questions and Wants of the Time. By RICHARD TUDOR, B.A., Curate of Helston.

Crown 8vo. (1860) 10s. 6d.

"The Decalogue occupies so prominent a part in the Service of the Church, that it demands our consideration, and yet we fear it is too often thought lightly of or explained away as being in many respects unsuitable to Christian times. This volume treats the subject more fully than we remember to have seen it done before; the author has met every objection, pointed out the particulars in which its rules admit of adoption to ourselves in the place of an exact obedience, and applied the whole to current opinions and feelings."—*Clerical Journal.*

WORKS BY CHARLES JOHN VAUGHAN, D.D.

Vicar of Doncaster, Chaplain-in-Ordinary to the Queen, and Chancellor of York.

1.
EXPOSITORY LECTURES ON THE REVELATION OF ST. JOHN THE DIVINE.
2 Vols. Crown 8vo. 15*s.*

2.
EXPOSITORY LECTURES ON ST. PAUL'S EPISTLE TO THE PHILIPPIANS.
Crown 8vo. 7*s.* 6*d.*

3.
EXPOSITORY LECTURES ON PORTIONS OF SCRIPTURE
Selected for the Seasons of EPIPHANY, LENT & EASTER.
Second Edition. 10*s.* 6*d.*

4.
THE BOOK AND THE LIFE:
Four Sermons Preached before the University of Cambridge, in November, 1862.
Second Edition. (1863) 3*s.* 6*d.*

5.
LESSONS OF LIFE AND GODLINESS:
Parish Sermons Preached in Doncaster.
Second Edition. Fcap. 8vo. (1863) 4*s.* 6*d.*

"It is impossible to speak too highly of these excellent discourses, which are as full of the truest spirit of Christianity as of wise and practical precepts for the conduct of a blameless life. They sound the **depths** of human nature. A more useful **book, or one** more fitted to be almost under **every** possible circumstance the guide and **support** of all earnest young people, could **not well** be conceived."—*The Press.*

6.
REVISION of the LITURGY.
Five Discourses.
Second Edition. 4*s.* 6*d.*

7.
MEMORIALS OF HARROW SUNDAYS.
A Selection of Sermons preached in the School Chapel. With Frontispiece.
Third Edition. (1861) 10*s.* 6*d.*

8.
ST. PAUL'S EPISTLE TO THE ROMANS:
The Greek Text, with English Notes.
Second Edition. (1861) 5*s.*

"A valuable book of original and careful and earnest thought bestowed on the accomplishment of a work which will be of much service and is much needed. We find in it a careful elucidation of the meaning of phrases by parallel passages, with a nearly continuous paraphrase and explanation by which the very different connection of the argument of the Epistles is pointedly brought out."—*Guardian.*

9.
NOTES FOR LECTURES ON CONFIRMATION.
With Prayers.
Fifth Edition. (1863) 1*s.* 6*d.*

This Work was originally prepared for use in Harrow School, and formed not only the basis of the Lecture but also of subsequent instruction and examination of the candidates for Confirmation in private.

"A complete manual of wholesome suggestions and instructions."—*John Bull.*

WORKS by JOSEPH F. THRUPP, M.A.
Vicar of Barrington, late Fellow of Trinity College, Cambridge.

1. INTRODUCTION to the STUDY and USE of THE PSALMS.
2 Vols. 8vo. (1861) 21s.

"Mr. Thrupp's learned, sound and sensible work fills a gap hitherto unfilled by any of its predecessors. It is the work of a painstaking and careful Hebrew scholar, of a sound English divine, and of an interpreter singularly fair and straightforward."—*Guardian.*

2. ANTIENT JERUSALEM.
A new Investigation into the History, Topography and Plan of the City, Environs and Temple. Designed principally to Illustrate the Records and Prophecies of Scripture. With Map, Plans and other Illustrations. 8vo. (1855) 15s.

"The object of the volume throughout is not merely historical or antiquarian, but it is to illustrate Scripture: and those who read it with this view will find reason to be grateful to the Author for the assistance it affords towards obtaining more clear and definite ideas of the various localities, with the names of which they are familiar, and which, from so many sacred associations and their spiritual and typical use, are invested with perpetual and universal interest."—*Literary Churchman.*

3. THE SONG OF SONGS.
A Revised Translation, with Introduction and Commentary. Crown 8vo. *cloth.* (1862) 7s. 6d.

The object of this volume is to unfold the meaning of one of the least appreciated portions of Holy Scripture. The conclusions of sober criticism will here be found to accord with the traditions of Christian teaching, and the more closely the Song is examined, the less compatible will its language and structure prove with any other theme than than that of the mutual love of the Incarnate Son of God and his redeemed Church.

WORKS by the Rt. Rev. G. E. L. COTTON, D.D. Lord Bishop of Calcutta.

1. EXPOSITORY SERMONS ON THE EPISTLES FOR THE CHRISTIAN YEAR.
2 Vols. Crown 8vo.

2. SERMONS AND ADDRESSES
Delivered in Marlborough College. Crown 8vo. *cloth,* 10s. 6d.

"Wise and affectionate and faithful religious counsels . . . There is the same reverence for the Word of God—the same anxiety to prepare young men for the theatre of life as in the sermons of Arnold—and much of the same sagacity in apprehending the boyish mind and adapting instruction to its want."—*Freeman.*

3. SERMONS:
Chiefly connected with Public Events of 1854. Fcap. 8vo. *cloth,* 3s.

THE PENTATEUCH;
Or, The Five Books of Moses. Translated into English from the Version of the LXX. With Notes on its Omissions and Insertions, and also on the Passages in which it differs from the Authorised Version. By the Hon. HENRY HOWARD, D.D., Dean of Lichfield. Crown 8vo. *cl.*
GENESIS, 1 vol. 8s. 6d.; EXODUS AND LEVITICUS, 1 vol. 10s. 6d.; NUMBERS AND DEUTERONOMY, 1 vol. 10s. 6d.

These books were primarily intended for the use of Candidates for the Cambridge Theological Examinations, but it was felt that they might be useful to other Students of Holy Writ: the younger Clergy in particular, who often after taking up the LXX. are tempted to lay it down again with a feeling of dissatisfaction and perplexity through meeting with discrepancies which they have not the means at hand or the leisure to reconcile for themselves; and yet there are few pursuits more useful to the Biblical student.

WORKS by the Rt. Rev. J. W. COLENSO, D.D.
Lord Bishop of Natal.

1.

ST. PAUL'S EPISTLE TO THE ROMANS.

Newly Translated, and Explained from a Missionary point of view. Crown 8vo. *cloth*, price 7s. 6d.

The teaching of the great Apostle to the Gentiles is here applied to some questions which daily arise in Missionary labours among the heathen, more directly than is usual with those commentators, who have not been engaged personally in such a work, but have written from a different point of view in the midst of a state of advanced civilization and settled Christianity. Hence they have usually passed by altogether, or only touched very lightly upon, many points, which are of great importance to Missionaries, but which seemed to be of no immediate practical interest for themselves or their readers. The views advanced in this book are the results of seven years of Missionary experience, as well as of many years of previous close study of this Epistle.

2.

A LETTER TO THE LORD ARCHBISHOP OF CANTERBURY

Upon the Question of the proper treatment of cases of Polygamy as found already existing in Converts from Heathenism.

Second Edition. 1s. 6d.

3.

THE COLONY of NATAL.

A Journal of Ten Weeks' Tour of Visitation among the Colonists and Zulu Kaffirs of Natal. With Map and Illustrations.

Fcp. 8vo. *cloth*, 5s.

"A most interesting and charmingly written book."—*Examiner.*

"The Church has good reason to be grateful for the publication."—*Colonial Church Chronicle.*

4.

VILLAGE SERMONS.

Third Thousand. Fcp. 8vo. *cloth.* 2s. 6d.

5.

FOUR SERMONS.

On Ordination and on Missions. 18mo. sewed. 1s.

6.

COMPANION TO THE HOLY COMMUNION.

Containing the Service with Select Readings from the Writings of the Rev. F. D. MAURICE.

18mo. *cloth, red leaves*, 2s. 6d.; *morocco*, 6s.; *paper edition*, 1s.

A COMMENTARY ON THE BOOK OF GENESIS.

For the Use of Students and Readers of the English Version of the Bible. By the Rev. H. C. GROVES, M.A., Perpetual Curate of Mullavilly, Armagh.

Crown 8vo. *cloth*, 9s.

In the course of the last thirty years much has been done to elucidate the text of the Pentateuch, to clear away the uncertainties and obscurities involving the Geographical and Historical notices contained in it, and to dispose of the objections which the disclosures made by the rapid advance of several branches of Physical Science were supposed to present to the statements of this part of Scripture. To bring the information on these various points within the reach of the general reader is the object of this Commentary; in the formation of which have been consulted the works containing the latest results of the investigations in sacred criticism and exegesis, in Biblical Geography and History, and in science considered in relation to religion

WORKS by J. McCOSH, LL.D.
Professor of Logic and Metaphysics in the Queen's University, Ireland.

1.
THE METHOD OF THE DIVINE GOVERNMENT
PHYSICAL AND MORAL.

Seventh Edition, 10s. 6d.

BOOK I.—General View of the Divine Government. BOOK II.—The Physical World; General Laws; Providence. BOOK III.—Man's Moral Nature. BOOK IV.—Reconciliation of Man and God.

"The work is of the compact, thought-elevating complexion which men do not willingly let die; and we promise such of our readers as may possess themselves of it, much entertainment and instruction of a high order, and a fund of solid thought which they will not soon exhaust."—*Hugh Miller*

2.
THE SUPERNATURAL IN RELATION TO THE NATURAL.

Crown 8vo. *cloth*, 7s. 6d.

Man discovering the uniformity of Nature—In what the Natural System consists—Mental Principles involved in our conviction as to the uniformity of Nature—The Natural a Manifestation of the Supernatural—The System in the Supernatural—The Evidences of Christianity.

"This work goes down to the very foundations of the controversy, and is characterised by deep and accurate thinking the results of which are clothed in a style brilliant and fascinating in no ordinary degree."—*Baptist Magazine.*

"A work whose scientific value as a contribution towards the defences of the Faith it would be difficult to overrate."—*Patriot.*

TRACTS FOR PRIESTS AND PEOPLE.

By THOMAS HUGHES, Rev. F. D. MAURICE, Rev. J. LL. DAVIES, J. M. LUDLOW, Rev. C. P. CHRETIEN, Rev. FRANCIS GARDEN, J. N. LANGLEY, SIR E. STRACHEY, HON. AND REV. W. H. LYTTELTON, RICHARD HUTTON, &c.

2 vols. Crown 8vo. 8s. each.

"A very important contribution to the religious literature of the day, throwing new light on many of the questions that are agitating us, and likely to be of good service in eliciting a hopeful result from the present panic.... We attach great importance to the honest treatment of these great questions in such works as this."—*John Bull.*

THE CHRISTIAN CLERGY OF THE FIRST TEN CENTURIES.

AND THEIR BENEFICIAL INFLUENCE ON EUROPEAN PROGRESS.

By HENRY MACKENZIE, B.A., late Scholar of Trinity College, Cambridge.

Crown 8vo. *cloth*, 6s. 6d.

It is endeavoured in this work to trace, during the first ten centuries of our era, the leading features of that mighty scheme by which the Christian religion was diffused through so many lands, and proclaimed in so many various tongues: neither the enduring remains of the constitution of Rome, nor the vigorous but shapeless energy of invading barbarism, can present to us more matter of interest or of instruction than the progress and influence of the Christian clergy during the earlier ages of their history.

ON TRUTH and ERROR.

Thoughts on the Principles of Truth and the Causes and Effects of Error. By JOHN HAMILTON, M.A. (of St. Ernan's), St. John's Coll. Cambridge.

Crown 8vo. *cloth*, 5s.

In order to assist the author's own researches after Truth, and to test his provings, he has been all along in the habit of writing a good deal, and endeavouring to put his views of Truth into every form he could think of, in order afterwards to be able to review and criticise himself. This he has endeavoured to do with that unsparing strictness which a man must value who is in pursuit of THE TRUTH—that truth which he is urged to seek by the highest assurance that when acquired "the truth shall make you free." This volume is composed of some of these writings. If they lead a few to seek the truth, under God's guidance, and to show how unspeakably more bright and glorious it is than they had conceived, or could conceive while shut up in the narrow circle of what is ordinarily called "the Christian Scheme," my object is attained.

THE WORK OF WOMEN IN THE ENGLISH CHURCH.

LECTURES TO LADIES

On Practical Subjects. By the Rev. F. D. MAURICE, PROFESSOR KINGSLEY, the Rev. J. LL. DAVIES, ARCHDEACON ALLEN, DEAN TRENCH, PROF. BREWER, DR. GEORGE JOHNSON, DR. SIEVEKING, DR. CHAMBERS, F. J. STEPHEN, ESQ., and TOM TAYLOR, ESQ.

Crown 8vo. 7s. 6d.

CONTENTS:—Plan of Female Colleges—The College and the Hospital—The Country Parish—Overwork and Anxiety—Dispensaries—District Visiting—Influence of Occupation on Health—Law as it affects the Poor—Everyday Work of Ladies—Teaching by Words—Sanitary Law—Workhouse Visiting.

"We scarcely know a volume containing more sterling good sense, or a finer expression of modern intelligence on social subjects."—*Chambers' Journal.*

THE DIFFICULTIES OF BELIEF

In connexion with the Creation and the Fall. By THOMAS RAWSON BIRKS, M.A., Rector of Kelshall, and Author of "The Life of the Rev. E. Bickersteth."

Crown 8vo. *cloth*, 4s. 6d.

The object of this Book is to remove some of those difficulties which have often haunted thoughtful and enquiring minds, when they reflect on the deeper truths and more solemn aspects of religion, both natural and revealed. The aim is not to awaken the sense of difficulty in their minds, but to relieve the depth of these shadows, where they have been felt already in their chilling and depressing power.

ON THE NATURE AND THE EFFECTS of FAITH.

Sermons on the Doctrine of Justification by Faith Only. With Notes.

By JAMES THOMAS O'BRIEN, D.D., Bishop of Ossory, formerly Fellow of Trinity College, Dublin.

Third Edition. 8vo. (1863) 12s.

This work, originally published in 1833 was out of print for thirty years, when a Second and enlarged Edition was published in 1862, which was very speedily sold off and the present Edition called for. The chief object of the work is to aid Theological Students in coming to right views upon the fundamental Doctrine, and of impressing upon them a due sense of its importance. In the Notes the author has taken great pains to give authorities from the Confessions of Protestant Churches and the writings of the eminent Protestant divines of the Reformation period for the statements contained in the work.

WORKS by R. C. TRENCH, D.D.
Dean of Westminster.

1.
SYNONYMS OF THE NEW TESTAMENT.

Fourth Edition. Fcap. 8vo. 5s.

The value of the study of the Synonyms of the New Testament as a discipline for training the mind into close and accurate habits of thought, the amount of instruction which may be drawn from it, the increase of intellectual wealth which it may yield, is great and well recognised. The words of the New Testament are eminently the στοιχεῖα of Christian theology, and he who will not begin with a patient study of these shall never make any considerable, least of all any secure, advances in this. This work is the result of patient study gathered during many years.

2.
HULSEAN LECTURES
For 1845—46.

Fourth Edition. Fcap. 8vo. *cloth*, 5s.

CONTENTS: (I) The Fitness of Holy Scripture for unfolding the Spiritual Life of Man—(II) Christ the Desire of all Nations; or the Unconscious Prophecies of Heathendom.

3.
THE SUBJECTION OF THE CREATURE.

Sermons preached before the University of Cambridge.

Fcp. 8vo. 3s.

4.
SERMONS
Preached before the University of Cambridge.

Fcap. 8vo. *cloth*, 2s. 6d.

WORKS by C. A. SWAINSON, M.A.
Principal of the Theological College, and Canon of Chichester.

1.
THE CREEDS OF THE CHURCH

In their Relations to the Word of God and to the Conscience of the Christian.

8vo. 9s.

2.
THE AUTHORITY OF THE NEW TESTAMENT:

The CONVICTION of RIGHTEOUSNESS: and the MINISTRY OF RECONCILIATION.

Three Series of Lectures delivered before the University of Cambridge, in 1848 and 1858. 12s.

3.
HANDBOOK to BUTLER'S ANALOGY.

With a few Notes. Price 1s. 6d.

———

CREATION IN PLAN AND IN PROGRESS.

Being an Essay on the First Chapter of Genesis. By the Rev. JAMES CHALLIS, M.A., F.R.S., F.R.A.S., Plumian Professor of Astronomy in the University of Cambridge.

Crown 8vo. *cloth*, 3s. 6d.

The course of the reasoning followed is intended to be conveyed by the title, *Creation in Plan and in Progress:* namely, that the creation, being a *work*, must have been, like every other work, *designed* as well as *executed*, and that this twofold view of it is *in the Scriptures*.

THE GENEALOGIES

Of our Lord and Saviour Jesus Christ, as contained in the Gospels of St. Matthew and St. Luke, reconciled with each other and with the Genealogy of the House of David, from Adam to the close of the Canon of the Old Testament, and shown to be in harmony with the true Chronology of the Times. By Lord ARTHUR HERVEY, M.A., Archdeacon of Sudbury, and Rector of Ickworth. 8vo. *cloth*, 10s. 6d.

The Genealogy of our Lord, as given by the Evangelists has been a subject of acknowledged difficulty and perplexity to commentators from the earliest days of Christianity. They comprise questions of history, of chronology, of law, of grammar, of criticism, of agreement between inspired writers, of harmony between the Old and New Testaments: in short they are difficulties of every kind which can beset a passage of Scripture. It is the object of this work to discover a solution of the chief difficulties by the author availing himself of the most sound and judicious explanations of former writers, and partly by some new matter which has been the result of his own investigations.

On CLERICAL SUBSCRIPTION

An Inquiry into the Position of the Church and the Clergy in reference

I. To the Articles; II. To the Liturgy; III. To the Canons and Statutes.

By the Rev. C. HEBERT, M.A. Crown 8vo. *cloth*, 7s. 6d.

This work contains a complete reprint of Dr. Lushington's Judgment in cases of Dr. Williams and Mr. Wilson, delivered June 25, 1862.

"A very useful manual of information to the various changes in our formularies of worship and belief. . . Mr. Hebert's temperate and ably-written volume will point out the historical facts which require to be examined before the practical part of the question can be approached."—*John Bull*.

PHILOSOPHY OF THE INFINITE.

A Treatise on Man's Knowledge of the Infinite Being, in answer to SIR WILLIAM HAMILTON and DR. MANSEL.

By the Rev. H. CALDERWOOD.

Second Edition, greatly enlarged. 8vo. *cloth* (520 pp.) 14s.

This work is intended as an illustration and defence of the proposition, that Man has a positive conception of the Infinite. It is an attempt, by a careful analysis of consciousness, to prove that man does possess a notion of an Infinite Being, and since such is the case, to ascertain the peculiar nature of the conception, and the peculiar relations in which it is found to arise.

CONTENTS: Belief in the existence of One Infinite Being—Province of Faith as related to that of Knowledge—Sir W Hamilton's Distinction of the Infinite and Absolute—Characteristics of Knowledge and Thought—Time and Space—Knowledge of the Infinite as First Cause—Knowledge of the Infinite as Moral Governor—Knowledge of the Infinite as the Object of Worship—Testimony of Scripture concerning Man's Knowledge of the Infinite.

CHRISTIANITY AGREEABLE to REASON.

IN ITS EVIDENCE, ITS DOCTRINE OF THE ATONEMENT, AND ITS COMMEMORATIVE SACRAMENT

By Rev. EDMUND MORTLOCK, B.D., Rector of Moulton, and late Fellow of Christ's College, Cambridge.

Second Edition. Fcap. 8vo. *cloth*. 3s. 6d.

This work presents a clear and summary vindication of the truth and reasonableness of the Christian Religion, level to the capacity of persons of ordinary understanding and attainments.

WORKS by FREDERICK DENISON MAURICE, M.A.
Incumbent of St. Peter's, St. Marylebone, London.

1.
ECCCLESIASTICAL HISTORY OF THE FIRST TWO CENTURIES.
8vo. *cloth*, 10s. 6d.

CONTENTS: The Jewish Calling—The Other Nations—The Sect Age of the Jewish Commonwealth—The Kingdom of Heaven—The New Society in Jerusalem, Samaria, and Syria—The Churches in Gentile Cities—St. James, St. Peter, and St. Paul—St. John—The Apocalypse—The Different Churches in the Second Century: Judea, Samaria, Syria—Churches in Asia Minor—Churches in Greece and Egypt—Churches in Italy and Gaul—The African Church—The Church and the Gods—The Failures of the Church in the Battle with the Gods—The Church and the Emperors—The Church and the Philosophers—The Church and the Sects.

2.
EXPOSITORY SERMONS
ON THE
HOLY SCRIPTURES.
Uniform in Crown 8vo. *cloth*.

1. The Patriarchs and Lawgivers of the Old Testament. Second Edition. Crown 8vo. *cloth*, 6s.
   This volume contains Discourses on the Pentateuch, Joshua, Judges, and the beginning of the First Book of Samuel.
2. The Prophets and Kings of the Old Testament. Second Ed. Crown 8vo. *cloth*, 10s. 6d.
   This volume contains Discourses on Samuel I. and II., Kings I. and II., Amos, Joel, Hosea, Isaiah, Micah, Nahum, Habakkuk, Jeremiah, and Ezekiel.
3. The Gospel of St. John; a Series of Discourses. Second Edition. Crown 8vo. *cloth*, 10s. 6d.
4. The Epistles of St. John; a Series of Lectures on Christian Ethics. Crown 8vo. 7s. 6d.
5. The Book of the Revelation of St. John. 10s. 6d.

3.
EXPOSITORY SERMONS
ON THE
BOOK OF COMMON PRAYER.
Fcap. 8vo. *cloth*, 5s. 6d.

4.
WHAT IS REVELATION?
A Series of Sermons on the Epiphany, with Letters to a Theological Student on
MR. MANSEL'S BAMPTON LECTURES.
Crown 8vo. *cloth*, 10s. 6d.

"If I succeed in inducing a few Christian Students and Christian workers to ask themselves what is Revelation; if I can convince a few serious doubters that what we call a Revelation of God, craves to be tried by the severest tests, is capable of meeting these agonies of the human spirit which our arguments can never meet—I have done what I meant to do."—*Preface*.

5.
SEQUEL TO THE ENQUIRY "WHAT IS REVELATION?"
With Letters on Mr. Mansel's Strictures.
Crown 8vo. *cloth*. 6s.

6.
THEOLOGICAL ESSAYS.
Second Edition. Crown 8vo. *cloth*, 10s. 6d.

CONTENTS: Charity—Sin—The Evil Spirit—The Sense of Righteousness in Men and their Discovery of a Redeemer—The Son of God—The Incarnation—The Atonement—The Resurrection of the Son of God—Justification by Faith—Regeneration—The Ascension of Christ—Inspiration—The Judgement Day—Personality and Teaching of the Holy Spirit—Unity of The Church—The Trinity in Unity—Eternal Life and Eternal Death.

WORKS by *FREDERICK DENISON MAURICE*—Continued.
Incumbent of St. Peter's, St. Marylebone, London.

7.
THE DOCTRINE OF SACRIFICE.
Deduced from the Scriptures.
Crown 8vo. *cloth*, 7s. 6d.

"My desire in this book is to ground all theology upon the Name of God the Father the Son and the Holy Ghost; not to begin from ourselves and our sins; not to measure the straight line by the crooked one. This is the method which I have learnt from the Bible. **There** everything proceeds from God; **He is** revealing Himself; He is acting, speaking, ruling. Next, my desire is to ground all human morality upon the relation in which man stands to God; to exhibit whatever is right and true in man, as only **the** image and reflex of the original Righteousness and Truth. I cannot base this morality upon the dread of some future punishments, upon the expectation of some future rewards. I believe the attempts to make men moral by such means have failed always; are never more egregiously and monstrously failing than now. I believe that they fail because they are in conformity with our notions, and not with God's purpose, as set forth in Holy Scripture. There I find God using punishments to make men sensible of the great misery of being at war with His will; showing them the blessed results to their spirits, to their bodies, to nations, to families, to individuals, to the father and the child, the master and the workman, to the persons who subdue the earth, and to the earth which they subdue from conformity to His will. There I find the Kingdom of Heaven set forth as the kingdom of righteousness and peace and joy in the Holy Ghost, which Christ, the only begotten of the Father, came **to** reveal; the kingdom over our spirits, the kingdom into which the poor in spirit who renounce themselves and trust in God, enter. There I find Hell set before me as the loss of this state, as separation from God, as the darkness into which those fall who love darkness rather than the light which has come into the world, and is shining into their hearts. There I am taught, that God by all His discipline and government here, is leading men to fly from the darkness and turn to the light; **and** that they are resisting His will when they prefer Hell to Heaven."

8.
LECTURES ON THE RELIGIONS OF THE WORLD.
CONTENTS.
PART I. Mahometanism—The Hindoo Faith. Buddhism—The Old Persian Faith. The Egyptian—The Greek—The Gothic.
PART II. Their Relations to Christianity.

Fourth Edition, 5s.

9.
SERMONS ON THE LORD'S PRAYER.
Fourth Edition, 2s. 6d.

10.
THE SABBATH, AND OTHER SERMONS.
Fcap. 8vo. *cloth*, 2s. 6d.

11.
LEARNING AND WORKING.
Six Lectures on Working Men's Colleges: To which are added Four Lectures on
THE RELIGION OF ROME
And its Influence on Modern Civilization.
Crown 8vo. *cloth*, 5s.

12.
DIALOGUES ON FAMILY WORSHIP.
Crown 8vo. 6s.

13.
CLAIMS OF THE BIBLE AND OF SCIENCE.
Crown 8vo. 4s. 6d.

MANUALS
FOR THEOLOGICAL STUDENTS AND GENERAL READERS.

This Series of Theological **Manuals** *has been published with* **the aim** *of supplying Books concise, comprehensive,* **and** *accurate, convenient* **for the** *Student, and yet interesting to the general reader.*

THE NEW TESTAMENT.

1. HISTORY OF THE CANON OF THE NEW TESTAMENT during the First Four Centuries. By BROOKE FOSS WESTCOTT, M.A., late Fellow of Trinity College, Cambridge. Crown 8vo. *cloth.* 12s. 6d.

"The Author has endeavoured to connect the history **of** the New Testament Canon with the growth and consolidation of the Catholic Church, and to point out the relation existing been the amount of evidence for the authenticity of its component parts and the whole mass of Christian literature. Such a method of inquiry will convey both the truest notion **of the connexion of** the written Word **with** the living Body of Christ, **and the surest** conviction of its divine authority."

"Theological Students—and not they only—but the general public owe a deep debt of gratitude to Mr Westcott for bringing this subject fully before them .... As a theological **work it** is at once perfectly fair and impartial, and imbued with a thoroughly religious spirit—and as a manual, it exhibits in a lucid form and in a narrow compass the results of extensive research and accurate thought."—*Saturday Review.*

2. INTRODUCTION TO THE STUDY OF THE GOSPELS. By BROOKE FOSS WESTCOTT, M.A. Crown 8vo. *cloth.* 10s. 6d.

"The worth of Mr. Westcott's volume for the spiritual interpretation of the Gospels is greater than we can readily express even by the most grateful and approving words. It presents with an unparalleled completeness—the characteristic of the book everywhere being this completeness—wholeness of view, comprehensiveness of representation, the fruits of sacred learning."—*Nonconformist.*

MANUALS FOR THEOLOGICAL STUDENTS—Continued.

CHURCH HISTORY.

1. HISTORY of the CHRISTIAN CHURCH DURING THE MIDDLE AGES. By CHARLES HARDWICK, M.A. Archdeacon of Ely and Christian Advocate in the University of Cambridge. Second Edition. With 4 Maps. Crown 8vo. *cloth.* 10s. 6d.

2. HISTORY of the CHRISTIAN CHURCH DURING THE REFORMATION. By ARCHDEACON HARDWICK. Crown 8vo. *cloth.* 10s. 6d.

COMPANION VOLUME TO HARDWICK'S CHURCH HISTORY.

HISTORY of CHRISTIAN MISSIONS IN THE MIDDLE AGES. By GEORGE FREDERICK MACLEAR, M.A. Crown 8vo. *cloth.* 10s. 6d.

THE BOOK OF COMMON PRAYER.

HISTORY of the BOOK of COMMON PRAYER. With a Rationale of its Offices. By FRANCIS PROCTER, M.A. Fifth Edition. 464 pp. (1860). Crown 8vo. *cloth.* 10s. 6d.

When the present series of Manuals was projected, it did not appear that any one of the existing volumes taken singly was available for the desired object. In the course of the last twenty years the whole question of Liturgical knowledge has been reopened with great learning and accurate research, and it was mainly with the view of epitomizing the extensive publications on the subject, and correcting by their help the errors and misconceptions which had obtained currency, that the present volume was published. The rapid sale of Four Editions may be taken as a proof that this work has been found useful to students and general readers.

"By far the best commentary extant .... As a manual of extensive information, historical and ritual, imbued with sound Church principles, we are entirely satisfied with Mr. Procter's **important** volume."—*Christian Remembrancer.*

By the same Author.

ELEMENTARY HISTORY of the BOOK of COMMON PRAYER. For the Use of Schools and popular reading. 12mo. *cloth.* 2s. 6d.

The Author having been frequently urged to give a popular abridgement of his larger work in a form which should be suited for use in Schools and general readers, has attempted in this book to trace the History of the Prayer-Book, and to supply to the English reader the general results which in the larger work are accompanied by elaborate discussions and references to authorities indispensable to the student. It is hoped that this book may form a useful manual to assist people generally to **a** more intelligent use of the Forms of our Common Prayer.

Printed by Jonathan Palmer, Sidney Street, Cambridge.